Praise for *The Lives of Campus Custodians*

"In this insightful volume, Magolda enters into the worlds of work of custodians who keep the spaces of learning and living clean, safe and welcoming for students, faculty and staff. Magolda's work is the first full-scale study of custodial work from the ground that I am aware of. His bottom-up documentation of custodians' realities and day-to-day experiences fills a very significance gap in the literature on higher education work. The organization of the book into three major themes—fear, fatalism and family—make much of what he learns applicable across other fields of work. Scholars and students of labor will find themselves in these pages, particularly in Magolda's insightful work on the 'family' of the workplace. His concluding section allows for a reinterpretation of the consequences of corporate managerialism on civility and community in higher education. Finally, Magolda is generous in sharing his methodological decisions and approaches in appendices that deepen the utility of the book for courses on labor, sociology, occupations, and higher education."—*Karla A. Erickson, PhD, professor of sociology and associate dean, Grinnell College*

"Magolda's goal was to create an 'interesting, accessible, credible, provocative, moderately disorienting, and educational' story. His ethnographic study of custodians at two higher education institutions has achieved that and more. In living their culture he came to appreciate the impact of the changing university on the 'least' of its members. Magolda uses this study of a university subculture to critique the trend toward corporatization in higher education. A critical read for everyone in the academy."—*Gretchen Metzelaars, PhD, senior associate vice president, Office of Student Life, The Ohio State University*

"Magolda's work promises to be one of the most important studies of our time, for higher education scholars have virtually ignored the lived experiences and contributions of members from the campus's invisible custodial caste. Through the use of casual conversation, storytelling and case studies, Magolda's writing is compelling, honest, and personal. His research stands as witness that the academy espouses inclusivity but does not enact it. This book is a must-read, a moral imperative, rooted in social justice."
—*Patty Perillo, PhD, vice president for student affairs and assistant professor of higher education, Virginia Tech*

THE LIVES OF CAMPUS CUSTODIANS

THE LIVES OF CAMPUS CUSTODIANS

Insights Into Corporatization and Civic Disengagement in the Academy

Peter Magolda

Foreword by Jeffrey F. Milem

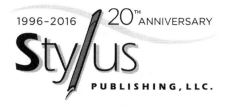

1996–2016 20TH ANNIVERSARY

STERLING, VIRGINIA

Published by Stylus Publishing, LLC.
22883 Quicksilver Drive
Sterling, Virginia 20166-2102

Library of Congress Cataloging-in-Publication Data
Names: Magolda, Peter Mark, author.
Title: The lives of campus custodians : insights into corporatization
and civic disengagement in the academy / Peter Magolda.
Description: First edition. | Sterling, Virginia : Stylus Publishing,
2016. | Includes bibliographical references and index.
Identifiers: LCCN 2015046955 (print) |
LCCN 2016009412 (ebook) |
  ISBN 9781620364604 (pbk. : alk. paper) |
  ISBN 9781620364598 (cloth : alk. paper) |
  ISBN 9781620364611 (Library networkable e-edition) |
  ISBN 9781620364628 (Consumer e-edition) |
Subjects: LCSH: School custodians--United States--Social
conditions. | College facilities--United States--Maintenance and
repair--Social aspects. | College personnel management--Moral and
ethical aspects--United States. | Work environment--United States.
Classification: LCC LB3235 .M25 2016 (print) | LCC LB3235
(ebook) | DDC
   371.6/8--dc23
LC record available at http://lccn.loc.gov/2015046955

13-digit ISBN: 978-1-62036-459-8 (cloth)
13-digit ISBN: 978-1-62036-460-4 (paperback)
13-digit ISBN: 978-1-62036-461-1 (library networkable e-edition)
13-digit ISBN: 978-1-62036-462-8 (consumer e-edition)

Printed in the United States of America

All first editions printed on acid-free paper
that meets the American National Standards Institute
Z39-48 Standard.

Bulk Purchases

Quantity discounts are available for use in workshops and for
staff development.
Call 1-800-232-0223

First Edition, 2016

10 9 8 7 6 5 4 3 2 1

For
Juanita "Pat" Denton (1923–2000)
and
Marcia Baxter Magolda

CONTENTS

PART FOUR: EDUCATION AND POSSIBILITIES

ACKNOWLEDGMENTS

This book includes my stories about campus custodians, tales probably different from ones you might expect. So, too, are my stories about and analyses of the universities where custodians work. Those to whom I owe the greatest thanks are the Harrison University and Compton University custodians. Although I do not mention them by name, I am certain they recognize who they are. Each custodian, I hope, will have the private pleasure of knowing the important contributions he or she made to this book. Spending sustained and quality time with them was the highlight of this undertaking.

These days, taking risks in higher education is the exception, not the rule. I am grateful to the Harrison and Compton University sponsors, administrators, and gatekeepers who took risks to allow me to experience their worlds of work. They granted me unbridled access to custodians and their work settings, accommodated my many administrative requests, and offered important insights. This book would not exist had it not been for their courage and support.

Nearly a decade ago Adolph Haislar, a colleague who spent his entire career as a campus administrator and custodian advocate, encouraged me to conduct this study. He assured me that I would have a great time and would get the education of my life. He was correct on both counts.

Sarah O'Connell and Liliana Delman, invaluable research associates, debriefed fieldwork outings with me. They also posed important conceptual questions and spent considerable time researching answers to them. Matthew Harley, Craig Berger, and P. Jesse Rine introduced theoretical possibilities and shared with me scholarly resources for which I am grateful. Celia Ellison, copyeditor extraordinaire, read numerous drafts of this manuscript. Her hyperattentiveness to details resulted in a reader-friendly document.

Ongoing and extended conversations about my fieldwork and findings with Lisa Weems, Carrie Miller, and James Bielo motivated me to think more sociologically and anthropologically. They also provided respites from writing. Kelsey Ebben-Gross read the entire manuscript and offered unvarnished and insightful feedback that I attempted to incorporate wisely. The book cover showcases Tom Hogeback's extraordinary photography talents; I am grateful for his support. John von Knorring, the president of Stylus Publishing, again took a risk when agreeing to publish this work. I admire his commitment to disseminating scholarship about marginalized enclaves in the academy, even so far specialized as custodians, even if the economic risks are great. Two close friends and colleagues, Jill Carnaghi and Paul Schimmele, encouraged and assisted me in every phase of this research. It is easier to do this kind of work with allies like them.

Finally, I thank Marcia Baxter Magolda, the quintessential life partner. She inspires, praises, critiques, and advises me. Marcia encouraged me to do this research "my way," even if the consequences burdened her, which they did. Thank you, Marcia.

FOREWORD

Peter Magolda and I share a few things in common. We've spent most of our professional lives working in colleges and universities. We followed a similar path to the professorate, having both worked as professionals in university residence halls before returning to graduate school to earn our PhDs and then moving on to our lives as faculty members who study higher education. Moreover, throughout our careers, we have been committed to critically assessing the role that higher education institutions play in either chipping away at or adding to the intense stratification we see in our society. Finally, we both spent time working with/as custodians in universities—with one key difference. My time working as a custodian occurred during three summers when I was an undergraduate at Michigan State University while Peter's time working with custodians occurred just before he retired from his career in higher education.

Peter's keen observations gleaned from his year of experiences working with custodians and listening to their life stories as he conducted this ethnography serve as the focal point of a critical assessment of the increasing corporatization and civic disengagement of higher education institutions— and what a marvelous critique it is. A central component of this study is a deep questioning of just how inclusive higher education institutions are.

The trend toward the increased corporatization of colleges and universities has been the focus of other important scholarship in higher education. For example, through their description of the emergence and consequences of what they term *academic capitalism*, Slaughter and Leslie (1997) and Slaughter and Rhoades (2004) document the impact that the increased corporatization of the academy has had on the nature of academic work, especially regarding its impact on faculty. Rhoades and Sporn (2002) suggest that one consequence of academic capitalism can be seen in the rise of a new class of worker in higher education, defined as *managerial professionals*, and they argue that this trend has had a negative impact on higher education by limiting faculty autonomy and faculty voice.

This book provides us with abundant evidence of the negative impact that increased corporatization (academic capitalism) has on those whose voices have been neglected or ignored in our studies of higher education.

By ignoring these voices, we fail to learn important lessons that we need to understand about ourselves and our work as educators. Peter documents how the efforts of mid- and upper-level administrators (or so-called managerial professionals [Rhoades & Sporn, 2002]) to economize, cut costs, and maximize profits have had a profoundly adverse impact on the professional and personal lives of those at the other end of the academic hierarchy. His analyses expose how highly stratified colleges and universities are and how this stratification silences key stakeholders and minimizes the role that they play in our institutions. Through the low wages paid and the burden of increased costs of health care and other benefits passed on to these workers, Peter shows how difficult it is for them to make ends meet, forcing many to take on additional jobs to support themselves and their families or to postpone or do without things that the rest of us would consider to be essentials (e.g., needed surgery). Moreover, he shows us how the concerns custodians have regarding their work environments are not raised because of the fear that they have of reprisal or dismissal from these jobs on which they depend. And, in spite of the many challenges faced by these silenced voices, Peter shows us how the colleagues who he came to know during his year of ethnography and to whom he introduces us in this book live their lives with great integrity, faith, and purpose.

In the preface to his book *A Different Mirror: A History of Multicultural America*, Ronald Takaki (2008) offers this explanation for his choice of title: "What happens, to borrow the words of Adrienne Rich, 'when someone with the authority of a teacher' describes our society, and 'you are not in it?' Such an experience can be disorienting —'a moment of psychic disequilibrium, as if you looked into a mirror and saw nothing.'" (p. 16) Through his thoughtful analyses of the experiences and life stories of the custodians in his book, Peter Magolda holds up a mirror to each of us and challenges us to think critically about what we see regarding the impact of recent trends in higher education and asks us to think critically about who we are and what our responsibilities are as educators.

In conclusion, I thank Peter for teaching me a difficult lesson I should have learned a long time ago about how little I really knew the professional custodians I worked with during my three summers in East Lansing. His book has helped me to "see" these colleagues in ways that I had not seen them before.

Jeffrey F. Milem
Ernest W. McFarland Distinguished Professor for Leadership in
Educational Policy and Reform
University of Arizona, Tucson
. . . and one-time custodian

References

Rhoades, G., & Sporn, B. (2002). New models of management and shifting modes and costs of production: Europe and the United States. *Tertiary Education & Management, 8*(1), 3–28.

Slaughter, S., & Leslie, L. L. (1997). *Academic capitalism: Politics, policies, and the entrepreneurial university.* Baltimore, MD: The Johns Hopkins University Press.

Slaughter, S., & Rhoades, G. (2004). *Academic capitalism and the new economy: Markets, state, and higher education.* Baltimore, MD: The Johns Hopkins University Press.

Takaki, R. (2008). *A different mirror: A history of multicultural America.* New York, NY: Back Bay Books.

PREFACE
"I See You"

For the past 39 years I have worked on college campuses as a student, student affairs educator, and faculty member. Needless to say, I have participated in thousands of icebreakers and acquaintanceship activities, and I abhor them. Revealing my favorite color is hardly the way I forge meaningful relationships with strangers. A common getting-acquainted activity involves answering the question, "Who do you most admire in the world?" I especially dislike this question for two reasons. First, I struggle to pay attention to participants' responses because I am too busy brainstorming a list of likely responses, like "Gandhi," "parents," "Rosa Parks," or a third-grade teacher. Second, sharing my true response, "Juanita 'Pat' Denton," who was a campus custodian, could mistakenly convey that I am mocking the activity. Although I seldom seriously analyze others' responses to this question, I am intensely serious about my response.

For the past 35 years Pat Denton has been on my short list of most admired people. Scott Adams wrote, "You don't have to be a 'person of influence' to be influential. In fact, the most influential people in my life are probably not even aware of the things they've taught me" (Muoio, 1998, para. 2). This quote echoes my unique relationship with Pat Denton before her death in 2000.

In 1980 I completed my master's degree and accepted my first full-time job as a residence hall director at The Ohio State University. My work commute involved exiting my suite on the first floor and taking the elevator to my office on the third floor. During my first day on the job I dropped by the housekeeping office to introduce myself. The housekeeping manager, Juanita Denton, was an African American woman in her midforties. Wearing a powder-blue smock that had a "Pat" patch embroidered on it, she immediately rose from her chair and gave me a big and unexpected hug. Her presence was commanding. She introduced me to every person in sight and concluded each introduction with, "Peter's our new director. You take care of him, you hear?"

Pat instructed me to follow her to the third floor because she wanted me to meet Oscar, the custodian who cleaned my office. Immediately after we arrived on the third floor Oscar approached and began to complain about overflowing trash in the lobby. Pat listened for a few moments to the rant, then interrupted: "Oscar, if students didn't make messes, you'd have no job. You understand?" Oscar's nod signaled that he did. Then Pat introduced us. "Oscar complains a lot, but he does good work. . . . This is Peter. He's the new director. You take care of him. You hear?" Oscar nodded to signal his agreement.

I took an immediate liking to Pat. Her pride in her work and concern for staff inspired me. She was highly relational and had high and unyielding expectations. She listened and spoke her mind. Her honest, straightforward, no-nonsense style, while momentarily jarring, intrigued and ultimately influenced me. An anonymous Japanese proverb reads, "Better than a thousand days of diligent study is one day with a great teacher." Despite my decades of diligent (and not-so-diligent) studying in formal classrooms, spending brief moments each day with Pat represented quintessential teaching and learning opportunities.

At the start of each workday I visited Pat. I learned to drink bitter coffee because it gave me a reason to extend our time together. I learned that the custodians knew as much, if not more, about the residents and the condition of the residence hall than I did. Pat provided me with invaluable daily updates. She taught me how to both challenge and support staff.

Over time our professional relationship morphed into a personal friendship. I learned about her family and she about mine. She loved working at a university and lamented that she never "got a proper education." She wanted her family to attend college. She reminded me to value my education, something I took for granted.

Pat and I kept in touch after I moved from Columbus and she retired. We would get together whenever I returned to Columbus. In November 2000 Pat called to matter-of-factly inform me she was nearing death. Her straightforward, "tell it like it is" style never waned, even in this context. I visited her the next day. En route to her home, I dreaded this visit. Once in Pat's presence, I did not want to depart.

A few hours later her daughter escorted me to my car. She confessed that 10 years earlier she neither liked nor trusted me. I nodded and replied, "I know. Your mother used to tell me you would say to her, 'Why does that White boy want to hang out with you? Something ain't right.'" We laughed, and I knew something *was* right. Pat died two days later. Arriving for her funeral I learned that her family listed me in her obituary as "her friend," and in the funeral program as an "honorary pallbearer." I treasure these recognitions.

In 2007, as a Miami University faculty member, I received a telephone call from a new student who began the conversation by saying, "You don't know me, but you knew my grandmother." Sunita, Pat's granddaughter, contacted me as soon as she arrived on the Miami University campus as a first-year student. I had not seen her since her grandmother's funeral. We spent much time together during her four years of college. In 2011 Sunita graduated with honors. Pat, my mentor, would be proud.

* * *

In 2008, 28 years after meeting Pat, I met Ludmila, a 75-year-old custodian who cleans my campus office. Most days I cross paths with Ludmila. Her oversized trash can on wheels bumping along the tile hallways announces her arrival long before we make visual contact. Over the years she has learned to subvert my "stay out of my way, I'm on a mission" work persona. As we approach she parks her trash can against the wall and greets me with a smile and hug. Regardless of my mood, interacting with Ludmila always improves it.

During her breaks Ludmila sits in a conference room adjacent to my office and reads Russian books from her homeland. Occasionally she invites me to join her and inevitably offers unsolicited health advice. I can't remember specifics about the hundreds of home remedies, diets, or exercise routines she has recommended, although I am certain my diet and health routines do not impress her. Yet her genuine concern for humanity and her passion for lifelong learning inspire me.

During an impromptu encounter in 2008, Ludmila inadvertently mentioned that she had earned a doctorate in Russian language. This news excited and embarrassed me. Questions flooded my mind: "Why would Ludmila conceal her educational accomplishments?" "How could I be so oblivious to her educational passions?" I asked why she never mentioned her terminal degree. She replied by shrugging her shoulders. I inquired if colleagues in our building knew about her educational accomplishments. She answered, "Not so many. It doesn't matter." I disagree.

A few months later Ludmila showed me a campus job posting for a Russian translator on a funded research project. Ludmila's broad smile conveyed her excitement about this opportunity that would allow her to use her Russian language and translation skills. She handed me a copy of her résumé and cover letter and solicited feedback. I gladly complied. She applied and, a few weeks later, received a generic rejection letter. Learning the news, I could not help but wonder if her status as a custodian influenced the decision. Do some members of the academy still believe wisdom is exclusive to particular professions or classes of people? I hope that things are not as they seem.

As I conceptualized a final major research project I would complete before retiring from the professorate, I wanted to learn more about campus custodians, since I have remained perplexed and annoyed that higher education scholars have virtually ignored this invisible campus subculture. My memories of Pat coupled with my weekly encounters with Ludmila influenced my decision to undertake this study. Both women cast a harsh light on cultural norms that make it difficult for custodians to share their wisdom about the academy with others, especially those with greater power, such as students, faculty, and administrators. Pat's reluctance to believe she was educated because she lacked credentials and Ludmila's reluctance to reveal her academic credentials illuminate negative byproducts of segregated and hierarchical universities.

Colleges and universities profess to be environments where those on the margins are important members of the campus community. But are universities really inclusive? Why do universities profess to value education, yet make it difficult for those on the margins, such as custodians, to "get educated"? Why do universities, in the education business, ignore sources of wisdom like Pat and Ludmila?

In this book I aim to answer questions such as these by recounting stories of the everyday work lives of custodians. The foundation for these stories is a year of fieldwork with campus custodians at two universities. "As anthropologists have come to know, culture can be invisible to its natives—so taken for granted that it seems unworthy of comment" (Nathan, 2005, p. 67). My fieldwork provided me unique opportunities to critically examine and question the espoused and enacted values of custodians, supervisors, administrators, faculty, students, and me. A particular focus is the influence of institutional culture and ideologies on members of the campus community, especially marginalized community members. These stories and analyses showcase acts of courage, resilience, and inspiration, as well as expose instances of intolerance, inequity, and injustices.

This book includes four parts. Part One provides background information about the research study (Chapter 1), research sites (Chapter 2), and the researcher (Chapter 3). Part Two focuses on the lives of custodians. This part describes custodians' diverse career pathways (Chapter 4) and recounts day-in-the-life stories about custodians (Chapter 5) and supervisors (Chapter 6). The next two chapters illuminate two issues that dominated our casual conversations and formal interviews: fear and fatalism (Chapter 7) and family (Chapter 8). Part Three discusses the corporatization of the academy and its influence on custodians (Chapter 9) and two negative byproducts of this corporatization movement: soiled educational aspirations and civic disengagement (Chapter 10). Part Four focuses on strategies for change by describing three case studies of fearless custodians working in corporate-like environments who remained civically engaged and committed to teaching and learning (Chapter 11). The final chapter (Chapter 12) includes research participants' and my reflections about ways to improve the quality of life for custodians. Appendix A includes information about the research methodology and methods. Appendix B discusses the influence of corporate managerialism on ethnographic research.

* * *

During a 2007 commencement speech at the Rochester Institute of Technology, former U.S. president Bill Clinton addressed an issue that is central to this book, one that influenced how I undertook this research. He said,

> In one part of the central highlands of Africa where I have been working on the AIDS Project, a typical greeting goes something like this when people meet each other. One person will say, "Hello" or "Good morning" or "How are you?" And instead of what we do in America when we say, "Fine" or "Fine and I hope you are, too," do you know what the answer is when someone says good morning, hello, or how are you? In English the answer is "I see you." You think about all the people in the world that we never see. I tell you half the world's people live on less than $2 a day. You may say, "I don't know any of them." If I say to you there are one in four people who will die from AIDS, TB [tuberculosis], malaria, or infections related to dirty water, you will say, "I don't know any of them." How many people do we not see? When we leave here today do you have any idea what job we are leaving for the people who are going to have to come in here and clean these chairs up and pick up after us? Do you have any idea how much they make or how they support themselves or their children, or if they believe anyone sees them? How you think about your life in relation to others will determine how you use what you know and what you do as citizens. (Saffran, 2007)

The stories contained in this book are my own. They are my attempts as an educational anthropologist; a college professor; and a White, middle-aged, American male to think about my life in relation to others. To the many custodians who graciously allowed me to learn from them, I say, "I see you."

PART ONE

THE RESEARCH STUDY,
RESEARCH SITES,
AND RESEARCHER

I

YOU MUST HAVE DONE
SOMETHING WRONG

The Right Kind of Wrong

"I never hauled trash with a professor before," declares Mone. I respond, "I've been on college campuses for 39 years, and I have never driven around a campus in a golf cart hauling trash."[1] Mone, a 58-year-old African American man, responds with a smile. He clears the passenger seat of the cart, throwing papers in the portable dumpster hitched to it, making room for me.

It is an unseasonably warm December afternoon on the Compton University (CU) campus. I grin at Mone as I contort my body into the passenger seat, quickly concluding that this vehicle was not designed for our two wide bodies. I instinctively reach for a seat belt. Not finding one, I discretely place my right hand on the roof of the cart to stabilize my ride. My flawed decision to wear a wool sweater instead of my coat is obvious to me as winds whip through the cart as it bounces along campus roads and sidewalks.

I ask Mone about the unusual spelling ("Moan") on the name patch sewn on his department-issued parka. He replies, "I got this coat a month ago, and it had my name spelled wrong. I just got it back this week, and they still spelled it wrong. I just kept it. By the time they fix it again, it'll be summer." I suspect that Mone's bright red floppy holiday stocking cap, with an "Obama" patch stitched on it, probably diverts people's attention away from the misspelled name on his coat. His postelection euphoria has yet to wane as he proudly pledges his allegiance to President Obama: "He's the man."

"We're taking a different route to the north end [a residential community]; this way is not as bumpy," Mone calls out. My innards appreciate Mone's thoughtfulness. Almost every 30 seconds a passerby waves or offers a greeting. Mone reciprocates by flashing his infectious smile. Mone's Friday afternoon optimism and enthusiasm are noteworthy, especially for a campus custodian wrapping up a long workweek.

"Lean in," Mone yells to me as we navigate a curb cut, moving from the street to the sidewalk. Mone's driving skills are honed; he seldom slows down or uses the brakes as he squeezes the cart through tight passageways and narrow paths. The noisy motor, city street traffic, and howling winds inhibit sustained conversation. I use our first stop, a residence hall loading dock, to learn more about Mone.

> I love my job. I like being outside. You meet a lot of people out here. It is better than being stuck inside cleaning dorms. It is a physical job, but I love my work. . . . It's no good out here if it's raining, really cold, or really hot. But, if the weather is really bad, I am allowed to go inside for a while. . . . They [the housekeepers] know when I am coming. I have to know when they are going to finish pulling trash. I don't like to go to a building twice. If I see trash, about four or five bags, I assume they are through.

Mone instinctively picks up the bags and tosses them with ease into the mobile dumpster as he continues his tutorial. "We'll separate the bags when we unload them. Some [bags] are recycle stuff and some are just trash." Mone verbalizes his look of surprise as I exit the cart and start loading bags into the dumpster, when he says, "Oh, I thought you were going to watch, not help me."

"Glad to help," I reply.

Reflecting aloud, Mone says, "You know, I do have a lot of students who work with me; they [campus administrators] call it *community service*. Community service? All I know is that if they have to work with me, they must have done something wrong."

We drive to an adjacent residence hall for our second stop. We work in tandem to quickly load the trash as Mone informs me that we will soon drop the bags in permanent dumpsters. At the drop site Mone reaches into the cart and retrieves two or three bags at a time, tossing them into either the trash or the recycle container. As I grab each bag Mone points to its appropriate destination and instructs me, "This one . . . that one." We resume our conversation as he activates the compactor attached to the dumpster.

> I see everyone—all different people. I speak, wave, and smile. This radio is my trademark. They see me with the radio. I know some are scratching their heads saying, "What's that old man doing driving around on that golf cart?" That's what keeps me going. I have to work.
>
> My rough days are every other Thursday. I have to make paper deliveries. Those days are the worst. In the morning, I have to go to about 10 buildings and put cartons of toilet paper in closets. . . . The hardest buildings are the ones that have steps. Going up those steps with heavy boxes

is hard. Sometimes I drive up on the lawn. I'm not supposed to, but at my age, you gotta do what you gotta do.

Mone provides a brief life history as the compactor continues to grind. I learn that, before working at CU, he worked as a short-order cook for over 20 years at several local restaurants. Mone liked restaurant work but disliked the long hours and minimal contact with people. When he started working in the residence halls at CU in 2000, he worked the graveyard shift for 18 months and then cleaned a residence hall during the day shift. Mone laughs as he explains how he got his current job.

One guy was driving the cart and a scrubbing machine fell off. Big mistake. Next thing I know, I got his job. That was a few years ago. . . . I like helping out around campus. I take shower curtains up to the buildings for every-one. They ask me to help and I say, "Sure." I have no problems with that. I do a lot of little stuff for them. One year we had a Christmas party. They all pitched in and bought me a snowsuit. It was fun. It had me in tears, because I didn't know they were going to do that.

Mone likes working the day shift as well as the option of working week-ends. He explains his daily routines:

I get home about 5:45 p.m. and eat. Around 7:00, I am asleep. I wake up about 8:30 or 9:00. I do some things, then eat again and go back to my room and sit down and fall asleep. I get up at 5:00. My commute is about 30 minutes. I catch two buses and a train. One bus is from my house to the Civic Center downtown. I get on the train and come out here. Then I catch a bus that takes me to the job. I get here around 7:15 or 7:30 each morning. When you catch a bus, you can't cut it too close.

He is even "okay" with his five supervisors. As he explains, "When they call, I do what they say." Happiness and pride in the simplicity of his job constitute his work philosophy.

Mone explains that his final task of the week is to replace trash bags in the containers located outside several residence halls. He parks near a residence hall, retrieves a box of industrial-strength trash bags tucked away behind the seat, selects a few bags, and jumps out of the cart. I study his swapping technique. During our second stop I again shift my role from observer to participant. We agree on a division of labor. Mone handles trash cans while I manage recycling containers. He instructs me how to tie knots on the lips of the bags to ensure that they do not fall into the can. As I quickly master these tricks of the trade, Mone jokes, "You got it. . . . You got a future in trash."

En route to our final stop, Mone abruptly yells, "Damn!" Initially perplexed, I notice that an SUV is blocking the curb cut, making it impossible to maneuver the cart onto the sidewalk. If the cart were not carrying such a heavy load (the dumpster and the two of us), I suspect Mone would jump the curb. Recognizing the dilemma, I hop out of the cart, grab a handful of bags, and head toward the cans located on a nearby plaza. Mone nods his head approvingly as he watches me execute my first solo assignment. Returning with four full bags of garbage in hand, I toss them into the cart's dumpster and plop down in my seat. Mone smirks and says, "Did you see the look she gave you?" as he nudges his head in the direction of a woman sitting in the SUV. Silence conveys my confusion. Mone continues, "Oh, I've seen that look. You must have seen that look. You know, they see you with trash bags and they give you that look—you know, you must have done something wrong if you got this job."

What's Wrong?

Later that evening during my seven-hour drive to Oxford, Ohio, I dictate notes about the trash run. Mone's repeated comment that someone "must have done something wrong," intrigues and troubles me. I concur with his premise that most people have preconceived negative perceptions about people hauling trash or dragging a mop and bucket around.

Paules (1991) argued that the media portrays service workers as "ignorant, incompetent, apathetic, lazy, and slow" (p. 9). Harris (1981) devoted an entire chapter to service workers titled, "Why the Help Won't Help You." He described service workers as impolite, apathetic, inept, and untrustworthy. These stereotypical perceptions about custodians are pervasive on college campuses.

"We defer to others according to their position; we may ignore, expect deference from, even act in an insulting way to those who are in lower positions than our own" (Charon, 2002, p. 64). Mone's comment, "I never hauled trash with a professor before," is his humorous way of deferring to a professor, someone he perceives as having more power. The SUV driver's facial expression of disgust is a reminder of the academy's omnipresent caste system. Custodians are acutely aware of and generally accept the ways that some individuals ignore or subtly accuse them of having done something wrong.

Mone recognized but did not accept *the look* or the belief that doing custodial work is an admission of "doing something wrong." His subtle and subversive actions symbolically communicated ways for universities to "do things right." Mone conveyed pride in his work as he crossed borders and regularly interacted with faculty, students, and staff—even those who gave him *the look*. He conceptualized his work as cleaning and so much more, such as making people smile and educating them.

Mone joked about a student whose disciplinary sanction for violating a university policy was to accompany him on trash runs. The implicit message is that when collegians really screw up, custodial work is the ultimate punishment. Despite the proliferation of university mission statements that proclaim institutional core values such as community, inclusion, respect, civic engagement, and equity, Mone's stories and *the look* are reminders that higher education remains hierarchical; segregated; elitist; and, at times, hardhearted.

Nixon (2011) noted, "Field observations enable researchers to gain a deep understanding of the ways in which individuals locate themselves relative to other individuals in society" (p. 135). Working side by side with campus custodians enlightened me about them and their interactions with others. During this particular four-day campus visit I interviewed more than a dozen custodians and worked three separate four-hour shifts. I collected custodians' life stories, inquired about their perceptions about higher education and campus subcultures, and solicited suggestions to improve their jobs and higher education. Most housekeepers, like Mone, had done most things right. The custodians with whom I interacted were the antithesis of ignorant, incompetent, apathetic, and slow. They were hardworking and dedicated staff with an acute understanding and acceptance of the ways that they are people positioned as "less than" when compared to other campus community members.

The custodians I met constituted a caring community whose moral values debunk stereotypes about service workers. I interviewed refugees, resilient individuals who did nothing wrong. The civil war in their Yugoslavian homeland dramatically altered their lives and limited career options after relocating to the United States. In fact, they did countless things right. They remained optimistic about their upended lives and did whatever was necessary to support their families. They spent hours talking with me about positive aspects of their lives, such as caring families, job security, friends, and faith. When I asked, they reluctantly revealed their hardships, such as low salaries or skyrocketing health care costs. Even interviewees who confessed that they had made some poor life choices, such as a teenage pregnancy or dropping out of high school, accepted responsibility for those choices. Ellison (1965) wrote, "I am invisible, understand, simply because people refuse to see me" (p. 7). Campus custodians, like Mone, are an invisible, marginalized, and powerless campus subculture—"a collective of persons differentiated from at least one other group by cultural forms, practices, or way of life" (Young, 1990, p. 43). Sweet (2001) discussed the dangers of insular and invisible campus subcultures:

> As a consequence of limited experience, privileged students at Ivy League colleges will likely have little insight into what life is like for the rural poor, and the rural poor have little idea of what life is like at an Ivy League college. Lacking this information, both groups will tend to rely on stereotypes, unrefined and often uninformed depictions of groups different from their own. Once a stereotype is accepted the tendency is to pay attention only to observations that fit this definition of reality and ignore observations that run counter to it. (p. 121)

Mone's comments provoke me to think differently and reflect on what I had "done wrong" in the past. As a former assistant dean of students in the 1980s, I was one of those administrators who mandated that judicial offenders pick up trash as a form of community service. My intention was to provide violators with a *teachable moment*. Mone helped me to realize the problems with my actions. What did custodians learn about administrators and judicial affairs officers? What did students learn about community service and custodians because of my mandate? In retrospect, I fear that I showed students that they needed to shape up or the university would punish them in the worst way possible: doing custodial work. I fear that I reaffirmed for custodians the stereotype of the clueless administrator. These ugly realizations made my journey home a long one.

Writing Wrongs

"When you think of the wisdom to be found on campus, you're likely to think of professors sharing the fruits of their decades of research on chemistry, classics, or quantum mechanics. You almost certainly won't think of the folks cleaning the bathrooms, washing the floors, and changing the trash bags" (Golden, 2009, para. 1). Golden's film review of Patrick Shen's (2009) *The Philosopher Kings* documentary, which is about eight campus custodians working at elite American universities, reminded readers that in the academy, learning occurs inside and outside of the classrooms, and faculty are not the only wise individuals capable of educating. Higher education must continually challenge stereotypical and debilitating misperceptions about custodians.

Shen's agenda influences the six overarching research aims of this study, which offer a unique organizational view and critique of the academy by

1. collecting, analyzing, and disseminating custodians' life stories;
2. documenting custodians' interactions with and insights about other campus subcultures and vice versa;
3. revealing how macro campus policies influence segregation, inequities, civic disengagement, and the quality of custodians' work lives;
4. providing a unique bottom-up organizational view of the academy;
5. illuminating how the gravitational pull toward corporatized universities influences organizational structures and administrative procedures; and
6. discussing ways for universities to initiate equitable and moral change.

Ethnographic fieldwork, such as my trash run, allowed me to learn about the Other and me. Fieldwork also provided me a unique vantage point to reexperience and reinterpret aspects about American higher education. When mopping a hallway in a campus gymnasium a few months earlier, I experienced a variation of *the look*—or what I call the *nonlook*. A faculty member walking to a racquetball court tiptoed around me without saying a word or even nodding in my direction. He acted as though he did not see me. For readers unfamiliar with my physique, discretely slithering around me with my mop and bucket in tow is a formidable task. Admittedly, he irritated me. Yet I knew these feelings would end when my fieldwork concluded. Custodians who experience *the look* are not as fortunate.

I not only experienced *the look* while both observing custodians and assuming custodial duties, but also frequently became the recipient of *the look* when I explained this research study to others. After a nonacademic friend learned that while on my yearlong sabbatical I would spend a few days cleaning with campus custodians to document their life stories and solicit their impressions of higher education and then write about the experience, he mocked my project: "Okay. You get a year off from work. You can do whatever you want. . . . You volunteer to clean toilets and then write about it. Really?"

Predictably, faculty colleagues had mixed reviews. The majority offered sincere affirmation for the study, conveying the urgent need for scholars to examine this invisible campus enclave. Some proponents acknowledged the merits of participant-observation studies and then joked that they were glad that someone else was doing this particular research study. Some colleagues couched their tepid feedback by sharing polite and analytic musings—making certain I recognized that they had my best interests in mind when conveying their criticisms: "I wonder if there is a more efficient, rigorous, and clean way (no pun intended) to learn about this subculture, like a survey, that wouldn't require you to do such extensive fieldwork." My interpretation is that they thought that neither the research topic nor the process was worthwhile and that I must have done something wrong to get to this point.

The custodians who participated in this research also expressed initial doubt about the study's merits. Their views gradually evolved, evident in the following seven stages of acceptance, a schema I devised:

Stage 1: Disbelief—"You're doing what?"
Stage 2: Enthusiasm—"Great idea."
Stage 3: Dumb Idea—"What can you possibly learn from talking to me? . . . You need to talk to . . ."
Stage 4: Appreciation—"Why don't people around here listen and ask me these kinds of questions?"
Stage 5: Relief—"This wasn't as painful as I imagined."
Stage 6: Skepticism—"Who would publish this book, and who would read it?"
Stage 7: Reciprocity—"If you actually get this book published, can I get a free copy?"

Fortunately, most research participants' rationales for participating mirrored Troman's (2001) findings:

> The motivations for respondents to become involved in the research were various. Some wanted their 'stories' to be told. Some wanted me to publish "findings" to alert policy makers about the "reality" of what was happening to teachers and schools; while some wanted to see their stories documented and, through reading, relate their experiences to others in similar circumstances. (p. 257)

Despite the varied reactions to and motivation for participating in this study, the overabundance of opportunities allowed to me to re-view and reinterpret American higher education through a custodial lens (as my custodial friends would joke, *from the bottom up*), which trumped the skepticism of colleagues.

My interactions with and observations of custodians led to a self-realization that occasionally I express a "You must have done something wrong" sentiment. When a colleague tosses a paper towel toward the trash can in a public bathroom, misses the can, and then jokes, "No problem, the janitor will get it," I am certain I invoke my version of *the look*, which conveys disappointment, disapproval, and disgust. When my research associates and I compare independent online library searches and all conclude that the educational research community has essentially ignored campus custodians, I am certain these colleagues were privy to my version of *the look*.

Self-analysis of *my look* exposes the ideology upon which this research agenda rests. Studying custodians is not simply a technical or rational task of researching an unexamined topic to fill a research void; it is a moral imperative rooted in social justice. Custodians are an invisible university subculture that should be seen. Similarly, universities' ideologies are also invisible. I want to reveal these hidden ideologies.

My interest in this topic stems from my belief that neither decision makers nor campus community members know very much about custodians or why they do what they do. Scholars occasionally reference custodians' meager salaries when conducting economic studies about living wages on college campuses (Epstein, 2005; Marks & Nermon, 2013; Van Der Werf, 2001). Frequently, university presidents explicitly praise custodians when delivering "It takes a village" speeches to ensure student success. Media feel-good stories about custodians who, for example, earn a college degree while working full-time are common (Ng, 2012). I also appreciate scholars who study campus culture and acknowledge service workers in their published works. For example, Kuh, Schuh, Whitt, and Associates (1991) reminded readers,

> People who play other roles in colleges and universities also make important contributions to creating an environment conducive to student learning and personal development. The work of librarians, trustees, secretaries, custodial staff, and buildings and grounds workers is important to making students feel welcome and comfortable and challenging students to do their best. (p. 181)

Kuh, Kinzie, Schuh, and Whitt (2005) devoted a paragraph to describing Ms. Rita, a service provider who goes *above and beyond* her duties running a campus coffee shop.

> She seems to know everyone on campus—by name! As we observed her for one 45-minute stretch, she had a personal greeting for almost everyone—encouraging some, cajoling others, and freely dispensing her own flavor of advice about students' academic performance and social life. She directed one student who reported that he had performed poorly on a recent test to "go and see the faculty member. . . . [He's a] good person [and] he'll be glad to speak with you." (pp. 170–171)

Sadly, these references are fleeting; the exception, not the rule. Bearman (2005) noted that in sociology and in everyday life, there is a "general distaste for the ordinary. Most people would indeed find it more interesting to study heroin addicts, gangsters, petty crooks, denizens of the subways, or prostitutes—the 'stuff' of much ethnographic work" (p. xii). Adapting Bearman's argument to the higher education research community, researchers are quick to study hookup cultures (Bogle, 2008), campus life in an age of disconnect and excess (Seaman, 2005), fraternity gang rape (Sanday, 1990), violence in Black Greek-letter fraternities (R. L. Jones, 2004), and race and gender wars (G. V. L. Kreuter, 1996). The dearth of scholarship on campus custodians leads me to believe that educational researchers perceive campus custodians as unremarkable and thus unworthy of study.

Anthropologically diverse tribes make up higher education, yet funded research about custodians is about as probable as a spotless public bathroom on an all-male residence hall floor on a Monday morning. During my fieldwork, custodians regularly shared extraordinary life stories and insights about higher education. These individual and potent stories are anything but ordinary, yet recounting and interpreting these stories is complicated. Rebekah Nathan (2005), when talking about what it was like for a professor to conduct covert research while pretending to be an undergraduate, discusses the challenges of studying and recounting research participants' stories:

> My personal experiences as a middle-aged woman cannot say anything directly about the "undergraduate experience." I am not 18 years old, not subject to the same pushes and pulls of that age group nor privy to their social interactions. As anthropologists learn in their overseas experience, one can never really "go native" or expect that one's own experience is indicative of the experience of others born in the culture. At the same time, it is the experience of living village life that offers the insight and vantage point needed to ask relevant questions and understand the context of the answers given. It is this that I hope to accomplish by becoming a freshman. (p. 15)

It would be foolish for me to try to convince readers that I "know" what it is like to be a custodian. I don't. I am not a custodian, although I am an intellectually curious visitor to their world and a grateful recipient of their labor. Gaining limited access to their social and work interactions was a privilege. As a result, I have a deeper appreciation of their joys and tribulations, a deeper understanding of my values, and a multifaceted understanding of the academy.

Duneier (1994) spent years studying a group of African American men who occupied a table at a cafeteria in Chicago. He challenged essentialized media-fueled stereotypes of Black men, illuminating an honest and decent citizenry, too often ignored and misunderstood. As with Duneier, fieldwork experiences afforded me opportunities to observe custodians, ask questions, and better understand the context of the answers they provide. A result is to challenge conventional wisdom and stereotypes about custodians. Perry (1978), when talking about society's disinterest in garbage collectors, noted, "Yet, if we primitively protectively try to shut ourselves off from this very fundamental, integral, and complicated part of society and its work, we lose the chance to learn something very important about our own way of life in

this country. . . . I wanted to present the work of garbage men as real and significant" (p. ix). Perry's goal mirrors my own.

I resist the urge to overstate the importance of studying campus custodians and offer grand prescriptions for innovation or structural reorganization to systemically reform higher education. That said, readers could easily draw implications from this book that have a bearing on these topics. Ultimately, I hope the stories and analyses do not evoke from readers a "You must have done something wrong" look.

Note

1. In compliance with the American Anthropological Association's commitment to protecting the privacy of research participants, I use pseudonyms for all participants, except Dolores, who appears in Chapter 11. I also changed the names of the two research sites and altered information about them to make it more difficult for readers to identify these institutions.

2

RESEARCH SITE INSIGHTS

Cleaning Insights

During my first week of fieldwork at Harrison University (HU) I learn about a specialized team of custodians working the graveyard shift who sanitize bathrooms each night using a revolutionary and environmentally friendly cleaning device, promoted by its manufacturer as "the greenest cleaning system on earth." I envision the crew wearing white jumpsuits, protective eyeglasses, and specialized rubber gloves and boots. En masse, they converge on a public bathroom. One team member has this state-of-the-art cleaning apparatus strapped to her or his back. The machine gun–like sprayer has the firepower to disperse with brute force cleaning solutions that annihilate bathroom germs and infections. Since I expect to be spending considerable time during this yearlong research study in campus bathrooms, this high-tech/no-touch cleaning system appeals to me, especially after reading *Nickel and Dimed* (Ehrenreich, 2002), which delineated the job hazards I would likely encounter:

> For those of you who have never cleaned a really dirty toilet, I should explain that there are three kinds of shit stains. There are remnants of landslides running down the inside of the toilet bowls. There are the splash-back remains on the underside of toilet bowls. And, perhaps most repulsively, there's sometimes a crust of brown on the rim of a toilet seat, where a turd happened to collide on its dive to the water. (p. 92)

My e-mail exchanges with Edgar, the crew coordinator, flushed my custodial Ghostbusters-like fantasy down the proverbial toilet, dismissing my perceptions about the crew, its work routines, and the techno-cleaning apparatus. Shit!

At 9:40 p.m. I arrive at HU's physical plant facility, a building tucked away on the outskirts of campus. En route to the entrance, I pass aging loading docks; rusted commercial trucks; leafless trees; and swaths of decaying leaves on soggy, dormant lawns. This unsightly location is a striking contrast to the remainder of the campus, renowned for its picturesque beauty.

I enter the eerily quiet custodial services suite and approach and shake hands with Edgar, a 50-something crew leader wearing a T-shirt and jeans. He turns and introduces me to the six staff seated around the table, including Edgar's spouse and daughter-in-law. One custodian poses a quasi-question: "You're a professor, and you're writing a book about us?" I can't tell what part of the question the inquirer finds more absurd—me being a professor or me writing a book about campus custodians. I resist the urge to clarify.

I listen to a conversation already in progress about the uncertain future of this cleaning crew. Rumor has it that management will disband this unit as part of a massive reorganization aimed at slashing budgets and staff, while bolstering efficiency and accountability. The custodians' raw feelings of anger, fear, confusion, pessimism, and relief due to current employment are on display. Usually HU's rising and falling fortunes seldom have much of an impact on custodians; they struggle in good and bad times. Yet, in this instance, custodians perceive the university's quest to become lean as *mean*.

At 10:00 p.m. each custodian clocks in and immediately exits the suite to begin a solitary night of cleaning between 20 and 30 bathrooms. On our way to a classroom building, Edgar shares his recent employment history:

> I started here first, back in 2004. My sister came in during the strike. She was hired off the street to help. That was 1999 or 2000. That's how I found out about Harrison. We [Edgar and his spouse] came here for the insurance and the college tuition for my son and stuff like that. The wages are no good. The benefits mattered to us. . . . Before I came here, I got pissed off at the factory. I was making over $13.00 an hour and I up and quit and went to work at Subway. I went from $13.00 to $6.21 an hour—that's how fed up I was.

Edgar pauses his story as he drives the truck onto the sidewalk and parks it a few feet from a building entrance. The "Physical Facilities" decal stenciled on the door ensures that this illegally parked vehicle is not ticketed. Edgar uses his ID to gain access to the locked building. The hallways are not quite pitch black, thanks to the emergency lighting. We wind our way down various hallways toward a custodial closet. He opens the door, and I get my first glimpse of "the greenest cleaning system on earth." And I'm underwhelmed. This $8,000 gadget looks like a cross between a power washer and a shop vacuum on steroids. I hope it cleans better than it looks.

Edgar cleans and replenishes chemicals for the machine at the conclusion of each shift, so it is ready to go. He backs the device out of the closet and explains its "best of" features. Since we will begin cleaning at the other end of the building and work our way back to the closet, our short walk allows our conversation to resume.

> Here people start at around $9.60 an hour. . . . What can you do? . . . It is a struggle. When I first started here, I was paying $6.00 every two weeks for insurance. Now I am paying $150.00. . . . Health care is what drew me here; now it is not as good. Together we [Edgar and his spouse] only make $48,000 a year, and that's before taxes. It's hard to get by.

The dismal local and national job markets make getting a better job unlikely for Edgar. With stagnant wages and rising health care costs, his safety net is dangerously frayed.

We arrive at a door on the third floor that reads "Men." Edgar knocks, cracks the door, and yells, "Housekeeping!" No one answers, so he props the door, plugs in the machine, then parks it against a wall. He does a 10-second tour of the room, pushing open the stall doors, flushing toilets, and picking up paper towels from the floor. I pull the plastic bag from the trash can, replace it, toss the bag in the hallway, and then watch Edgar and the machine do their thing.

Edgar pulls the trigger on the wand, and a steady and powerful stream of clear water sprays onto the walls, sinks, toilets, and urinals. He spares the ceiling and mirrors. The only things he touches with his hands are the toilet seats while raising them. He drenches the surfaces and flicks a switch. Then the wand sprays an odorless, frothy cleaning solution, blasting dirt and water onto the floor. He turns the water switch to "off" and switches the vacuum switch to "on." The standing water instantly disappears. Edgar wipes clean the mirrors, unplugs the machine, and wheels it to the adjoining women's bathroom. We finish in 14 minutes flat.

He repeats the exact cleaning routine in the adjacent bathroom. "I'm fine. I carry two or three T-shirts in the summer to survive the heat," Edgar remarks. I suspect he is responding to me staring at his sweat-stained shirt. After cleaning another four restrooms, following an identical routine, Edgar declares, "Six down, 20 to go; break time." We purchase soft drinks from the vending machine and relax in a classroom, a brief reprieve from the joyless monotony.

As Edgar cleans the next restroom, I stand in the hallway and put my phone's calculator to good use. Edgar and his spouse each clean 26 bathrooms each night, 5 nights a week, 48 weeks a year. In total, they sanitize 12,480 bathrooms annually, for a combined income of $48,000. Edgar scowls after hearing my analysis. This evening, I am learning the arts of high-tech toilet cleaning and resiliency.

After sanitizing all 12 bathrooms in the building, we return to the custodial closet to empty the tank and replenish the machine with chemicals and fresh water. Edgar carefully attaches a hose to the bottom of the tank to drain its contents into a utility sink. The sludge and stench combination is utterly disgusting. I award a C– grade for the machine's aesthetics and an A for effectiveness.

Next up is cleaning the physical facilities building's eight restrooms, which are too small for the machine. We revert to old-school cleaning techniques and retrieve mops, chemicals, and towels from a nearby closet. Cleaning bathrooms the old-fashioned way is hard and hardly glamorous. These quasiprivate facilities are cleaner than the public restrooms in the previous building. Still, at this point, there is no respite in sight.

Edgar talks about his family, especially his two sons and his four grandchildren. Finding time to spend with them is complicated. He and his spouse leave home at 9:30 each evening and work until 6:00 each morning. After returning home, Edgar sleeps, while his spouse takes their son to school. Edgar arises around 2:00 p.m. and prepares supper and then picks up his son from school. He rests from 5:00 p.m. until around 8:30 p.m. before preparing for another evening of work.

Edgar makes explicit the hardships he will encounter if the department changes his work schedule so that he begins work at 4:30 a.m.:

> I have a 16-year-old son. He's old enough to drive, but he still has to complete a driver's education course before he can get a license. The course costs about $400. My wife and me won't have the money until we get our tax return money back early next year. What am I supposed to do when I am working and he needs a ride to school?

"Good question," I murmur under my breath.

As Edgar prepares to meet his spouse and daughter-in-law for a sanctioned 2:00 a.m. lunch break, he describes the best part of his job:

> I can't tell you how good it feels for someone to come up to you and say they appreciate what you do. I appreciate it when people don't look at you or treat you like you are a lowly old janitor. Most of the kids on campus are great. A lot of kids come up to me and tell me that they appreciate the work I do. Dr. Gary in the science building is great. I loved the library staff. Dr. Speck in the business school, he is one of us; he is there for the people.

I intend to return tomorrow night to shadow Edgar during the second half of his shift. Secretly, I hope he allows me to commandeer the machine to fulfill my custodial Ghostbusters fantasy.

Research Sites

This chapter includes background information about the two primary research sites, HU and Compton University (CU). Sweet (2001) argued, "A serious analysis of comparatively trivial social events, such as a hockey tournament or a cockfight, may actually offer more information about a culture than a detailed study of a notable trial, a public election, or even laws passed by governments" (p. 92). I concur. Edgar's ordinary tale of work includes essential demographic information about the research site and research participants, highlights unique aspects of the culture (e.g., contested issues and policies), and raises questions that warrant further investigation.

After concluding this observation, I posed the following questions in my journal: How should HU allocate its increasingly scarce resources? Is addressing service workers' concerns part of the HU mission? Does the not-so-picturesque locale of the Department of Physical Facilities, located on the outskirts of campus, symbolically convey HU's investment in physical plant workers in general and custodians in particular? Is HU a good place to work or the only place to work? Why don't managers seek input from workers before modifying policies? What prompted the union strike and how was it resolved? Is living from paycheck to paycheck unique to Edgar or reflective of most custodians? Why do workers appear agitated and fearful? Are stagnant salaries a campus-wide or custodial departmental issue? Does the low starting salary suggest that recruiting and retaining the best possible custodians is a low priority?

To answer the aforementioned questions, the remainder of this chapter includes demographic information about the two sites and historical interludes that provide contextual information about custodians and their universities.

Harrison University

HU, a public university, resides in a rural midwestern college town east of the Mississippi River. This residential campus, surrounded by corn and soybean fields, is an hour from two major cities. Unique institutional claims to fame include a commitment to undergraduate teaching; one of the highest retention and graduation rates in the country; and high student involvement in both its liberal arts curriculum and comprehensive cocurriculum, such as community service and leadership development. Enrollment hovers around 16,000 students (14,000 undergraduates and 2,000 graduate students). Undergraduate enrollments have increased during the past five years despite the escalating cost of tuition and room and board ($25,000 for in-state undergraduates and $38,000 for out-of-state undergraduates), which is the highest public university tuition and room and board rate in the state.

Two distinct in-house custodial operations coexist at HU. Custodians working for the Department of Physical Facilities (DPF) clean academic and administration buildings, and custodians employed by Auxiliary Services clean residential, recreational, and dining facilities. (The Auxiliary Services custodians did not participate in this study.) The DPF, funded by HU's operating budget, oversees custodial, maintenance, utilities, engineering, trucking, and architectural services for over 200 buildings on the 2,000-acre campus. DPF's custodial staff includes a director, a senior supervisor, 6 shift supervisors, 3 support staff, and 112 employees (108 full-time custodians [96.4%] and 4 part-timers [3.6%]). Of the custodians, 41 are women (36.7%); 71 are men (63.3%). Ninety-nine percent of the custodians are Caucasian.

Two factors that influence these demographics are the starting salaries ($9.60 per hour) and the rural campus locale. Most custodians live within 20 miles of campus (only a few live within the town limits since real estate near campus is exorbitantly inflated). The swath of the county where the campus resides is mostly White. Most non-White residents live in larger municipalities, at least 20 miles from campus. Because there are many low-paying jobs in these cities, recruiting prospective custodians from these areas is a long shot. Because HU promotes staff from within, rarely hiring supervisors and managers from outside the university, the management team is exclusively White. This trend is unlikely to change anytime soon, unless HU dramatically alters its hiring norms.

The state's budget allocation to HU has steadily declined over the past decade, resulting in fewer and less predictable revenue streams. Despite HU's stellar academic reputation and numerous national accolades, it remains trapped in a constant state of economic and fiscal turbulence. Local and statewide fiscal uncertainty as well as targeted campus cost-cutting measures have disproportionally harmed custodians.

In 2013, to avoid another year of deficit spending, DPF combined two shifts of custodial workers into a single daytime shift and blurred the distinctions between building custodians and groundskeepers. Proponents of this new policy argue that combining shifts and workers saved HU over $100,000. The new policy also improves departmental communication and efficiency and allows managers to more easily redistribute staff each day to counter rampant absenteeism.

One custodian summarizes opponents' concerns. "When they [grounds-workers] come inside [for example, to replace absentee custodians] they will do things that we don't want to do. When we go out [to replace absentee groundsworkers], we will do what they don't want to do, like weed pulling and mulching. This can't be good for morale. I was hired to be a custodian, not a groundskeeper." The downsizing of staff over the past several years and constant threats of outsourcing have resulted in an increase in work responsibilities and a decrease in job satisfaction.

Two major incidents that occurred during the past decade profoundly influenced worker-management relations and staff morale. First, consider the incident in 2009 when, for the first time in its history, HU laid off 64 workers in good standing at the university. HU also eliminated an additional 150 jobs through staff attrition and terminated a disproportionate number of custodians. Suddenly, the perception of job security that existed for nearly two centuries evaporated. Job layoffs fueled feelings of betrayal that persist.

The second, and more serious incident, that fundamentally altered custodian-management relations was a 13-day campus-wide strike in 2004. It was HU's first and only strike and involved campus dining, custodial, and maintenance workers. At the time, service workers' salaries were the lowest of all public universities in the state, while HU had the highest tuition of all public universities.

For two weeks, picket lines, rallies, demonstrations, hunger strikes, and even a tent city took center stage on campus. Strikers had no previous experience in matters such as these, did not have access to a strike fund, and had already lost over $200,000 in wages, which virtually ensured that the walkout would be brief and unsuccessful. When the strike ended, the workers accepted the university's 1% wage increase proposal; striking workers could no longer afford to hold out. One retired senior administrator, centrally involved in the strike, provides some historical context:

> For years there has been a feeling that all staff, faculty, union, and nonunion folks were treated the same. So all raises were the same—that was the philosophy of the administrative structure back then. Being in the union did not give you more pull to get more money. Our union membership was always about 25%. We had the policy that you did not have to pay union dues, but they would always represent you because of the contract and by law. A lot of people would say, "Why should I pay, if they are going to represent me anyway?" The union, as a result, did not invest a lot here. Unions, as you know, are their own businesses. . . . They probably said that since not everyone is paying we are not going to allocate significant resources and assign someone on campus. It was always locally run by the people here.

Another retired senior administrator's retrospective sensemaking of the strike affirmed this analysis:

The union is getting very little money from this campus. The nonuniversity union leaders they sent here were not strong. They are rough, hard, scrappy people, but could not get the fervor here. People [custodians] were suspicious of them. That strike hurt the union. It was an example of not getting anything. The big hurt was the layoffs that came later.

A decade later, custodians continue to express strong feelings about this watershed incident. Two women offer their rationales for shunning the union:

Worthless strike. . . . We don't have a strong union. They do not stand up for their employees. If I get myself in trouble, I will get myself out of trouble. I don't need anyone to speak for me. I can speak for myself. If we had a strong union, I would not mind being in it. But they went on strike and ended up getting what the university initially offered them before the strike.—Woman One

I was originally in the union but I got out of it the year we went on strike. Back then it was $22 a month for dues. Now it's $36 a month. Who can afford that? . . . They didn't even pay those people in the union when they went out on strike.—Woman One

The union needs members like HU custodians, and the custodians need advocates like the union. Yet custodians' lack of confidence in their union's ability to represent them and the high monthly dues make reconciliation unlikely. More recently HU custodians report feelings of powerlessness, lacking trust and confidence in both their university and the union. These dynamics breed fear and feelings of fatalism. One administrator explains,

Now, you have a fear factor. Employees have a fear of senior administrators because they don't know them. Most people I talk to say that if you raise concerns, they will blackball them and they will be out of here. Staff believe that administrators keep notes of what they do, how they drive trucks. They think the university wants to get rid of them.

Custodians' most intense criticisms and fears are all about outsourcing, an idea that HU's vice president for business and finance publicly advocates. Custodians are keenly aware that the university recently outsourced its motor pool operation, recycling center, and health center. As one custodian sarcastically notes, "They're getting good at it." Custodians worry that if HU outsources their jobs, they are in trouble. Even if the external cleaning agency retains them as employees of a private company (independent of HU), they would lose several treasured benefits, such as the tuition waiver.

Private companies could also unilaterally reduce work hours, making custodians part-time employees ineligible for health care benefits. Outsourcing would make custodians virtually disposable.

The worldwide economic recession, statewide reductions in educational subsidies, and local efforts to protect faculty have prompted HU to take dramatic action. Custodians argue that these decisions have disproportionatly harmed them. The layoffs in 2009 brought to the surface the realization that custodians neither respect nor trust their university and unions. These incidents remain a constant reminder for custodians that, in the academy, "Anything goes." Life can change suddenly and dramatically.

Compton University

CU, a private, medium-sized institution, resides in a major midwestern metropolis west of the Mississippi River. This residential campus is a posh oasis surrounded by gritty neighborhoods. Annually, 30,000 applicants compete to be one of the 1,600 undergraduates admitted each year. The ratio of applicants to admitted students speaks volumes about CU's elite reputation and student body. Its 12,000 full-time students (6,000 undergraduates) include over 4,000 residents who reside in the 30 residence halls cleaned by the custodians participating in this study. Annually, national associations rank CU as a top-20 undergraduate university. It has been highly successful in securing externally funded grants each year, making it a premiere university for professional and graduate education. The steep $50,000 annual tuition is a sound investment for students, even in a wobbly job market. While the national economy in 2012 traumatized American higher education, CU remains a prosperous and thriving anomaly.

Compton University's custodial services are decentralized and include dozens of discrete campus cleaning units. Some are unionized and others are not. Some hire university employees. Other external cleaning services hire nonuniversity employees. Tuition dollars fund some housekeeping units; auxiliary operations subsidize others.

The Department of Housing (DOH) oversees all custodial services in the residence halls. Over the past two decades it has embraced three management models. Prior to 1995, Compton's DOH contracted with a national agency to clean the residence halls. The cleaning company underbid the contract and failed to provide basic services. A senior CU administrator described the dire cleaning conditions at that time:

> Workers did not show up on Mondays because students made messes on the weekend. Nobody wanted to clean up Monday's mess. There was con-

stant turnover of nameless faces in the community. . . . They [custodians] needed to be respected more.

In 1995 the department shifted from an external cleaning vendor to an in-house cleaning operation. CU supported the change but feared that if the DOH hired a CU custodial staff and the in-house housekeeping experiment failed (necessitating CU to again outsource cleaning services), then CU, the DOH, and its custodians would be adversely affected. To minimize this risk, CU created the Octagon Cleaning Company (OCC), an independent, although affiliated, custodial company. The DOH then hired a CU employee as director to oversee all OCC operations, although custodians were OCC employees. This management model allowed the OCC to customize and easily modify custodial job descriptions, hiring practices, work expectations, benefits, and staff evaluation procedures. A senior administrator notes several risks with this model:

> There were people around the table [who] were worried about unioniza-tion. But they said they were willing to let us run our own housekeeping program, but they did not want them to be university employees. My heart said they should have been, but my head said that not making them CU employees made good business sense. . . . I knew there would be complica-tions, but I didn't know what they would be. I said I would take it on, but I needed to find someone to run it. Then I am going to look at the highest pay scale in the city for that type of work and we are going to surpass that. I wanted a great benefits package.

To remain competitive with other campus housekeeping operations, and to avoid unionization, the OCC regularly monitors and regularly adjusts cus-todians' salaries and benefits. Over the years threats of unionization flared, but the OCC enhanced custodians' salaries and benefit packages, such as free access to campus events and recreation facilities, cheaper cell phone service, and public transportation passes that squelched unionization chatter.

Lance, the director of custodial operations, had extensive background in hotel management, which influenced OCC's commitment to quality customer service. This notion of customer service shapes custodians' job descriptions, responsibilities, and evaluation procedures. Daily, OCC custo-dians follow lockstep procedures for cleaning; supervisors inspect buildings several times each week to ensure that custodians meet expectations.

Hiring and retaining an ethnically diverse staff has been a high prior-ity for the OCC. Since it was an independent entity, it had the freedom to design and implement its diversity initiative with minimal institutional oversight. In 1996 the DOH forged a unique alliance with city agencies that provided job training for immigrants new to the city. Lance explained this collaboration:

> I had worked for a major hotel chain in St. Paul that hired many Chinese, Vietnamese, and African housekeepers. Diversity was an asset. When I came here, diversity was not that intentional. One goal, when I got here, was to hire a diverse staff. Since CU personified diversity, I wanted to do my part. I contacted a local agency that supported families seeking refuge in the United States. This was during the Gulf War. Of my first three hires, one was from Pakistan and two were Iraqis. These people were the neatest staff. About three years later, the Yugoslavian war started, and this was one of the main places where Bosnians came. I hired a few; they were outstanding people and staff. As the department grew, they [Bosnian staff] knew family and friends who wanted to work as housekeepers, so we hired many of them.

Ironically, over a 16-year period, OCC's highly successful diversity initiative yielded a homogeneous staff. Because of OCC's word-of-mouth hiring norms, most Bosnian and Serbian custodians encouraged family members to apply for vacancies. Candidates whose family and friends worked for OCC understood the job expectations and relished the opportunity to work with family. These factors contributed to OCC's unusual homogeneous demographics and unusually high retention rates. For example, of the 72 CU employees, 56 (77.7%) were Bosnian or Serbian refugees. Lance cites data to clarify the benefits of his hiring practices:

> Back in 1997, I had about 30 employees, and eight are still here [26.6%]. Sixty percent have worked here over five years; over half of the 70 current staff have been here 10 years or longer. During my early years, I was averaging far less turnover than CU. Initially I had 15, 20, 22% turnover. It gradually dropped to 15%, 7%, and now 3%. In the hotel business, the turnover rate is about 98%.

Two major incidents during the past decade significantly influenced the department's practices, accomplishments, and challenges.

The first major incident was in 2005 when, CU students staged a three-week sit-in as well as a hunger strike to protest the low wages of service workers, which included custodians. The goal was for these workers to earn a fair wage, which signals respect and acknowledges their value to the university. The protesters' mantra was, "Everyone is more successful when people are paid a living wage."

The negotiated resolution stipulated that CU would allocate nearly a half-million dollars to improve the salaries of service workers. CU also agreed to monitor outside contractors that hired historically low-wage earners. CU did not agree to protesters' demands that the university only do business with unionized workers. The settlement did not result in the university meeting students' demand that all CU staff earn a living wage (between $10 and $12 an hour), but the university's concessions were significant. From the perspective of protesters and university negotiators, the final pact was a reasonable and acceptable alternative to the status quo. Service workers received an immediate 50-cents-an-hour raise and another 50-cents-an-hour raise the following year. Starting salaries for all service workers also increased. Improved morale was a predictable outcome.

The second major incident that dramatically shaped the DOH and its custodians occurred in 2011. A new senior business/finance officer commissioned a study to assess the benefits and liabilities of nonuniversity corporations owned by CU (e.g., OCC). In 2012 the university incorporated the OCC. As a result, all OCC employees became CU employees.

Contrary to national trends that typically initiated actions such as these to save money, CU's decision to dissolve the corporation and hire OCC staff cost more than $400,000, which resulted in a larger personnel budget. The decision was intended to address staff inequities and inconsistent personnel practices. This consolidation transformed the OCC from an independent "ma and pa"–like business to a campus corporate-like department. The DOH had to modify most of its policies to align it with CU's human resources mandates, which were more formal, elaborate, and rigid. Predictably some staff struggled to accept these changes. One supervisor captured the sentiment of staff during this transition period:

> Any time there is something new there is distrust or questioning. To their credit, they have grown and adapted, changed, and evolved. This group has done better with change than I have experienced in other organizations. Some people say they don't like the changes. Maybe we don't either, but that is the way it is. I try to tell them there are also benefits, even to changes that we don't agree with. . . . It depends on how long they are here—older people feel safe that they can voice their concerns. The new employees or if they don't know the manager well will not likely say anything and they will be frustrated. . . . You always have to deal with change, and it has a bad impact on morale and longevity.

As CU employees, custodians had access to a tuition stipend. Custodians who expressed no interest in this substantial education benefit lamented the loss of the OCC benefits package that had lower health care premiums and more flexible vacation and sick leave benefits. The influence of the worldwide recession was far less traumatic for the CU community than the sit-in was.

TABLE 2.1
Compton University and Harrison University Institutional and Custodial Profiles

Institution Characteristics	Compton University	Harrison University
Type of institution	Private	Public
Campus locale	Major city	Rural college town
Enrollment	12,000 students (6,000 undergrads)	16,000 students (14,000 undergrads)
Tuition	$50,000 for undergraduates	$25,000 for in-state and $38,000 for out-of-state
Operations	University managed/ funded through auxiliary operations	University managed/ funded through university's operating budget
Custodian Staffing Profiles		
Custodians	73 (22 men/51 women)	112 (71 men/41 women)
Administrators	2 (2 men)	2 (2 men)
Supervisors	7 (1 man/6 women)	7 (5 men/2 women)

Both incidents shaped the department's ethos and its custodians' attitudes and behaviors. The corporate creep, which has been under way since 2012, coupled with institutional reorganizations has many custodians worried about the security of their job.

Table 2.1 summarizes the institutional and custodial staffing profiles for CU and HU.

Historical and Political Insights

During a national fiscal crisis in the 1970s, government funding of higher education began to decline, so universities forged relationships with private corporations and foundations to offset shortfalls. Colleges and universities have solicited corporate funding throughout the history of American higher education, but in the wake of the 1970s' crises, efforts to turn directly to private, corporate sources for funds intensified (Rosow & Kriger, 2010). A similar trend reemerged in 2008.

When the economic tsunami washed over them in 2008, almost every institution of higher learning, from the Ivy League to the community colleges, feared that it was in trouble. States cut back their funding, while endowments plummeted. Though each school handled the loss of income in its own way, their early responses indicate that the current crisis will only intensify many of the deleterious trends. . . . Administrations usually acted unilaterally, sometimes by implementing long-sought strategic plans without consulting their faculties. Most strove, it is true, to avoid laying off tenured and tenure-track faculty members and instead resorted to hiring freezes, tuition increases, pay cuts, and reductions in everything from pension contributions to trash collection. (Schrecker, 2010, p. 225)

Policy changes aimed at responding to the lethargic worldwide economy affected almost every higher education institution. In 2015 entrepreneurialism continues to be tightly woven into the fabric of American higher education. "Behind ivied walls and on leafy quadrangles, administrators and professors acknowledge this new reality. Higher education is changing profoundly, retreating from ideals of liberal arts and the leading-edge research it always has cherished. Instead, it is behaving more like the $250 billion business it has become" (Hammonds, Jackson, DeGeorge, & Morris, 1997, p. 96). Businesslike concerns continue to dominate the academy. Huber (2000b) affirmed this assertion:

Heavily influenced by the attention from the corporate world and increasingly cut off from public sector funding, the university is running itself like a corporation, seeking profits through formal and informal close relationships with other corporations. (p. 107)

HU and CU both represent a new and different kind of academic institution emerging in the late twentieth century, heavily influenced by entrepreneurialism. As American universities grappled with shrinking public support, declining state and federal funding, uncertain federal research grants, and institutional retrenchment (Zusman, 1999), a popular "solution" was to transform universities from nonprofit corporations guided by scholars and students into corporations tightly managed by a small and elite cadre of administrators whose primary responsibilities were to generate revenues and cut costs. This new kind of university assumes characteristics of profit-making organizations, manifested in capitalist ideals such as entrepreneurialism.

HU is much further along than CU regarding implementation of corporate practices to cope with the changing times. The transition from the more relaxed and fluid OCC practices to CU policy and procedures has been met with cautious uncertainty. CU's status as a private university makes it easier to form and dissolve the OCC, bargain with custodians, and resolve campus unrest. HU, a public university, has far more state-imposed constraints.

HU funds and closely monitors the DPF, limiting and slowing down problem-solving strategies. CU's first-rate academic reputation guarantees that it will meet its enrollment targets each year, ensuring that students will fill the residence halls, making these revenues generated by an auxiliary operation available to enhance housekeeping services. HU has fewer and less predictable revenue streams, which makes funding existing and new services unlikely.

CU's decentralized custodial operations led to a multitude of custodial organizational structures. Competition among units necessitated that each unit adjust employee salaries and benefit packages to remain an appealing place to work. If other campus custodial units offer more attractive packages, custodians will likely apply for work in that unit. HU's two custodial services (both managed by the vice president of business and finance) are a monopoly. The lack of competition, inexperienced custodians acting as their own advocates, and a hobbled union left them very little leverage when negotiating with the university.

Campus locales influence institutions' capacity to hire and maintain diverse staffs. CU, in the heart of a major city of over three million residents, had a far greater probability of hiring a qualified and diverse staff than HU, because of the latter's rural setting. As these brief comparative analyses reveal, history and context matter if one is to understand the contemporary experiences of campus custodians and the universities that employ them.

Insights Unseen

CU and HU are in transition. CU's senior administrators' concept of transformation is different from that of HU's senior administrators. Likewise, CU and HU custodians' views about transformation differ from those of their respective institutions. These differences lead to different answers to the questions posed at the start of this chapter, such as: How should HU allocate increasingly scarce resources? Is addressing service workers' concerns part of HU's mission?

Downsizing, subcontracting, and *outsourcing*—terms more commonly associated with American corporations—have made their way into campus administrative planning, which calls into question the nature and social function of higher education. Times are changing, and they must. How universities manage change has dire consequences for the academy and its diverse stakeholders, as Nelson (1997) noted:

> As universities struggle with increasingly constrained budgets, the temptation to make ends meet by exploiting more vulnerable employees grows daily. Industry meanwhile provides a handbook of relevant strategies and

techniques: make paying workers as little as possible a basic managerial principle and goal; deny employee benefits anytime you can get away with it; disguise your responsibility for the most abused workers by subcontracting for their services; during contract negotiations offer nothing until frustration peaks, then make generous salary and job security offers to long-term employees on condition they agree to decrease their numbers through attrition; establish multiple tiers for compensation, hiring all new employees on substantially lower salaries; break existing unions and fight recognition for new ones. (pp. 3–4)

The remainder of this book examines how HU and CU manage change and the perils that inevitably accompany it.

3

COMING CLEAN

Ethnographic Origins and Milieus

Life experiences influence our identity and how we act. Weis and Fine (2000) summarized findings from a research study about crime that they conducted in Buffalo, New York and Jersey City, New Jersey. One question they posed to research participants was, "If the President were to come to your city to hold a town meeting, what problems would you want him to pay attention to?" (p. 3). "Crime" was the near universal response. An in-depth analysis of data refuted respondents' seemingly homogeneous view that nearly all city residents feared violent crime. Depending on their race, gender, and class, participants differed about which crimes were the most serious, as well as who perpetrated the most serious crimes. African American men expressed concern about state-initiated violence (e.g., police harassment and entrapment). Conversely, White men highlighted escalating street violence, mostly perpetrated by men of color. Domestic or home-based violence concerned African American women more than street violence or state-initiated violence. White men trusted police and viewed them as protectors from and responders to crimes. In contrast, people of color, as well as some White women, distrusted police. These enclaves viewed police as perpetrators of crime and corruption. Modifying a popular idiom best captures the essence of these revised findings: *Crime and criminals are in the eye of the beholder.* Past experiences influence one's contemporary beliefs. Understanding researchers' life stories is essential to understanding how they make meaning of their findings. This is true of me.

In this chapter I recount stories—a potent way of *coming to know*—that reveal how life experiences influenced and still influence my interest in this topic as well as my interpretations. Stories challenge ways of knowing by connecting events, actors, storytellers, and readers to each other. Narratives guide behaviors and frame not only how people make sense of the past but also how they see themselves in the future. Storytelling fosters learning by acting as a springboard for action (Witherell & Noddings, 1991). I strive to recount memorable and meaningful tales, not an antiseptic and bloodless report about custodians and me. I strive to depict complex phenomena in authentic ways, while remaining self-analytical, political, aware, and honest. Harrison (2002) revealed some of the perils associated with storytelling:

> Most curriculum designers, researchers, and theorists are slow to embrace the use of storytelling because it tends to break the mold of traditional thinking. It is somewhat different—possibly even suspect. The subjectivity in narrative causes both a sense of freedom and uneasiness—freedom in that some of the rules are relaxed and the writer has some license but uneasiness because of believability (credibility of source, text, and events). (p. 73)

Stories, as Ganz (2009) noted, "are what enable us to communicate values to one another" (para. 7). In the remainder of this book I tell my stories of listening, interpreting, and retelling custodians' stories. "We are storytellers. Perhaps more than anything else, it's what makes us human" (Glauberman, 2013, para. 1).

I favor stories for four reasons. First, the stories are interesting, educationally potent, and seldom told. Second, stories refute one-dimensional conceptualizations about custodians by contesting common, stereotypical janitorial characteristics, such as being undereducated and disinterested in current events. Third, stories provide glimpses of what higher education looks like from the vantage point of this invisible campus subculture. Finally, stories reveal insights about issues that need to be reformed and transformed. While telling stories, I scrutinize, not simply report. I resist presenting one-size-fits-all findings that are nothing more than common sense on stilts (e.g., custodians are underpaid and underappreciated). Narratives influence behaviors and shape how we see ourselves now and in the future (McAdams, 2006). In this chapter I focus on life stories that influence how I interpreted my fieldwork and my proposals for change.

Storytelling as a mode of "re-presentation" (a) challenges ways of knowing; (b) connects the events, actors, storyteller, and readers to each other; (c) teaches and fosters learning, and (d) acts as a springboard for action (Witherell & Noddings, 1991). These narratives describe custodians' experiences and include my own reflections and interpretations.

The Subjective "I" and "Eye"

My research is neither neutral nor objective. Value-free research is a myth and an impossibility. Thus, it is essential for readers to know who I am, what I believe, and how I act. Being attentive to and explicit about one's life experiences and the "subjective I" (one's subjective thoughts and feelings) is crucial in qualitative research in general and ethnographic research in particular. Madden (2010) noted,

> There is a need to account for the inevitability of the ethnographer's influence on the research process and to manage the tension between objectivity and subjectivity in order to produce better portraits of the human condition. Dealing rigorously with reflexivity is an important aspect of contemporary ethnography. In this vein it is appropriate to say something about the person who brings you this encounter with ethnography. (p. 2)

This desire aligns with that of Banda (2014), who wrote,

> Glesne and Peshkin (1992) argued that researchers must make known who they are in the context of the study under investigation and make explicit the "subjective I." This includes the experiential and interpretive stance within which researchers situate their studies (Jones, 2002).
>
> Being explicit about life experiences and subjectivities as a researcher is crucial in qualitative research. My life experiences reveal, among other things, the epistemological premises (Saldana, 2011) that influence every phase of my research. According to Saldana (2011), an *epistemology* is broadly defined as "a theory of knowledge construction based on the researcher's worldview—how his or her lens on the world and ways of knowing it focus and filter the perception and interpretation of it" (p. 82). My values, attitude, and beliefs about the topic under exploration (Saldana, 2011) are the basis of epistemological premises. Essentially, revealing my identity, background, experiences, and values allows readers to weigh my role in the conduct of the study, as well as the understandings gained from engaging with participants, data and setting (Fossey, Harvey, McDermott, & Davidson, 2002). (p. 17)

Four short tales reveal how my life experiences, work contexts, identity, and values inform and influence the subjective eye through which I view campus custodians (Saldana, 2011). I heed S. R. Jones's (2002) advice that urges researchers to "make known who they are in the context of the study under investigation. . . . This includes the experiential and interpretive stance from which all phases of the research are approached and conducted" (p. 463). As hooks (1994) noted, "Without our voices in written work and in oral presentations there will be no articulation of our concerns" (p. 105).

Dirty Albert

In 1960 my parents, brother, sister, and I moved from the Bronx, New York, to Wildwood, New Jersey. My father had finished pharmacy school and opened Magolda's Pharmacy. We lived two blocks from the Atlantic Ocean in a two-bedroom bungalow. My grandfather lived a few blocks away. Since he was retired and an able handyman, he built a playhouse in our backyard. I spent my youth in and around this structure.

A favorite pastime was peeking out a side window hoping to catch a glimpse of our mysterious next-door neighbor, "Dirty Albert," who lived in a shacklike structure a few hundred yards behind our neighbor's street-side home. Albert wore tattered clothes; he had a straggly beard and unkempt hair. Rumor had it that he seldom bathed, because his house had no indoor plumbing.

Dirty Albert was my childhood Boo Radley. In *To Kill a Mockingbird* (Lee, 1960), Arthur (Boo) Radley was a neighbor of Atticus Finch and his two children. Radley, according to rumors, was a shadowy, unapproachable, and scary loner. My father, possessing at least one of Atticus Finch's qualities, respected Albert. He was the only person I knew who refused to call him "Dirty Albert." Unfortunately, I was too young to appreciate and emulate my father's wisdom and respect.

Like Atticus's children, Jem and Scout, I became preoccupied—almost obsessed—with Dirty Albert. I would spend days looking out the playhouse window hoping to catch a glimpse of him. I learned from neighbors' gossip that Dirty Albert was an unmarried, retired Scandinavian sailor who would be gone for weeks at a time. I wanted to meet him, yet I feared the encounter. One day I intentionally threw a baseball onto his porch to get a closer look. Another day, I stole a fork and knife from our kitchen. With the utensils in hand, I ran from our backyard to Albert's house, placing the gifts on the porch and then running as fast as I could back to the safety of the playhouse. My reflections on this incident led me to conclude that Albert captured my attention because he was different. My fascination with *difference* (the Other) still persists.

Like Jem and Scout, I eventually had a face-to-face encounter with Albert. I unexpectedly passed him on the street one day. To my surprise he said, "Hello, Peter," and smiled. I momentarily froze. I had no idea he knew my name. I said, "Hello, Mr. Albert." From that moment I no longer feared him and wanted to be Albert's friend. Unlike Boo, Albert did not save my life, yet he provided an opportunity for me to interact with and learn from the Other and (years later) recognize my privilege.

Daisy

The great flood of 1962 temporarily washed away Wildwood, New Jersey, and my parents' dreams of the good life. I remember waking up with my brother one morning and noticing that the Atlantic Ocean was in our living room. We immediately woke up our parents, who were unaware that a hurricane-like storm had engulfed us (life without cable television and the Internet surely complicated crises at that time). We stood in ankle-deep water in our living room and watched trash cans, cars, and trees float down the street.

A few hours later my grandfather arrived in a small motorboat and transported us to safety. We took up temporary residence in a nearby relative's home for a few days, before moving to the grammar school gymnasium for refuge until we could return home. As a six-year-old, living in a school gymnasium, spending 24 hours a day with my playmates, and sleeping on cots was living the good life. Unbeknownst to me, the flood had wiped out my father's pharmacy. My father's uncle loaned him money to pay storm-related debts. The storm forced us to move to a suburb of Philadelphia to live with my mother's parents.

Eighteen months later, we moved to Stratford, New Jersey. My mother's parents helped us purchase a house. My father worked six days a week as a pharmacy manager for a grocery chain. My mother taught at the local school. Sunday was the only day of the week my family was together, so we attended church and family gatherings.

Each June, the day after the school year ended, my mother, sister, brother, and I packed up the family station wagon and headed to Wildwood. We lived in our old home, which was only habitable during the summer because of the lack of heating. My mother managed a business during the week, and my father visited every Sunday. Each Labor Day, we would repack the station wagon and return to Stratford, so that my mother could resume her teaching responsibilities and we would resume our schooling.

My parents' intense year-round work routines aimed at supporting our family worried my grandmother and aunt. Both lived in suburbs outside of Philadelphia, and they were the only people I knew who were "rich." After months of my grandmother pestering my mother to slow down and seek help from others, my mother hired Daisy, an African American domestic who also cleaned my grandparents' home. Daisy was the first African American with whom I had ever spoken face-to-face.

Daisy lived in Philadelphia. Twice a month she took several trains and buses to arrive at our New Jersey home. My mother's Friday night ritual was as predictable as Daisy's Saturday morning travels. To prepare for Daisy's visit, my mother would hurry home after school and start at one corner of the house and clean each room from floor to ceiling. My mother worried about what other people thought about her family. In this instance, cleaning the house before Daisy arrived increased the probability that Daisy would perceive us as a clean family. In retrospect, these actions also increased the probability that Daisy recognized at least one of my family's many dysfunctions.

Each Saturday afternoon after Daisy finished cleaning, my father drove Daisy to the town's main highway so that she could catch a bus to Philadelphia. Unfortunately, one Saturday, Daisy missed her bus, so my father ended up driving Miss Daisy home. I accompanied him on the trip. My family had an automobile ritual to ensure our safety as we traveled the mean streets of Philly. Once we exited from expressway ramps to the dangerous neighborhood streets, we would lock our car doors. In the days before cars automatically locked, my mother, father, brother, and I (my sister sat in the backseat between my brother and me) locked each of the four doors of our station wagon in sequence. Hearing the *click, click, click,* and *click* assured us that we were safe and secure. On this late Saturday afternoon, as we exited the Schuylkill Expressway ramp, I immediately locked my door and looked to my father and Daisy to follow my lead. They didn't. Daisy and my father gave me one of those "What's wrong with you, child?" looks. Shortly thereafter, we arrived in Daisy's neighborhood.

To say Daisy's row house was in total decay would be an understatement. At age eight, I did not understand hardship, but I witnessed it that afternoon. Those days I had many hazy questions that drove me crazy, like, "Why would my mother clean our home and then pay someone to clean it the very next day?" and "How could Daisy, who cleaned houses for a living, live in such a dirty old house?" My curiosities about the Other and perceived injustices persisted.

Victor

In high school I worked in a nearby apartment complex; essentially I was a janitor. My supervisor, Victor, was a Vietnam veteran. Victor used his military benefits to learn the heating and air-conditioning trade. He was a thorn in the side of management, but his trade skills made him indispensable, especially working in a complex with aging and low-quality heating and air-conditioning units. Victor knew he was indispensable, and he made sure that management knew it as well. In my world, I wanted to challenge my teachers' authority but never mustered the courage to do so. I secretly admired Victor's confrontations with and indifference to those in power.

I remember sitting in the shop listening to the crew gossip about residents. It was the first time I encountered divorced older men who boasted about their sexual conquests. It was the first time I had met a veteran who enjoyed killing as well as condemning the war. It was also the first time I regularly interacted with elders who trash-talked college and college graduates. I was in a different, intriguing world.

My coworkers berated and ridiculed the college-educated district manager as well as college-educated residents (who didn't know how to perform tasks like resetting a tripped circuit breaker). I had little in common with my coworkers, but they fascinated me. When they harassed me, I seldom worried, because Victor was my guardian angel.

Although I never explicitly talked with Victor about my future, I suspect he assumed I would finish high school and work full-time at the apartment complex. My coworkers' disdain for college—a post–high school option I was considering—probably contributed to my reluctance to discuss my career possibilities. Coming of age in New Jersey at age 16 and working as a custodian seemed like the good life. I would have a free apartment and utilities, drive a company truck, roll out of bed at 7:30 a.m. and clock in at 8:00 a.m., save enough money to buy a car, and learn a trade from Victor (so that I could rebuke management if necessary). College, too, seemed like a path to the good life. Either option was acceptable during these ambivalent times.

One summer weekend before my senior year of high school, my father and I planned a day trip to a nearby university, which meant I would miss work. I tried to be evasive about the reasons for my absence, but I felt compelled to tell Victor. Upon hearing the news, he responded, "Soooooo, you wanna be a college boy?" Publicly he mocked me. Privately he encouraged me to pursue this option. I chose college and felt like a traitor. No matter how many times I look back and try to make sense of that decision, my rationale for attending college remains a mystery. Becoming a card-carrying member of either the educated or working-class caste made me uneasy—a feeling that remains with me nearly 40 years later. Fitting into socially constructed categories continues to make me uneasy.

Tony

In 1988 the Miami University Freshman Reading Program (as it was called back then) invited all new students to read a book the summer before they matriculated to college. After convocation, which took place the day before the first day of classes, faculty would meet with small groups of students to discuss the book, modeling a seminar discussion and subtly socializing new students to what faculty termed the *life of the mind*. My role as assistant dean of students was to ensure that the residence hall staff persuaded residents to attend the convocation and the seminar. As an insider I knew that an insufficient number of faculty had signed up to facilitate the discussions on the selected book: Robert Pirsig's (1974) *Zen and the Art of Motorcycle Maintenance*.

During the summer of 1986 I encountered Tony, a custodian who worked on campus, and we discussed Pirsig's book. Tony had a long ponytail and a "Who gives a shit?" attitude. Most importantly, his incredible grasp of the book impressed me. Our brief discussion prompted me to completely rethink the small-group discussion agenda that I had been contemplating for weeks. Recognizing his passion and understanding of the text coupled with the need for more facilitators, I asked if he would consider cofacilitating my seminar. He countered, "If you could get me out of my shit job for a few hours, I'd do it."

The following Monday I discussed the possibility with my department chair. She advised me to consult with Tony's supervisor, which I did. I liked the idea of a custodian coleading an academic discussion; I thought the scene would both disorient and educate new students, which is a great way to begin a college career. Tony's supervisor denied my request. His rationale had something to do with opening up Pandora's box. Whatever. Tony seemed unfazed and mildly amused by the outcome. Doing things differently and enacting Miami University's espoused values, such as diversity, community, and egalitarianism, was easier said than done.

Lessons Learned

Moffatt (1989) reminded qualitative researchers that too much reflexivity makes for wearisome reading. Heeding this warning, I have recounted four stories that taught me invaluable lessons about life. From Albert I learned that I gravitate toward the Other, and that by interacting with those who are different I could overcome fear and learn respect. My interactions with Daisy reminded me of my privilege, and that before I critique the Other, it might be prudent to critique one's self (and in this instance, one's family). Victor taught me that I could learn from people with whom I ideologically disagree and that education is not confined to the classroom. I learned the art of resistance and that wisdom exists in unusual places. Tony reminded me that a caste system persists in higher education, no matter how often members of the academy try to suggest otherwise. These life encounters challenged what I had been socialized to believe was "normal" as it related to housing, family, careers, and teaching and learning. My remembrance of things past is not necessarily the remembrance of things as they were; memory of these encounters is not as lucid as it appears in print, yet the memories influence the research interests, fieldwork, interpretations, and convictions contained in this book.

PART TWO

THE CUSTODIAL LIFE
Family and Fear

4

PATHWAYS TO A
CLEANER['S] LIFE

Career Immobility

In the Compton University (CU) housekeeping break room, a middle-aged African American man sits alone at a table. Because we are the only two people present, I introduce myself and explain my research study. His response is predictable: a forced smile and a polite "Hmmm." Harold is a job candidate for the night-shift custodial vacancy. He fiddles with his crumpled sport jacket, which hangs awkwardly on his body, as he confesses to being unemployed for nine months. Harold is polite and guarded. I surmise he wants to avoid saying something that will jeopardize his candidacy, unaware I have no influence on the hiring process.

To calm Harold's nerves, I convey harmless background information about the interview. When I casually mention that six women supervisors will conduct his interview, Harold looks straight at me with bugged-out eyes and whispers, "Oh, Jesus!" Neither of us knows what to say so we silently gawk at each other. Moments later, a supervisor appears and escorts Harold to the interview. I wish him well and then murmur to myself, "Oh, Jesus."

Custodial candidates like Harold want to work and recognize that hundreds of other individuals also covet these low-paying jobs. Applying for a job online is especially intimidating for not-so-tech-savvy candidates. They must submit extensive life histories and undergo extensive background checks as part of the application process. And candidates wait, sometimes months, for a reply. During interviews, finalists must confess past sins, explain their unemployed status, and then convince decision makers of their competence and excitement about cleaning up after others. During an impromptu conversation, a supervisor participating in Harold's interview

41

provides insights into proverbial land mines that candidates must avoid during a job interview:

> When hiring people, I need to know they can do it. It is a challenge to work at night alone. I want someone who wants and likes the position. I want someone who wants to do this for a couple of years. . . . You have some people who think they are going to find gold and jewels, and instead they find nasty stuff when you follow after people. We try to mention so many times that each shift is 12.5 hours. They work nights, weekends, and holidays. . . . Some people are overqualified. Some come from medical fields, like nursing. I ask them, "Why do you want to do this?" Usually they are struggling in life and need something now. When they get a chance to leave, they do.

Candidates must convey that they are eager to work, but not desperate; eager about cleaning, but not too enthusiastic; qualified, but not overqualified; and independent, yet highly receptive to supervision. Candidates recognize that the "technical skills that janitors need to master are few and simple. Much of their work requires no particular mechanical knowledge, while mastery of the remainder of their work requires only a few weeks training on the job" (Gold, 1964, p. 3). Candidates know that there are many qualified individuals, and the odds of getting (what universities deem as) an "unskilled job" (that supposedly anyone can do) are against them. Getting a job is anything but easy.

"I have neither interviewed nor heard of a janitor who as much as suggested that he had ever aspired to be a janitor. Without exception, all janitors interviewed were either 'forced' into the occupation by the necessity of earning a living, or 'somebody talked them into it'" (Gold, 1964, p. 39). Nearly 50 years after this sociological research study about janitors, every participant in this campus custodian study affirmed Gold's claim. Participants never aspired to be custodians; life circumstances dictated it.

In this chapter I report on research participants' responses to two questions I devised and posed while working with them: "What life experiences influenced your decision to become a custodian?" and "What factors influenced your decision to work on a college campus?" To answer these questions, I present stories about two Harrison University (HU) and two CU custodians' pathways to a cleaner's life.

Upward Mobility

For many research participants, the pathway to custodial work was uneventful and predictable. They needed a job, possessed the requisite qualifications, did not mind cleaning up after others, and concluded that they could earn a sufficient salary to provide for their families. They applied to become campus custodians, and universities hired them. Getting a job represented upward mobility. Monroe and Chip traveled this pathway.

Maid My Own Way

Monroe, a 50-something African American woman, graduated from high school and wanted to enlist in the military. During her physical she learned that she was pregnant, which disqualified her from military service. She needed a job and accepted an offer to clean hotel rooms.

> I started here [CU] in 1997 but I've been housekeeping for 24 years. I liked doing it as a kid. That's all my mom had us doing was cleaning—spring cleaning and summer cleaning. And I enjoy doing it. When I applied for my first job in 1988, my oldest son was four months old. I started to do a quiz and found out that I liked working with people. So I started cleaning at a hotel, and I met a lot of different people. They're from different places and stuff. When I started I was making $3.10 an hour. . . . I worked there for two years. Once I left, I went to a bigger hotel and earned more money.

As we stroll down a long residence hall corridor during a tour of her work domain, Monroe acknowledges almost everyone with whom she makes eye contact—"Afternoon. . . . Mornin'. . . . Hi." She augments these verbal greetings with nonverbal gestures such as a nod of her head or a flick of her finger. Almost every recipient responds to her greeting and warm smile. Monroe is both a residence hall custodian and an ambassador for the Department of Housing. Between greetings, she spot cleans as we stroll through residence halls. She picks up trash that almost made it into hallway wastebaskets; she polishes community kitchen stovetops while explaining how to "detail a kitchen." She even straightens flyers haphazardly posted on bulletin boards. Monroe shares with me the best parts of her job:

> I enjoy coming to work every single day. I have my days, you know, when I have issues and such. I get over it. I might have disagreements with managers, but I get over it. We know this is a workplace and we have to communicate. I get along with all the housekeepers. I was never suspended on my job. I was never written up for discipline. I never lost my job. I do a good job. The kids are the single thing that keeps me coming back. Being a mother, I love kids! I want somebody someday in my shoes, looking out for my kids. Overall everything's fine.

Monroe, a single "mama" of three, arrived at CU in 1997 after working at several local hotels. While on the job, she immediately forged strong bonds with residents and found her calling. She explains, "They need a mother away from home. And I felt like I was that mother figure." Monroe's family upbringing and the importance that she places on family influence how she approaches work.

> I was born and raised around here. In my family there were 12 of us; now there are 10. My sister passed and my brother was killed. I have a brother and sister who live in California. Eight of us live here. I lost my dad in 2008. He and my mom were together for 43 years. When he passed, it took a big chunk out of our lives. He was a good man. He was not only a father to us; he was a father to people who didn't have fathers. He had an open door to any and everybody, even people on the streets who were selling drugs and things. If he thought he could help, then he would. If they were selling little things he would buy them, even though he didn't need them. He wanted to support them so they wouldn't rob or steal. That was the kind of person he was. My parents instilled those [values] in us, and that's how we are. A lot of people take kindness for weakness. We never said "no" to no one.

Around noon, we suspend the tour. In the break room Monroe retrieves her "dinner leftovers" stored in a community refrigerator as I munch on a wrap I purchased from a nearby dining hall. As Monroe unpacks her food containers, she wipes the tabletop as she explains her commitment to work:

> As a single parent working, I just had to do it. There was nobody there to help me. I knew what was important. I just organize myself. . . . Before my father passed, he helped out a lot. I never had to worry about a babysitter; my dad did it. When my dad passed, it was hard, but it was good that my kids weren't itty-bitty babies anymore. I was never going to get them to the bus stop, because I had to be at work before then. My son got an evening job, which helped me out a lot. My dad was a construction worker; when it rained and snowed and he couldn't work, he helped out a lot. But the majority [of] the time it was on me, Mama. I made a way. My kids appreciate me for that. They never went without. They knew Mama got up and went to work every day, and they appreciated that. They didn't know what Mama was paid, but they knew they would get what they needed.

Seventeen years later after arriving at CU, Monroe continues to make her way, providing CU residents what they need, while getting what she needs.

Janitor in a [Conun]Drum

I struggle to make myself comfortable in this tiny utility closet that Chip has converted into his man cave/office. The mostly 1970s-ish desks, chairs, and file cabinets (that I suspect he salvaged from the building during previous renovations) along with a mini refrigerator and microwave fill the compact space. The proximity of cleaning chemicals to snacks on the nearby table does not appear bothersome to Chip. I intentionally ask him an open-ended question to begin our interview: "What is it like to be a custodian?" My goal is to allow him maximum degrees of freedom to talk about what matters most. Chip complies with gusto:

> One Sunday evening, we were sitting down at the house. It was the start of summer. Dad said, "What are you doing this summer?" I said, "I plan to lay around and watch television." He told me that I started my job Monday morning. My dad and his friends worked at the school. I said, "I don't want no job," and he said, "You start Monday morning." And I did. I worked at Winterville [High School] for six years while I was in junior and senior high.

Chip began with this 1970s story to explain how he got a job as a custodian at HU. After working six years as a part-time janitor while attending junior and senior high school, he desired full-time work. Since there were few employment opportunities and his only work experience was as a janitor, Chip applied to be a full-time custodian at HU. In 1977 the hiring process was simple. Chip explains, "I lived about 10 miles from the university. I got a ride, applied, and went back home. Forty-five minutes later I got a call and they said, 'You start on Monday.' It took me 45 minutes to get a job." According to Chip, this $2.78-an-hour job was his best and only option.

"Turbulent" best describes Chip's first three years as an HU custodian. Chip's ever-worsening alcohol and other drug dependencies created drama. By 1981 Chip divorced his wife and quit his job. Chip enlisted in the military to "straighten out" and start anew. He expected the military to provide him structure and discipline to address his substance abuse problems. While in the military these problems persisted.

> I got into a lot of alcohol and drug problems. I wanted to get away from drugs and alcohol, so I joined the army, not realizing that there was still a lot of drugs and alcohol in the military and [they were] cheaper. It was a bad time back then.

In 1983 Chip returned home without a job, but with a goal of redemption. Trying to "right some wrongs of the past," Chip retook the civil service test and reapplied for a custodial job at HU. He was 26th on the list; six months later, HU rehired him. The university's decentralized and primitive personnel record keeping at that time worked to Chip's advantage.

I came back to HU, since there were no other options. From 1977 to 1980, I admit, I was a lousy custodian. They told me this. They did not want me back. When I got out of the army I started church. I quit drinking alcohol and met my second wife. We have been married 20 years. I did the civil service test and then got hired back on at Harrison. I worked for six months before they realized that I was the Chip who was the bad custodian. I guess I ruffled a few feathers when they found out.

They called me in and wanted to know what happened to me. I said, "I got off the alcohol; I got off the drugs. Now I have a family to support. I can't be the Chip of years ago." They told me back then I was a sorry worker. I said, "I agree." I told them they had to let me keep working. I wanted to prove to them I had changed. My boss was confused. He said he heard I was a drinker and a drugger. I said, "I was!" I told him, "I started church. I got a family to support. I have to man up. The Bible says, 'A man has to work or man does not eat'. . . I have to take care of my family."

In 2013, more than 30 years after HU rehired Chip, he remains a custodian—drug-free and taking care of his family—working each day to continue to tidy his messy life.

* * *

Shipler (2005), when writing about the working poor, identified life circumstances that influenced some unemployed individuals to consider jobs like custodians. "They [the working poor] entered it [the job market] burdened by their personal histories of repeated failure: failure to finish school, failure to resist drugs, failure to maintain loving relationships, failure to hold jobs" (p. 122). Monroe and Chip both entered the job market with some heavy burdens and self-inflicted wounds. Chip's drug and alcohol addictions contributed to his troubles during his first full-time job, his unceremonious stint in the military, and his divorce. Monroe's teenage pregnancy squashed her aspiration of enlisting in the military and complicated efforts to find employment that would allow her to manage work and home responsibilities. Despite limited job skills and employment options, Chip and Monroe, like many custodians, "did what they had to do," which provided them jobs, economic stability, and satisfaction with life.

Downward Mobility

For some research participants the pathway to custodial work was unexpected and disappointing. Circumstances outside of their control resulted in the loss of their jobs. They reluctantly applied to become campus custodians, and universities hired them. These jobs represented downward mobility. Kathyleen and Anna traveled this pathway.

Maid of Honor

Finding campus parking on this windy autumn evening is a breeze. I exit my car and enter a dilapidated campus recreation building on the HU campus. Knowing it is Kathyleen's break, I pause outside the custodians' break room and peek inside to make certain I don't interrupt her daily ritual of a dinner phone conversation with her spouse. Kathyleen, a 56-year-old woman seated at the table, looks up and invites me in.

Health updates trump work chatter. Kathyleen's recent consultation with a cancer specialist dominates our conversation. She begins, "That darn spot on my lung. I wish they would have caught it earlier." She appears both worried and determined. "I've come so far. I'm going to fight this." In 2012 Kathyleen had part of her lung removed. She was off work for eight weeks but is now working full-time and balancing work, health, and family demands. She recites upcoming health appointments, which will require her to miss work. Fortunately, the Department of Physical Facilities and her direct supervisor have been highly supportive throughout this health crisis.

> I go for a PET scan tomorrow and see my radiologist on the 30th. . . . In December before Christmas I went in and had a CT scan done. I saw my surgeon and oncologist. . . . The PET scan is the one that tells the story— the one I do tomorrow. That will tell if the radiation does what it is supposed to do. I am nervous and not. My radiologist told me—he said, "The key is to keep that positive attitude." He shared a story about his uncle, who was a judge. He found out he had cancer and went through the treatment and everything. He worried himself sick—"Was the cancer coming back?" or "Am I going to get it again?" He started to drink heavily and it killed him. You can be worried and concerned to an extent, but you can't let it control your life. We have no guarantees in life. We can walk out of here and that could be it. . . . We'll see how it goes.

Kathyleen's mix of optimism, realism, and stamina is noteworthy. A few days earlier I worked a four-hour shift with Kathyleen and deemed the experience exhausting. The thought of managing her intense daily responsibilities—an eight-hour work shift, chemotherapy, cancer consults, and family responsibilities, and still allocating time to rest—is overwhelming. Glancing at the clock we both know that the end of the 30-minute dinner break is approaching. We rise and walk across the hallway to the custodial closet. Inside, Kathyleen clips a mop head to a handle and hands it to me as she explains the Rube Goldberg–like contraption that dispenses the appropriate amount of soap and water into a bucket. As it fills, Kathyleen provides some background information about her brief custodial career:

> I started here about two years ago, July 2010. I was a substitute for a lady on maternity leave. I worked days, coming in at 4:30 and clocking out at 1:00 a.m. In September a couple people quit. A supervisor approached me about the possibility of coming to work full-time. I told her I would get back with her the next morning. I wanted to talk to Jack [Kathyleen's spouse] about it. I called the next morning to let them know I would.

Kathyleen pushes our buckets into the hallway and then retrieves six "Caution, Wet Floors" signs. She gives three to me and keeps three. We walk down the long and wide corridor, strategically situating signs at intersections and entryways to warn visitors of potential hazards. Kathyleen shows me how to effectively and efficiently wring out a mop and reminds me to not leave too much water on the floor. We return to the closet to retrieve mops and buckets. Evening mopping duties commence as Kathyleen mops one end of the long hallway and I do the other.

Working solo, I begin with small mop swipes, using the terrazzo floor patterns as guides. I mop around the industrial welcome mats, trash cans, and recycling bins, trying to be as meticulous as Kathyleen. I nod to the tennis coach as he enters the building; he reciprocates. Gradually I establish a rhythm, swabbing the hallway from wall to wall. I inadvertently park my bucket in front of a locker room door. A woman exits, and the door bumps the bucket. The jolt causes a few waves, but no spillage. It is a rookie mistake I hope not to repeat.

This work is not terribly complicated, but my back is throbbing. I wonder how Kathyleen, who is 56 years old, copes with these daily physical demands in addition to her cancer treatments. Custodians like Kathyleen live in a world of pain managed by Anacin. Numerous screaming children in karate attire running down the hallway disrupt my thoughts. I hear from afar Kathyleen kindly and firmly asking the children enrolled in an after-school program to slow and quiet down, explaining that they could slip and fall. I model her message and demeanor as I educate the karate kids at my end of the hallway.

Kathyleen and I eventually complete our independent mopping assignments. Not surprisingly, she mopped more of the hallway. Our mission accomplished, we return to the closet. She deadlifts each bucket to empty the filthy water into the antiquated industrial sink. She seemingly effortlessly squeezes remaining water from both mops and then hangs them neatly on the wall as she continues her story.

> I never did go to college. I graduated high school in 1974. I was in the vocational part of it. Then it was called "secretarial training." I started working in September 1974 at an automotive parts factory. They made radiator caps. Back then it was a booming business. . . . I started part-time doing data entry. . . . I ended up working there for 34 years. I was a keypunch operator. . . . We had a big tabulator computer. . . . That stuff got phased out and then we got a mainframe computer. We switched disks depending on whether it was payroll, accounting, or whatever they wanted to process. You take one disc out and put another one in. . . . Over the years I became the operations manager. The company was all across the world. Everything was dispatched to the help desk. I was the one who routed requests. That's what I took care of.

Kathyleen explains that the company had been sold numerous times during the past decade. An investment company bought it in 2008, and administrators had assembled employees to announce the sale and assure them that there would be no changes, only business as usual. With her duties supervising the help desk, Kathyleen had access to several messages discussing staff terminations. Because of this insider knowledge, she knew it was only a matter of time before she would lose her job. The week before Thanksgiving in 2008, the company fired her. She explains, "I was devastated. I went into a meeting and they had a severance package for me. They extended my insurance for three or four months. My pension was still good, although I couldn't draw on it yet."

Kathyleen grabs an oversized push broom, a trash can, and a coal shovel and heads toward the exit. Once outside, the swirling winds make our next task of sweeping the parking lot a formidable challenge. Each time we fill the can, we work in tandem to extract the bag from the can, tie its opening shut, and haul it to the dumpster. During our 30-minute "sweep," we fill five trash bags as she explains unemployment intricacies and realities.

I learn Kathyleen was out of work for 17 months and collected unemployment during that time. To continue to receive benefits, the employment agency mandated that each week she apply for at least three jobs and complete online vouchers. During her 17-month work gap, Kathyleen had only a handful of face-to-face interviews. She speculates on the reasons companies appeared disinterested in hiring her: "My problem is I have no college degree. My age is probably a borderline hindrance. And my previous salary is a hindrance, since I had to list my current salary. There were a lot of red lights."

Kathyleen regularly applied for jobs at HU, which was about seven miles from her home, and she regularly received rejection letters.

> One of them [an HU job vacancy] was like running a switchboard. I had all that experience and had switchboard operators reporting to me, but it didn't do any good. The rest of the jobs were custodial jobs. Finally, one of those rejection letters came back and it ticked me off. I called HR. I said, "I have a question here. I'm applying at HU and I have 34 years of experience in one place. How can you go and tell me that I don't qualify to do a custodial job? Something's not right here."

At Kathyleen's former job she earned over $22 per hour. At HU, the starting salary for custodians is approximately $9 an hour. A few days after she called, HU invited Kathyleen to a job interview, which resulted in an offer. She assessed the situation: "I don't know if it took me being a you-know-what to get the job. But I wasn't mean. Come on. Maybe they thought I was overqualified."

We return to the closet to exchange our shovels and brooms for two dry mops. I follow Kathyleen to a nearby men's locker room. She opens the door and yells inside to announce her intent to enter. Hearing no concerns, she enters and dry mops the room. She uses a small dustpan and brush to scoop up dirt and dust. Before she exits, she checks to ensure that there is sufficient toilet paper in each stall and soap in each dispenser. The room is spotless, but the crumbling walls and faded paint distract me from appreciating Kathyleen's work. On the way to the break room Kathyleen reveals strategies she undertook to offset her low wages.

> Life throws a lot at us. . . . I started here at nine-something an hour. I did the first phase of the job enrichment program [a skills program that if completed results in a salary bonus and modest raise]. The first phase included five different courses: English, math, computers, first aid, and CPR. I have taken college classes at a community college, and I had 34 years of experience. I gave HR a copy of my resume. I also gave them a transcript of my grades.

HU waived the computer, English, and math courses, leaving CPR and the first-aid course as required courses. Kathyleen liked the first-aid course but dreaded CPR. She successfully completed the entry job enrichment program and received a onetime $1,500 bonus and a modest raise. Her health problems prohibited her from enrolling in the intermediate job enrichment program. She reflected on this experience: "Now I am making $10.30 an hour. . . . You know, they did not credit me for my 34 years of experience. I started at the bottom. It was depressing to look at my last paycheck there and my first paycheck here. I made more than double at my old job. I was making over $20 an hour."

We continue to converse as we wander the hallways, retrieving almost full trash bags from containers and replacing them with new ones. Despite Kathyleen's obvious health challenges, the intensity she devotes to the physical labor and mental aspects of her job is inspirational. She has many reasons to complain and be bitter, but she resists these urges. She looks ahead rather than remain fixated on the past.

Kathyleen works from 3:00 p.m. to 11:00 p.m., Mondays through Fridays. When she returns home she showers, watches TV, and eats a snack. Around 1:30 a.m. she retires and arises at 9:00 a.m. Each workday her free time is between 9:00 a.m. and 2:00 p.m. She schedules her personal and cancer-related appointments early in the morning, since many doctors' offices are over an hour away.

Usually we work and talk, except when talking about family. It is then, and only then, that she momentarily ceases work to focus exclusively on what matters most to her. Kathyleen retrieves her cell phone and shares family photographs. Her oldest son is married and lives about four miles from Kathyleen. Her middle child is enrolled at a nearby university, and her daughter lives at home. She proudly shows me numerous photos of her children and spouse as well as the three cars that he has restored. Working at a job for which she is overqualified and underpaid is all about providing for family. From Kathyleen's point of view, this is not an "important" thing—it is everything.

Maid in America

Minutes after the CU custodians have clocked in for their morning shift, the break room is nearly empty. Most of the 80 custodians are going to their residence halls; a few custodians linger in the nearby laundry room collecting supplies. For the most part, only supervisors remain. Anna, one of six supervisors working the day shift, has agreed to allow me to accompany her on her morning routine. She fiddles with the key cabinet, looks over some notes she retrieved from her nearby desk, and updates the giant whiteboard that includes announcements for staff: "Please bring in your e-mail/phone number so we can update our emergency contact list, Thank you." "Shower curtain exchange, Zone C, starts Wednesday." She briefs her supervisor about her morning agenda before shifting her attention to me. As Anna approaches, she inquires, "Ready?" I nod and discard my coffee cup into the recycle bin as we exit.

For most custodians, history and context matter. Anna began our day-in-the-life walk-and-talk tour with a story about her first days in the United States, a prerequisite for her before talking about her current custodial work:

I got here to [the United States] in September 4, 1997. Four days later we were in [an] empty apartment with only two blankets and a couple of books for my girls, so that they would not get bored. We decided to walk outside to see what was going on. We lived in a not-nice neighborhood. That's where the Immigration Center sent us. They said, "You're going to be here." They paid three months of rent for us. We walked outside, and some guy in a car stopped and said, "You need job?" By watching movies, I knew what "job" means. My husband says, "Yes," but I say, "No." He took him in a car. My husband was crazy. Where is he going? . . . He ended up getting a job at a big restaurant across the street, washing dishes. It was right there, three minutes from our apartment. He was lucky.

Our first stop is to check on a residence hall room with a foul odor. On the way to the building, Anna multitasks, which is part of her DNA. She straightens entryway mats, wipes fingerprints off glass doors, and checks her phone for messages as she continues her coming-to-America story:

It was tough for us. I came with $200, three girls, and a husband. . . . We had two sponsors; one was a cousin. We came here because he got moved here. You have to go where the sponsor is. . . . That guy's brother lives here as well. He invited us to his house. I met [her friend] Meredith there. So I asked her where she worked. She said, "Some school. It's a college. I clean some rooms and bathrooms." She did not speak English either. It is interesting how things worked out.

Before securing employment, Anna took the necessary time to ensure that her family was safe and adjusted to their new surroundings. She describes this orientation process:

When we got here in 1997, they [friends] showed us a cheap grocery store. They had really bad bread that had a terrible smell. It was weird. We could not eat it, and we were hungry. One night my husband was working as a dishwasher at that Italian restaurant, where you need an appointment to eat there and it's not cheap. My kids were reading the same books over and over again, and I was sitting there waiting for my husband. I was waiting, 8:00, 9:00, and 10:00. I did not have a phone to call him. I did not know where he was. I was walking around the apartment thinking he was dead. At 11:30 he comes in and comes upstairs. The kids were sleeping. He has baskets and plates. The big Italian restaurant owner gave us leftovers. I wake up my kids and we had meatballs and Italian bread. Finally, we had real bread. We were so happy.

Anna describes that night as her family's "Christmas." Her children were happy, just like the characters in American movies she had been watching since she was a child.

As we exit a dingy stairwell and power walk down a long residence hall corridor, Anna recounts a story about her CU job interview. Meredith, the friend who was a CU employee at that time, encouraged Anna to interview for a vacancy. Anna studied graphic design in Yugoslavia but knew that she would be unable to secure a graphics job in the United States because she lacked confidence in speaking English. Being a custodian was a job that Anna could accept as she honed her speaking skills.

Meredith gave Anna directions to CU, and Anna arrived on campus at 7:30 one morning. She walked aimlessly around campus. Campus community members, trying to be helpful, sent her from building to building. When she finally located the housekeeping office, it was empty. She returned home later that afternoon without meeting the housekeeping supervisory staff. At home, her spouse greeted her by saying, "Are you crazy? Where have you been all this time?"

We finally arrive at the foul-odor suite. Anna's investigation reveals that a student preparing for the semester break unplugged his mini refrigerator and left open the door but failed to discard the perishable items inside. Some of the rancid items seeped into the carpet, which was the origin of the stench. Anna, the consummate problem solver, notified suite inhabitants that a carpet-shampooing team would clean and deodorize the carpet later that evening.

Back at the housekeeping suite, Anna continues her story. I learn that a week after her first trip to CU, Anna and Meredith traveled together to campus, and Anna interviewed with Lance, the director of custodial operations (Meredith translated during the interview). Lance offered Anna a job. Anna quickly connects her downwardly mobile job with a desire to ensure that her children experience upward mobility in the United States:

> When we came here we had three kids, three daughters. I had one, then twins. It was a struggle, but we made it. Now, one daughter is 29 and living in New York City working in the fashion business, in charge of commercials. The twins are 27. One finished college in Texas and has a degree in journalism. She now works for [a] national furniture corporation, and she gets good discounts. The other twin wanted to be an interior designer or architect. . . . She's still looking for something really exciting to do. She wanted to be a flight attendant, but she was not tall enough. Now she is in the medical field and wants to be a nurse practitioner.

Bringing closure to our conversation, Anna jokes, "I don't know what Lance saw in me, but God bless him. He hired me."

* * *

> Hundreds of thousands of middle-class families plunge down America's social ladder every year. They lose their jobs, their income drops dramatically, and they confront prolonged economic hardship, often for the first time. In the face of this downward mobility, people long accustomed to feeling secure and in control find themselves suddenly powerless and unable to direct their lives. (Newman, 1988, p. ix)

Both Anna and Kathyleen had been living comfortable lives while working satisfying jobs and providing for their families. Without warning, through no fault of their own, both individuals watched their careers suddenly vanish and their modest incomes and labor mobility evaporate. Parnes (1954) defined *labor mobility* as "(1) the ability to change jobs, or move into or out of the work force; (2) the willingness to pursue such moves when opportunities arise; or (3) actual movements between jobs, or into or out of employment" (p. 13).

For Kathyleen, the sale and merger of the company where she worked for 34 years resulted in her losing her IT administrator job. After an excruciating 17-month unemployment odyssey, she reluctantly accepted a job as an HU custodian. For Anna, the Bosnian-Croatian war necessitated that her family members flee their homeland and start anew in the United States. Anna's lack of social networks, intense pressure from local immigration staff to get a job as soon as possible, her lack of confidence speaking English, and her need to provide for family influenced her decision to accept CU's job offer. Anna and thousands of other refugees who had enjoyed successful careers or lives in their home countries arrive in the United States each year to unknowingly and automatically become members of an invisible, downwardly mobile subculture:

> The downwardly mobile are a very special tribe. Some are heroes who find ways to rise above their circumstances; others are lost souls, wandering the social landscape without direction. But almost all are deeply sensitive to the lives they leave behind. They spend hours reflecting upon what their old world meant and what the new one lacks. (Newman, 1988, p. x)

It is unlikely that Kathyleen and Anna would characterize themselves as heroes or lost souls. Instead, they presented themselves as ordinary people doing what is necessary to cope with extreme and unexpected life events.

With Herculean strength they reluctantly accepted their downward career trajectories and strove to cope, while never forgetting their past. They did what they had to do.

The Allure of Custodial Work on College Campuses

Getting a job was the highest priority for Monroe, Chip, Kathyleen, and Anna. Monroe needed to earn a paycheck to pay bills and support her new child. Chip needed a job after being discharged from the military. Kathyleen suffered the consequences of long-term unemployment and would do almost anything to get back on her proverbial feet. Anna needed a job sooner rather than later to satisfy her immigration sponsors and resume providing for her family.

When asked, "What factors influenced your job search process?" two themes emerged: locale and social networks. Working close to home was nonnegotiable. Individuals need to be relatively close to home to minimize commuting costs and in case family emergencies arise. Yet working in a neighborhood near one's home was unlikely. Because HU is in a rural town with inflated real estate prices, most custodians live in lower-cost housing developments in the surrounding counties and commute 15 to 30 minutes to and from work. Because CU is in the heart of a major metropolis, affordable housing near campus was atypical. Most CU custodians live 7 to 15 miles from campus and use public transportation or automobiles to travel to and from work.

Custodians' worlds of work and home are starkly different. In an ethnographic study of doormen in New York City, Bearman (2005) noted, "The neighborhoods that they [doormen] leave from and return to differ remarkably from those they work in" (p. 19). This is especially true for HU and CU custodians. They live and work in very different worlds, geographically and culturally far apart. For campus custodians seeking employment, locale matters. And if they are fortunate enough to get a job, the cultural differences between work and home are often dramatic.

Social networks were a second factor that influenced custodians' job search. Getting a job necessitates having a sponsor to assist with the application and selection processes. Granovetter (1974) found that professional, technical, and managerial workers use three approaches to learning about jobs: (a) formal means (e.g., advertisements, employment agencies), (b) personal contacts (e.g., friends), and (c) direct application (e.g., simply writing directly to an employer). The majority of workers in Granovetter's study reported that learning about a job through personal contacts resulted in higher-quality insights and was more useful than information gained through formal means

or direct application, because "a friend gives more than a simple job description" (p. 13). Granovetter's findings align with Bearman's (2005) study of
New York City doormen: "Less than a handful of the doormen in our sample
heard about their job from an advertisement. . . . The vast majority of doormen in our sample got their jobs through relatives and friends" (p. 49).

Custodians in this study, similar to participants in Granovetter's (1974)
and Bearman's (2005) studies, relied on social networks to learn about and
gain insider insights about the job during the application and selection processes. Anna's friend, Meredith, informed her about the CU job vacancy, and
then scheduled and translated during the interview. Friends of Chip and Monroe encouraged them to apply, communicated job expectations, and offered
positive endorsements about the university. Kathyleen was one of the only
research participants who applied for a job without the support of insiders.

Social networks are also prevalent in CU's custodial department. These
networks not only disseminate custodian vacancy information to family and
friends; but also vouch for the organization, conveying to candidates that the
department and the job are okay. If custodians had neither connections nor
sponsors, they seldom applied for jobs. This networking criterion, like the
work-home proximity criterion, limits job prospects.

The question, "Why did you opt to work for a university rather than for
industry?" elicited numerous responses. The most common responses were:
(a) job security; (b) job autonomy; and (c) health, education, and retirement
benefits.

Job Security

> We suspect that one of the central determinants in working-class life is the
> striving for stability and security. External and internal factors promote
> instability and insecurity. Chief among the external factors [are] unemploy-
> ment and layoffs. (Miller & Reissman, 1961, p. 91)

Most custodians know that they will not be highly paid employees, regardless of the organization that employs them. Although custodians aspire to
get jobs and earn honest wages, job security is more important than salary.
Monroe moved from cleaning hotels to campus residence halls because CU
offered her about the same wages, but greater job security. CU's numerous
failed attempts to outsource custodial services ensured that the university
would continue to hire staff to provide these services, enhancing job security
for custodians like Monroe.

HU remains one of the largest employers in the county and has a reputation as a fervent advocate for custodial staff, protecting their jobs even

in tough economic times. In the old days, word on the street was that if a custodian worked hard, he or she would never get rich but would have a job. A retired senior administrator responsible for physical facilities during an interview revealed the ways that locals learned about HU's commitment to job security:

> Universities that are in rural areas are different from metropolitan schools. The isolation factor means you can't talk to someone [at HU] without figuring out that they are related to someone else who works here. Many farmers in the region started applying here in the 1930s and '40s. The farming area around here had big farm families. They had to look for better jobs. They came to HU, and they ended up in physical facilities. They figured that since they can fix a baler, they could do this kind of work. Like Ted—his grandmother worked here, his mother worked here, his brother works here, and his son will probably soon work here.

In 2001 Ben (an HU custodian) had worked as a manager at a nearby factory for 28 years before accepting an offer to work as an HU custodian. He also took a significant cut in pay. At the time, HU's impeccable reputation within the county influenced Ben's seemingly irrational career move:

> In 2001, they [factory owners] were starting to have some bad times. They were getting rid of managers. I was 49 at the time. It seemed like it was time to make a switch. There wasn't a lot of opportunity and job security. . . . So, I decided to leave. Things were tight there, but they tried to talk me out of it. They told me to take some time off, but I told them I wanted a different opportunity. So I came here as a custodian. I was starting out at $7.50 an hour. I had plenty of money saved up. It was a lot less than I was making, but I needed security.

Positive endorsements from generations of low-paid but satisfied staff appealed to Chip. For Kathyleen, being unemployed for 17 months elevated the importance of finding a job that would provide job security, even though her take-home pay was half of what it was at her former employer. A few months after starting work at HU, Kathyleen's former employer contacted her to see if she was interested in applying for a vacant job. She explained,

> The network manager had contacted me. He asked me if I was interested in getting a job back there. He told me about the job and told me who was retiring. I said, "Sure, I'll come in." I went in to play it out to see what it was like. I interviewed with two guys I worked with for years. It had changed so much. There were very few familiar faces left. They brought in a lot of external people. I could've had the job, although I don't know what

the starting pay would've been. I figured it would not be close to what I had when I got out of there. The interview was on a Friday. I went back home and talked to my husband, kids, and my parents. There was something that just didn't feel right. My husband said I could do whatever I want and he would support me. He did say he thought it would be a mistake if I went back. He said there's not one person there who is secure with their position. There are different things that I saw going on, or things I was hearing, that didn't feel right. . . . That weekend I decided I wasn't going to do it. I sat down and sent an e-mail to the two guys who interviewed me. I thanked them for their time and consideration.

Despite many negative aspects of her job, Kathyleen concluded that HU was a less risky option than her former place of employment. For HU as well as CU custodians, long-term job security is the primary reason they favor custodial jobs on college campuses.

Job Autonomy

A major finding from Paules's (1991) ethnographic study of waitresses revealed that, despite extensive regulations, waitresses found ways to become autonomous and free from external constraints while on the job. Like Paules's waitresses, campus custodians also work in highly regulated environments. They know interference from managers when they see it and value the autonomy that contributes to job satisfaction and retention. Chip understood his supervisor's expectations and appreciated the autonomy provided him, even if things went terribly wrong.

My third night here, I was told to mop up black marks on the floor. He [supervisor] showed me my closet. I mixed up some cool water, ammonia, and mixed it in with bleach. It started to smoke. I took a whiff of it, and it felt like an elephant was on my chest. I had just invented chlorine gas. I did not know about it, because I was not trained. My supervisor walked in and said, "Oh, my God, what have you done?" I poured it down the drain. My metal mop bucket was hot. He told me to never do that again.

Chip lived and learned, which suited his style. Chee-Chee (a 64-year-old African American custodian at CU) tells a story that captures the autonomy desires of many custodians:

I do the study areas. I clean seven bathrooms on Thursday and six on Tuesdays and Fridays. On Wednesdays I have four; that is my easy day. Wednesday I do my detailing. I also vacuum 13 suites on Tuesdays, Thursdays, and Fridays. I play around with the kids. The students are cool. I speak to them every day, and they speak to me. They see me coming down the hall dancing. They don't know what music I'm listening to. They ask me what am I listening to today? I let them know. . . . Today I listened to R. Kelly and Ashanti. I dance all day. . . . I had one supervisor who did not like it. She told me I should only put one earplug in. I told her, "No. You are not in this building all day with me. You come every now and then. When you come, I take out my buds and listen to what you have to say. Other than that I keep both of them in." I haven't had any problems.

Some students I teach how to cook, some I teach them how to wash; you know. One day I got tired of a girl crying and I walked down the floor and sat down with her. I told her, "I don't want to be nosey or anything, but I notice you have been out in the hallway crying." I told her, "All you need is a hug."

Chee-Chee understands her supervisor's expectations and wants to be left alone to exceed those expectations. Management regulates where and when she cleans and sets quality standards, while supervisors conduct numerous scheduled and unscheduled weekly inspections. For most custodians like Chee-Chee, these work parameters are acceptable, provided management allows them the independence to complete tasks without feeling micromanaged. Custodians know that the environments that provide them freedom to, for example, listen to music and interact with residents (aspects of work not included in the job description) distinguish this campus job from cleaning jobs in industrial settings.

Job Benefits

Benefits—in particular health care and tuition—are of utmost importance to campus custodians. From their vantage point, a bad job with health care and tuition benefits is better than a good-paying job without them. Because many custodians are members of large families that incur extensive and expensive health care bills—and these family members also want to attend college, but do not have the financial resources—benefits make campus custodian jobs at HU and CU superior to nonuniversity custodial opportunities. Chip talked about how health care benefits help him financially and improve his health:

In 2002, I had a gastrointestinal bypass. I was hurting so bad. I thought I was dying. I went to my doctor. He said, "Chip, you are a candidate for a stroke and heart attack." I weighed 327 pounds. I would lie in bed and fear I would not wake up. . . . I would fall a lot. I asked my doctor if something was wrong with my equilibrium. He said, "I don't want to sound rude, but you can't see your feet and that is why you fall when walking." I had a

55-inch waist. I would work 30 minutes and sit down for 10. I had constant pain. My feet would hurt.

They would ask me what size uniform I would like. I would say, "Medium." They would say, "Seriously?" I would say, "I would *like* a medium, but I *need* a 4X." Now I am down to a large. I had another [surgery] in 2004 where they gave me a tummy tuck. The second one was worse than the first. It worked okay. I was out that time for three weeks. I can now play with the grandkids. Harrison [HU] put out a lot of money. I got three checks in the mail from Anthem [health insurance company]: $14,000, $10,000, and $75,000. I had to hand deliver them to my doctor. All I had to pay was $500 out of pocket.

Joanne, a CU custodian, shared a similar story, highlighting not only the financial support but also the emotional support of coworkers and CU. After being diagnosed with cancer, she underwent surgery and six weeks of radiation, which her health care benefits covered.

I continued to work every day while I was doing my radiation. I would leave the last hour of the day to get my radiation and then I would go home. After the radiation, my body—here to here—[pointing to two places on her torso] was black and blue because of the radiation. I had to have a wet towel on it at times to keep the skin moist. I needed to make sure that when I moved, the skin would not tear. I put cream on it at night. My treatment was in the heart of the summer. It was hot; we were in hot dorm rooms. I had to inspect rooms. I had to freeze towels and take them along with me. It took about three months for the skin color to come back.

People here were great. They would see me and it would be emotional. They would pad me up with cold towels.

Custodians wanted jobs that provided assistance to reduce the costs of health care and provided emotional and institutional support (e.g., time off for medical treatments).

Harrison University provides a tuition waiver for all employees. An excerpt from the staff handbook details the scope of this benefit:

For eligible full-time administrative and instructional staff, their spouses or domestic partners, and dependent children (includes the natural-born or adopted child of the employee, and the stepchild of the employee who is claimed by the eligible employee as a dependent for federal income tax purposes), the benefit is equal to 100% of the undergraduate or graduate instructional fee.

After a probationary period, full-time custodians receive a tuition waiver that allows them and select members of their family, after three years, to attend

HU for free. At the start of my CU fieldwork, custodians did not have access to a tuition benefit because they were Octagon Cleaning Company (OCC) employees. After CU dissolved the corporation and bestowed on OCC custodians university employee status, the university provided this benefit to them.

The importance of family for each custodian showcased in this chapter is obvious, and having the opportunity to work to provide the next generation with opportunities to remain healthy and attend college are the most precious of all benefits that make campus custodial life a satisfying career.

Left Behind and Losing Ground

Custodians want to work and traveled various pathways to this career. Some, like Monroe and Chip, used the job to develop work skills while earning a living. Custodians like Kathyleen and Anna coped with their downward mobility and provided for their families. Despite the lack of status associated with this job, they focused on aspects of the work that offset the low status and low wages. Although the pay was seldom great, they had job security, which comforted most. While the work is dirty, their jobs provide an opportunity to be independent, which is starkly different from factory work, where many custodians started their careers. Benefits that subsidized health care and education made tolerable the less desirable aspects of the job.

Being employed is, as many participants noted, "a blessing." Yet embedded in the "I am lucky to be employed" discourse is a stealth discourse that expresses feelings of being left behind and losing ground, which breed fear and fatalistic tendencies. For example, HU's long-standing tradition of ensuring workers' job security, even in tough economic times, ended in 2009, when, for the first time in its history, the university laid off employees in good standing, including custodians. Veteran custodians lament that, years ago, collegiality and respect reigned as supervisors clarified job expectations and then provided custodians the freedom to complete their work. Interviewees describe their contemporary relationships with supervisors as more strained, intrusive, and formal. Bosses rein in workers' independence and autonomy to stave off senior administrators' threats of outsourcing. Over the past five years, custodians' individual contributions to health care costs have continually risen while their salaries have remained flat.

Feelings of being left behind and losing ground are common and troubling for custodians. They like their jobs and remain nervous about the future. They fear losing their jobs to outsourcing and escalating work demands. Concurrently, custodians express fatalistic feelings, believing their destiny and their status within the community are fixed and they are powerless to alter their destinies.

Job security, benefits, and autonomy are primary reasons custodians gave for opting to work at a university rather than in industry. Yet in uncertain economic times, each workday they experience greater job insecurity, the erosion of job benefits, and the loss of autonomy. These dynamics coupled with the need to stay close to home make the job less appealing and make it more difficult to recommend these custodial jobs to family and friends.

5

THE CUSTODIAN LIFE

Mr. Clean

Stuck in a McDonald's drive-through in a mini–traffic jam at 4:05 a.m. is no way to start the day. How can there be three vehicles in line ahead of me in the middle of the night? Noticing that two trucks have Harrison University (HU) parking tags hanging from their rearview mirrors, I surmise that they, too, are getting breakfast before beginning work. Hearing the whistle of an approaching train, I hope it will pass by the time I get my sandwiches and coffees. And it does, avoiding another delay. This chapter provides glimpses into the lives of campus custodians while on the job.

I arrive at Dudley Hall at 4:20 a.m., and I park next to Samuel's pickup truck. I retrieve our breakfast from the passenger seat and hustle toward the building's loading-dock door. Samuel is waiting and grants me access to the locked building. Recently, campus police assumed responsibility for remotely locking and unlocking buildings, which is a task Samuel no longer has on his daily to-do list.

Samuel greets me with a smile, while eyeing his watch to ensure that he clocks in within the permissible boundaries (i.e., 4:23 a.m. to 4:30 a.m.). Clocking in too early yields a verbal warning; being late results in a written reprimand. In his early 50s, Samuel looks like he could be 30 years old, especially in his custodian uniform, which includes dark blue twill matching slacks and shirt (which includes an embroidered "Physical Facilities" logo patch). Despite clocking in a few moments ago, Samuel has been working for 90 minutes, cleaning two bathrooms and three offices. Most days he arrives at 3:00 a.m. to get settled and complete some of his duties before building occupants arrive around 7:30.

Samuel summons the elevator and then uses his ID card to activate it. He explains, "They are locked until 7:00 a.m., and you need an ID to swipe to get to the middle and upper floors." Moments after we enter a third-floor workroom, Samuel drops to his knees to scoop up some hole-punch residue on the floor. I assume that today is not the designated day to vacuum this room.

As Samuel tidies the conference table, I differentiate the three spray bottles—an all-purpose cleaner, a stainless steel cleaner, and a germicidal toilet bowl cleaner—on the top of his fully stocked custodial cart. The bottles are in close proximity to two rolls of paper towels, cleaning pads, a can of WD-40, and miscellaneous tools. Different sizes of trash bags hang on the cart's handles for easy access. The medium bags look like they will fit the ones I need to replace in the hallway trash cans, so I grab two and make the switch. Samuel continues to thoroughly dust the office furniture. Before entering the third-floor men's room, he enters and exits two nearby offices to empty the trash.

The cleanliness of the men's room (which has not been attended to for nearly 16 hours) surprises me. Samuel explains that, in most administration buildings, virtually the same people use these facilities, making them cleaner and easier to maintain than, for example, bathrooms in classroom or athletic buildings that serve a more transient population. As we negotiate a division of labor, I wash my hands, which elicits a puzzled look from Samuel. In this context, washing is unnecessary before returning to work.

Samuel assigns me the easy tasks of wiping the window ledges, mirrors, sinks, counters, and soap and paper towel dispensers. He agrees to sanitize the stall walls, doors, and handles. Inside each stall he kneels on the tile floor to wipe behind each toilet, leaving no germ unchallenged. I think to myself, *I don't clean my home as well as Samuel cleans this public restroom.*

As Samuel disinfects the yellow-stained tile floor near the urinals, he lets out a sigh of frustration, then offers an explanation: "We have to use these green [environmentally safe] cleaners. Like, the mirror spray does not really clean, it just streaks. I am always experimenting, but these are not as good as the old stuff." From Samuel's perspective, a streaky mirror or dull stainless-steel water fountain reflects poorly on him, which weighs heavy on his mind. As we exit, he reaches into a trash can and retrieves a few paper towels out of it rather than simply replacing the bag. He explains, "I usually replace about 20 to 25 bags a day; I don't replace them unless they're really full."

We return to the lower level, and Samuel hands me a vacuum. I start at one end of the hall as he tends to some tasks in a custodial closet. This commercial-grade machine works wonders on the crunchy autumn leaves ground into the entryway mats but is mostly ineffective in sucking up some glitter that found its way onto the floor from Halloween decorations posted on an office door. When Samuel returns, I mention a worn-out and stained carpet in one conference room at my end of the hall that needs to be replaced. I obviously and unintentionally strike a nerve with Samuel; he exhibits a moment of frustration. "The carpet-cleaning crew hasn't been in here for months, and I don't have the equipment to clean it right. It probably should be replaced, but it probably won't." The Department of Physical Facilities does not seem as invested as Samuel is in the upkeep of Dudley Hall. As we walk down to the end of the hallway, Samuel retrieves a putty knife from his cart to scrape up residual glitter from the space where I just vacuumed. He smiles, but I know deep down I failed his impromptu inspection.

While I am vacuuming, a physical facilities driver drops off ice-melting salt in the loading dock area, a reminder that winter is approaching. Samuel decides to move the salt later in the morning, since his most pressing task is cleaning offices before occupants arrive in a few hours. We enter and exit three offices, emptying trashcans and dusting desks, chairs, tables, and credenzas. In one senior administrator's office, Samuel carefully places a birthday card and small wrapped gift (a snow globe) on her desk as he departs. Samuel rattles off the birthdays of several longtime administrators. And then I wonder, *Do these staff members know the date of Samuel's birthday?*

It's 6:00 a.m. and time to clean a nearby campus chapel. Samuel inherited this daily 90-minute cleaning ritual as a result of a recent custodial downsizing initiative. He shakes his head as he explains this part of his workday. "I would just rather stay here and keep cleaning. They're [supervisors] always trying to cut costs and add work for us." Outside, the campus has yet to awaken. The only sign of life is several construction workers loitering on the street, apparently unfazed by the damp and windy weather.

Standing on the chapel porch I notice that the indoor lights are shining through the stained-glass windows. Samuel assures me that nobody is inside; "People just leave the lights on at night and there is no timer [to turn them off]." *So much for campus energy conservation*, I think to myself. Inside, Samuel hangs his coat in the vestibule and then opens an office that includes a private bathroom. Samuel explains that wedding parties use this space to get dressed and remain out of sight before nuptial ceremonies. We quickly dust the furniture and spot clean the bathroom. Samuel retrieves a printout from his pocket, unfolds it, and then announces that there is only one wedding scheduled in November. The university requires that a custodian be present for all weddings. Samuel gets first crack at working these events, providing him with coveted overtime opportunities. He elaborates on his wedding duties:

> It's the easiest work I do. I show up before the wedding, make sure everything is clean. Afterward I go in the meditation room downstairs and I listen to the wedding, unless they need me. Then I clean up after everyone leaves.

Inside the sanctuary, we do a cleanliness assessment. I immediately notice the dirty pew cushions; upon closer examination I realize these threadbare cushions are clean, but in dire need of replacement. Noticing me scrutinizing the cushions, Samuel interjects, "I put in a work order to replace them, but it probably won't happen." Again, Samuel's standard of quality exceeds that of those with the authority to replace the cushions.

Samuel hands me a vacuum, and I clean the entryway and altar, the only carpeted spaces on the main floor. Samuel dry mops the hardwood floors, effortlessly maneuvering around the narrow pews and wide aisles. Afterward he straightens items on the altar. His regimented and disciplined routines are hard to disguise.

Next on the agenda is cleaning the basement. The stairwell feels like a sauna, and I immediately begin to sweat. This morning the steam heaters are working overtime. We arrive at two small bathrooms; neither is big enough for both of us to clean, so Samuel decontaminates these spaces. A sweat-stained shirt is his reward for a job well done.

The larger space resembles most church basements—mismatched chairs strewn about the room. The freckled white linoleum floor makes it appear perpetually dirty. I dry mop these wide-open spaces as Samuel spruces up the meditation room. Then he opens the emergency exit to assess the level of leaf accumulation in the underground stairwell. He offers his appraisal: "It's okay. I can rake them on Friday."

I organize the hodgepodge chairs into pods and move the leftover ones to the perimeter of the room. It looks much neater, but I suspect after the first meeting of the day the room will return to a disorganized state. The heat is so intense, I remove my sweater. It's 6:45 a.m., and I am already ready for a shower and nap. Samuel declares, "We're way ahead of schedule," so we proceed to a dilapidated choir loft for a break. Almost every custodian has a hideout. If I were Samuel, this would be my sanctuary.

With the chapel lights dimmed and daylight barely penetrating the stained-glass windows, it is eerily serene. We sit on a church pew, and I stare into the darkness as Samuel thanks me for cleaning with him. We sit silently for a while, and then, without prompting, Samuel speculates about his upcoming hernia operation. He expects to be off work from late December to mid-January to recover from the medical procedure. He purposefully schedules the surgery between semesters so that he will use 88 rather than 120 sick leave hours (because campus is closed the week between Christmas and New Year's Day). His medical worries have begun to mount.

> I wanted to do it [the surgery] then, so that no one has to clean for me. I don't like being off and having someone else clean for me. . . . I am worried about paying for it. I know someone who had to pay $4,000 [out of pocket] for the same operation. I have to talk to them [hospital

administrators] about payments. I don't have that kind of money. I hope they have a payment plan. . . . If I can get through this operation, then I am going to lose $36 each paycheck because of higher health premiums that start next year. That's going to put a big hurt on me.

Samuel's fears are real, and his disdain for the Affordable Care Act is unmistakable. He rattles off alarmist talking points that flood conservative talk radio, condemning changes to national health care policy. I refrain from challenging his assumptions. I sense Samuel wants to just "get by," but local and national health care costs and policies jeopardize this modest goal.

Samuel raises a second concern, which is the recent change in his work hours. For decades Samuel worked the 4:00 p.m. to midnight shift, which he deemed ideal. He arrived on campus midafternoon, which allowed him sufficient time each day to interact with building occupants before they departed around 5:00. The building would usually be minimally occupied from 7:00 p.m. to midnight, allowing him to clean without having to work around students and staff. His current work shift begins at 4:30 a.m., which requires him to be more strategic about cleaning since most of the building is occupied from 7:30 a.m. to 1:00 p.m. (the end of his shift). Samuel provides a succinct reason for the change: "There's a lot of absenteeism, and they [management] want to move everyone to the same shift so they can move people around to clean for people missing."

This mandated change, which occurred with minimal input from custodians, has also decreased the quality of Samuel's home life. On workdays, he arises at 11:30 p.m., showers, drinks a cup of coffee, does housework, listens to the radio, then departs for campus. He arrives approximately at 3:00 a.m. (90 minutes before the university allows him to clock in). He uses an office computer to check his e-mail (since he does not own a computer). He provides a rationale for working 90 minutes each day without pay:

> I get my work done early so that when the people come in, I won't be in the way or making a whole lot of noise. . . . If I had an office job, I would not want people to be in my way saying, "Excuse me, can I get your trash?"

After work, en route to the farmhouse he shares with his mother, he tends to errands. Upon returning home after his 17-mile, 35-minute commute, he and his mother tend to farm duties. Most afternoons he watches local television or listens to the radio. Without expensive cable television and Internet service, electronic entertainment options are limited. Samuel's mother cooks dinner at 5:00 p.m., and he stays up for a few hours before taking one final nap from 8:00 p.m. to 11:30 p.m. He appraises this lifestyle:

It is a crazy schedule. During the week I don't get much sleep. Friday, it hits me. I'm zapped. I lounge around pretty much. Saturday I sleep in later, until 7:00. It is different from the week. I help my mom if she has errands, like I go to the store or bank.

Morning has broken; the sunlight filling the chapel signals that it is time to end the break and return to Dudley Hall. We gather our belongings and make a stop at a nearby dumpster to deposit a bag of trash. The Dudley Hall parking lot is almost full; for the majority of the campus community, the day has begun. Inside, a woman approaches Samuel and warmly greets him. He reciprocates. This exchange prompts me to ask him about staff relationships. He replies,

> I try to respect them as much as possible. When I talk with people in the building, it is pretty much small talk, no major stories. . . . I try to keep it as short as possible. I really don't get too personal. I listen to them talk about their family life, if they bring it up. That's fine—like grandkids or something like that. I don't want to keep them from work.
>
> I am not on their level. I am kind of way down low at the bottom, below the secretaries. That's where I am. I do the most menial tasks. The secretaries are pretty important. They have to get things organized for the dean. They take phone calls and messages. What do I do? I just sweep floors, clean bathrooms, wash some windows, and say, "Hi." That's it.

I disagree with Samuel's perspective but refrain from debating with him. Inside a mechanical closet that Samuel has commandeered into an office, he restocks his cart with trash bags and paper products for the second half of his shift and describes his family's longtime affiliation with HU:

> My mom and dad worked here. My mom was a librarian, and my dad was a custodian. Both retired in 1990. My mom was 60 and my dad was 68 when they retired. I knew about HU from them.

When Samuel graduated from high school, he enrolled at HU for two semesters, then dropped out. "It didn't work because I was not that good at it." Afterward he worked at a lumberyard, and in 1982 he enlisted in the navy and was discharged in 1986. Between 1986 and 1988 he worked odd jobs, then returned to HU as a custodian.

Samuel props the door open to keep an eye on hallway happenings. He looks up and greets a woman dressed in a Halloween costume. He then opens the refrigerator and retrieves a container that includes two donuts. "Do you want one?" I decline the offer and instead take some Halloween candy from his desk. The work shift is half over, and we have yet to cross paths with Samuel's supervisor. I inquire after her whereabouts.

She leaves me alone because she knows I will do my work. She's good to me. The people she knows that don't do their work, they get watched and asked questions. In the old days when I first started, over 20 years ago, one guy did not come in for about a week, and the manager let him slide. Now, you could not slide like that. If we clock in late, even five minutes, we get wrote up. If you get in more trouble, they hold it against you. It's a way to get rid of you. I hear if you do something bad, it stays on your record permanent, but I am not sure.

Monthly, Samuel's supervisor formally inspects his work. She evaluates the cleanliness of the bathrooms, hallways, public areas, and stairways and generates two evaluation summaries that he must sign; he keeps one copy and returns the other to her. Consistently his evaluations exceed departmental expectations.

Although Samuel is satisfied with his current boss (and vice versa), this was not always the case. He explains:

My old supervisor wanted me out of Dudley Hall, because I was here for a long time. He did not like that I was friendly and they [the occupants] liked me. . . . He wanted me to do more work. If someone were out sick, he'd send me to do their work. He worked me to death. He knew I would do both jobs good.

Samuel also offers a respectful critique of coworkers. He likes working alone, so that he does not have to respond to his peers' perceptions that he is too conscientious or has unreasonably high standards. "They get jealous if your floors look better than theirs. Here, I have control over how the place looks and I don't get dragged down. I want to do it right; that's what I am paid to do." Although he prefers to work alone, he relishes interactions with Dudley Hall occupants—his surrogate family. Samuel explains,

Christmastime they have a breakfast for me and give me a card that has a check with money in it. The cards say something like, "Samuel, thanks for what you do." It's nice. I just don't want complaints. If they are not complaining, I guess I am doing a good job.

Samuel retrieves from his desk a Campus Community Service Award certificate and explains its significance:

I got that award in 2004. The ceremony was in the campus center. And when I got the award, Dr. Richards [the vice president who nominated him] told me that the students gave me a standing ovation. I didn't notice. I told him, "I didn't know that." I was kind of focusing on the words they were saying about me, not the people. It was a surprise to me, really. I was the first custodian to get that award. My manager came to the ceremony; my mom was there, too. For being a custodian, I guess it's not too bad. I'm lucky enough to be in a building where the people respect the building. They try to keep it clean. And they're not really snobs.

Samuel justifies his supervisor's lax management style by reminding me that Dudley Hall occupants provide him regular feedback. "Really I get inspected every day, because of the people in the building. If something is not right they will complain. Here, they tell me first, before they call over to my boss. I like that a lot better." While Samuel appreciates his autonomy as it relates to his boss and his positive relationship with Dudley Hall administrators, he laments the changing culture of the department:

Today, they [management] want more for less. And they want people to be more businesslike. They don't want a friendly atmosphere. I don't think they really want people to be friendly with each other. That's the way I view it. They think you get less done if you feel good and talk to people more. I say, if you are pretty well done with your work, why not be friendly with them and see how they are doing, instead of just work, work, work?

. . . They don't really care about you, like helping you plan for your future. When I retire I couldn't live off just my retirement money. I'd have to do something else. I don't think Harrison provides any financial planning for us. . . . They have workshops on campus, but I'm not really sure. I don't know much about this.

With the building in full operation, Samuel and I venture out into the hallway to continue cleaning, being intentional to disturb occupants only minimally. We move the sidewalk salt to a storage room and stock the supply closets on each floor. We vacuum a conference room, dust framed photographs that line the hallways, and then return to the chapel for a cleanliness check. Samuel drops by to visit with support staff throughout the building to ascertain if they need anything before he departs for the day. I use this time to generate a list of aspects of the job that Samuel deems satisfying: his boss, Dudley Hall administrators, his salary ($17.39/hour), overtime pay ($25/hour), and predictable and regimented work routines. I also list areas that concern him: rising health care costs, additional work responsibilities, a less friendly campus atmosphere, his lack of influence, inhumane work hours, infrequent raises, and minimal retirement counseling.

Before I depart, so that Samuel can enjoy his 30-minute (11:00 a.m.–11:30 a.m.) lunch break without the burden of me being present, I ask about Samuel's postwork agenda. He explains that he is going to a nearby grocery to buy a birthday cake for his mother. I inquire about his mother's favorite cake, and he replies, "She really likes chocolate cake, but I will only get it if it is on sale." Samuel is constantly monitoring his expenditures to make certain he is living within his means. This verbal exchange reminds me of my privileges, and I am privileged to have crossed paths with Samuel.

An All-Purpose Cleaner

Awake, I prepare for my daylong fieldwork with Ajla and Kichelle, the two women responsible for cleaning a living-learning residence hall on the Compton University (CU) campus. Because the residence hall classrooms need to be cleaned by 8:00 a.m., Ajla starts work a few hours before her coworkers. It's almost 6:00 a.m. The November sun has barely risen above the grand window in the lobby, and I am enjoying the tranquility. The lobby is empty except for a woman clutching a laptop computer and dragging a blanket. She nods in my direction, and I reciprocate.

A loud *click* precedes the unlocking of the main door, which alerts me that someone has used an ID card to gain access to the building. Suddenly the door swings open, and Ajla enters, offering an enthusiastic greeting. Her hair is tucked away under her white stocking cap, which is both functional and fashionable. A stylish leather jacket hides her university-issued microplaid polo shirt. Her ID card, clipped to a lanyard hanging around her neck, sways as she moves, reminding people that she is a university employee. She sits down next to me, and my informal orientation commences. First she tells me, "This job worked out because it starts at 6 o'clock in the morning, and I wanted a job where I could get started early so I can get home early and spend time with my family."

Ajla then shifts from an overview of her cleaning responsibilities to an overview of her parental-like responsibilities, which are not included in her formal job description:

> I talked to the kids. When the parents drop the kids off, I kind of tell them like, "Don't worry. I'm going to take care of them." I make sure they do what they're supposed to do. This year I have wonderful kids. I do. They are so open and so bright and so nice. They also are neat and clean. I cook for them, like around the holidays. I cook at home, and then I bring them in some Bosnian food. They love it. They asked me to do it again. I promise the kids I'd get them some more food before winter break. I'll make time.

Of the 56 Yugoslavian-born custodians working for CU's Department of Housing (DOH), approximately 85% have a good or excellent command of the English language. Yet, when speaking English, their confidence lags behind their competence. As a result, most conversations tend to be deliberate and somewhat stilted. Ajla does not fit this conversational profile. Her communication style is fast-paced, fluid, enthusiastic, and highly informative. I struggle to keep up with the pace of her stories. Glancing at her watch, she jumps up and declares, "I better get downstairs and start cleaning. . . . I've got a lot to do." I follow Ajla as she swipes her ID card on a nearby card reader, allowing us access to an adjacent wing of the building. The lower level includes numerous discrete spaces: classrooms, restrooms, study rooms, custodial closets, a computer room, a laundry room, a television lounge, and even a billiards room.

As we clean a classroom, it appears that the nightshift custodians pushed the chairs and desks to one end of the room when waxing the floor. I follow Ajla's lead as we rearrange the furniture, erase the whiteboards, dust the computer workstation, and replace trash bags. Once Ajla is satisfied with the condition of the room, we move to an adjacent classroom and start again. As Ajla vacuums, I read the label on a cleaning solution bottle: "Removes blood stains, grease, wine, liquor, oil, glue, coffee, pet stains, paint, hair dye, food stains, and berry juice." This manufacturer has brilliantly marketed this product to universities, where there is never a shortage of these stains—especially coffee and liquor. Ajla finishes vacuuming and then resumes her storytelling:

> I met a faculty member [who teaches in the living-learning center]; she's such a good person. She leaves me little sweets or something, and she leaves me a note. She tells me that I work hard and smile all the time. She says, "How you do it?" I tell her I learn from my daughter at home; she's in college. I know sometimes she can go crazy, especially this time of year, with final exams. I learned to just leave her alone. She doesn't need to clean up or anything. That helps here.

Inside a study room, Ajla vacuums, and I study the artifacts piled high in the recycling bin—pizza boxes, ecofriendly takeout containers, disposable coffee cups, newspapers, and even a pair of sneakers. Ajla takes the mess in stride and tackles it with zest. As a connoisseur of collegians, she espouses her theories about them:

> I have a student up on the fourth floor. His name is Alfred. Every time I would clean his bathroom, which was around 1:00 in the afternoon, he would just be getting up. I would say to him, "You are just like my

daughter. Why don't you schedule your classes early and then you have the afternoon for yourself?" He would say, "You're right, Ajla. I'm glad to do that next year." We joke and laugh—and I know he won't. I want students to feel like they're at home. They spend a lot of time here [residence hall]. This is their life right now. It's important to try to get them to relax. It's their classes that are most important here. They usually say, "Hi." But they don't need to say, "Hi," if they don't want to. I feel like making them feel relaxed is a good thing. It's good for us, too. You know, we have parents come in and say, "We appreciate all that you do." I feel like the kids are like my kids.

Ajla's daughter is a commuting college student. Ajla appraises her daughter's college. "It's a very nice campus and has very nice faculty. . . . The people there made the campus nice for her. I'm trying to do the same thing here." Ajla supports others, because others have supported her.

Conversing with custodians about current work experiences inevitably includes historical primers. Custodians' life experiences influence their present. Ajla is no exception.

I was born in February 1974. We married in 1993. It will be 20 years in February. We came here [the United States] in 1999. Me and my husband thought things in our country would be better. We thought everything would change, but it didn't. We decided to come here mostly because [of] my kids.

My husband was a sergeant in the army. In 1994, August, he saw one of his friends being shot. He went to help him—to get out of the crossfire. He got shot in the arm and two times in his leg. The last shot was in his back. He now limps and has back problems. He's healthy now, considering.

Ajla's husband believed it would be better to remain in Bosnia; she disagreed.

When my girl was two years old, we just had potatoes to eat, nothing else. No salt or no oil, you just boil or bake them. She was a chubby kid. Kids were starving, and she was starving, too, but she was chubby. She came in the kitchen one day and said, "What we eating?" It was like baby talk, and I said, "Potatoes." She said, "Potatoes again?" It was funny and sad. I couldn't provide her a better meal.

Ajla offers a rationale: "Hey, what are we going to do? We got two kids. We don't have work. All the factories and companies are closing. Everything's destroyed." After weeks of deliberation, they agree to relocate to the United States. She raises her voice to clarify the magnitude of this decision: "That is not a life. That is not a life. I am young. I am strong. I have to do what's best for my family."

Yet drama and sadness followed Ajla and her family to America. While Ajla's mother was visiting, an inebriated driver struck and killed her. Ajla reflects on the hit-and-run experience:

> It happened six years ago, and I still stand at the door waiting for her to come in. You know, like her just walking in a house and me doing her hair. This was a very hard period for me. I waited a long time to be with her. I waited a long time to do things with her, like go shopping. All of a sudden she was taken away from everybody.

Pain and hardship have no geographic boundaries. For Ajla, dramatic and traumatic life events such as these help her to put into perspective her work challenges, which accounts for much of her optimism and satisfaction on the job.

While cleaning the television room, the conversation shifts to a lighter topic: entertainment, a welcome respite from our war and death discussions. I erroneously assumed that Ajla's Americanized children tutored her about popular culture, but her socialization to the United States began long before she moved to America.

> When I was in high school—you know, when I was a teenager—I was thinking with my hormones, not the brain. I was madly in love with Axl Rose, you know, in Guns N' Roses—that was before he had all those surgeries. I took English and dancing classes in Bosnia while in high school. I always loved American movies. I had a Lifetime TV station that I never turned off. I love Lifetime movies and scary movies. In Bosnia, past midnight I would watch the scary movies, and my mom would go nuts. She would yell at me, "Go to bed, you have school in the morning." I would tell her, "I'm watching this vampire movie first."

The cleaning tasks are rather ordinary and not particularly taxing. We dust desks, wipe windows, scrape chewing gum from underneath tables, haul trash, scrub sinks, vacuum furniture, shine lamps, disinfect toilets, restock paper towels, and replenish soap reservoirs. As I wipe the recycling bin with Terminator One-Step Disinfectant and squirt Totally Awesome All-Purpose Concentrated Cleaner and Degreaser into the sink, I doubt the credibility of these claims. I ask Ajla, "Can you really terminate germs in one step?" and "Is the cleaner and degreaser really awesome?" Shaking her head from side to side is her only response; she understands sarcasm.

We shift our energies from cleaning public spaces to hauling trash. Admittedly, cleaning classrooms and bathrooms is hard work and at times gross, but collecting and consolidating trash bags and then hauling them to loading docks is literally risky business. Garbage responsibilities expose custodians to dangers and health hazards.

The department's industrial-strength clear trash bags mask broken glass that can easily puncture a bag as well as a custodian's arm or leg. Ajla coaches me about how to hold the bags away from my body to avoid injury, yet enacting this advice strains my aging upper body. In the recycling room I wrestle with a heavy bag of trash that I am struggling to insert into an empty bag to keep the original overstuffed bag from ripping open. In this battle royale, the bag is winning. As we consolidate trash I posit that students consume less during the week and more during weekends, making Mondays the most challenging garbage-hauling day. I share my consumption theory, and she gives me a "whatever" look. I surmise that, for Ajla, finishing this "garbage in/garbage out" ritual appears to be of greater interest than garbage consumption theorizing. Ajla's Type A personality is unnerving at this early hour. Efficiency, solving problems, and staying busy are what matters.

> I find it funny, but really it's crazy. It's just me. I'm hyper. Once we got here [United States], my first year I help in the school, I find a job, then I open my business. My husband was working for a company that made dog food. It was an easy job for him. After being here a few years we took money out of my husband's 403(b) retirement to buy a franchise. And I started a commercial cleaning franchise. I clean 11 buildings now. My customers are now part of my family. I do stuff for them and don't charge them. They come to visit. They appreciate me. It's not about the money all the time. These people are nice human beings.

Ajla explains that she has her family, and all members are in good health. She describes herself as financially comfortable, not rich. "Having family and friends around, if I cry, they come cry with me. If I laugh, they laugh with me. I am 38 years old, but I still feel young. I have a young spirit."

The Grim Sweeper

> I guess the students like me because I smile and I talk to them. That's what I do. Every day I speak to them and find out how they're doing. I ask how school is going. I asked if they are doing their work or playing. I pretty much talk to them. The RAs [resident assistants—undergraduate staff assigned to each corridor] are pretty good overall. Some of them talk to you. Some of them are [a] little too busy, but that's okay. Howard lives in the same building as where you stay [I was living on campus while doing fieldwork]. He's full-time and oversees the buildings and the RAs. He walks

the building and makes sure everything is all right. He takes control of the students if they're not doing what they're supposed to do. Like if they are drinking—he be on them.

Kichelle—an African American woman and a 16-year veteran CU custodian—works in the same residence hall as Ajla. Like Ajla, relationships matter to Kichelle. Getting to know students and staff consumes a large part of her workday, despite the absence of these responsibilities on her job description and performance inspection form. Kichelle's relationship with me also matters. She allows me to get to know her, and like a skilled anthropologist, she expects to get to know me. Her quid pro quo persona provides me opportunities to ponder my motivation for and approach to my fieldwork.

Because Kichelle lives about 15 miles from campus and uses public transportation to get to and from work, she usually arrives about 30 minutes before clocking in. Each morning, she and her coworker Diane watch television and chat in a lounge adjacent to an on-campus eatery. Knowing her schedule, I temporarily suspend my work with Ajla and travel across the quad to hang with Kichelle. As expected, she is in the lounge watching the local news. Today the topic du jour is an ungrateful daughter.

> My daughter is in eighth grade and will be in high school next year. Oh Lord, she's already trying to be beside herself. She thinks she's grown. She's lazy. She used to be good, like cleaning her room. She has been doing it since she was a girl. Now, she's getting lazier and lazier.

This mini rant prompts Kichelle to offer a more measured and thorough reflective interlude about her daily struggles as both a custodian and a single parent.

> My son is 20. He is out of town right now. He's been in trouble here, so I sent him out of town. He was hanging out with the wrong people. I'm trying to keep him away from that. He's with my sister in Kansas City. My son understands my concerns, but at times he doesn't listen. You know they don't listen sometimes. But he gets it. I pretty much hope so. My sister doesn't have any kids, but she knows how to talk to him.

Kichelle expects her son to return home in a few months; she intends to move as soon as she can find an affordable foreclosure home. Keeping her children out of harm's way is always on her mind.

> I pretty much stay on them to help them stay away from trouble. I don't drink and I don't smoke. I don't party or anything like that. I pretty much

go to work and go to church. And then I go home. I shop at the stores. I pretty much don't go anywhere, for real.

Kichelle sets the bar high for straight talk and expects me to do the same—quid pro quo. I smile, anticipating that she is about to ask a question—and she does. "Peter, why you do this study?" I pause for a few moments to compose a cogent response. I convey that my research agenda has centered on so-called underdog campus subcultures, and I have a deep respect for the many custodians on my campus who are on the margins. When I mention that custodians are invisible and their stories should be told, Diane and Kichelle nod in agreement. I hope they interpret my response as honest, neither self-serving nor virtuous. Kichelle's insistence on learning about me reminds me that ethnographic work is contingent on participants talking about themselves. The exchange makes me realize that I must overcome my disdain for talking about myself and reciprocate—quid pro quo.

After a moment of silence, Kichelle poses a follow-up question: "Peter, why do you travel so far from home to come here?" I highlight differences between HU and CU (HU is public, and CU is a private university). After this comparative analysis, I reveal something I had not shared with others. Only a handful of universities agreed to participate in this study; because CU granted me access, it became a research site.

I thought it was my turn to ask Kichelle a question, but she corrects this misperception by posing a third question: "Peter, what does your wife think about you being so far away for so long and sleeping in a dormitory?" I reply, "Marcia is a faculty member who also does educational research, so she gets what I do." Her wry smile suggests that she is mostly satisfied. Quid pro quo—I use this silent pause to pose a follow-up question: "What do you do outside of work?" She laughs aloud and replies,

> At home I don't really have to clean because the house is pretty much clean. I fix my bed before I leave for work in the morning. I pretty much don't have to do much except the wash. I pretty much have everything done. During the week I don't like to cook, so I get something along the way home. I get my daughter something, too. I be tired on the weekdays; I go home, lay down, and rest. I read the Bible and Scriptures. My family— we have prayers on Sunday, every Sunday. We meet at my sister's house, which is about 10 minutes from me. My family's kind of close. My daughter has to go where I go. Sometimes when I'm at home, I'm down and stressed and start to cry, but I never let my daughter see me cry.

Sensing that it is almost time for Kichelle and Diane to clock in, I pose a final question: "Do many CU people know your life story?" Kichelle takes a deep breath, exhales, then replies,

No. They never ask. Students sometimes will ask, like, "How many kids do you have?" They also ask me how long I've been here. Maybe it's because we are strangers and they don't want to talk to us. Once you have relationships with students they talk to you. The people I work with don't know me. Like Lance and the higher-ups, they do kind of know, like, that I have kids and stuff.

I wait in the television room as Diane and Kichelle descend into a stairwell to clock in at the satellite office located in the basement. About 10 minutes later, Kichelle returns and we walk across the quad and swipe into her building. Because it is too early to begin cleaning suites, Kichelle tackles her public area responsibility of cleaning hallways, stairwells, a kitchenette, a multipurpose room, a storage room, a laundry room, trash/recycle rooms, and two guest suites. Kichelle devotes 45% of her time to cleaning public spaces and 45% to cleaning residential suites. The remaining 10% centers on maintaining her housekeeping closets.

Kichelle's work pace is a bit slower than Ajla's, but her workflow is more predictable. I watch intently as Kichelle removes lint from dryers, chisels crusted macaroni and cheese from a kitchenette stovetop, and consolidates and organizes trash bags. As the morning unfolds, Kichelle and I encounter an increasing number of residents as they travel to and from classes. Almost every resident offers a greeting. Despite vast social and cultural differences, Kichelle effortlessly interacts with students. Although she does not know the name of every resident, she knows each one by sight.

Around 10:30 a.m., we enter a student suite and begin cleaning. There are several suite configurations, but each suite includes a hallway, two common bathrooms, and multiple bedrooms. The sheer amount of stuff in the students' private rooms (often visible from the suite hallway) surprises me. Clothes are piled high in laundry baskets, and trash is overflowing in most cans. The bathrooms are even more cluttered. Electronic toothbrushes; a blow dryer; mascara brushes; toothpaste; boxes of tampons; contact lens solution; and multiple bottles of shampoo, conditioner, and mouthwash cover nearly every square inch of counter space.

Kichelle makes use of her many different spray bottles to tackle each unique mess she encounters. She switches from a tub-cleaning gel for the shower to an all-purpose cleaner for the sink. I watch her step into a shower and scrub the shower walls with both hands. She tackles the soap scum, making her a prime candidate to develop carpal tunnel syndrome (which her health care benefits will not likely fully cover). "This is not the worst one for today," she predicts.

Leaving a "custom-designed sticky note" for residents is an option if custodians encounter extreme clutter. Kichelle rarely issues these tags. Today she knocks on two bedroom doors to find residents who can help her declutter public spaces so that she can resume her cleaning responsibilities. Two women exit a bedroom and profusely apologize for the mess. As we work in unison, I wonder how supervisors evaluate the quality of custodians' work in contexts such as this one. It seems unfair that custodians' job performances are contingent on residents' capacities to respect and maintain their living spaces. I make a mental note to raise this observation/concern with the director.

As Kichelle cleans, I calculate the value of the electronic equipment that is in plain sight, which includes a desktop computer, a laptop computer, an oversized flat-screen TV, and a musical keyboard. I estimate that there is nearly $4,000 of equipment in this space. The extension cords plugged into every visible electric receptacle would horrify a fire marshal. Somehow Kichelle devises creative solutions to clean around these hazards. As we pack up, Kichelle announces that it is time for a break.

In my world as a professor, I determine when it is appropriate to take a break. When relaxing, I neither proceed to a designated space nor worry about how others will interpret my inaction. Nor do my supervisors designate an official starting and ending time for the respite. If I need a break, I identify an appropriate time and take it. I don't apologize for periodic escapes from work responsibilities. Watching Kichelle prepare for a break reminds me that, as a custodian, preparing to relax is anything but relaxing. Knowing when a break begins and ends is easy; managers set these parameters, and most custodians comply. Yet for custodians like Kichelle and Ajla, it is important to relax in private. Custodians who showcase their sanctioned leisure activities in public spaces can inadvertently reinforce stereotypes that custodians seldom work or frequently slack off. Today Kichelle, Diane, and I move to a locked lounge. Since the door has a key-card device, any *click* signals that a visitor is entering, which is an invaluable mode of early warning.

Kichelle and Diane engage in a humorous "Can you top this?" exchange of noteworthy morning adventures. Kichelle turns the television station to *Family Feud*. We collectively guess and critique the most popular responses to questions the game host poses, which, for me, is both enjoyable and humbling.

Cleaning another suite is the next task. This space is cleaner and less cluttered, yet the cleaning routines are almost identical to the one we deployed in the previous suite. I begin to memorize bathroom routines: Remove items from around the toilet, flush and add cleaning solution, clean the exterior of the toilet, clean the toilet seat, clean the inside of the toilet bowl, wipe drips and spills. While there is less clutter, the two women chatting in the hallway and the one woman occupying the bathroom create a traffic jam that Kichelle artfully works around as she chats with them. In approximately 20 minutes this makeover is complete, much quicker and easier than the previous one.

After lunch we enter our first men's suite, which stinks. The building's high-tech climate-controlled ventilation system is no match for the room's disgusting locker-room odors; my only recourse is to breathe through my mouth. The contents of the various suite rooms visible from the hallway remind me of American collegians' unswerving allegiance to materialism. The abundance of possessions that I can see—gaming consoles, a state-of-the-art television, top-of-the-line basketball sneakers—symbolically conveys residents' economic privilege and what counts as entertainment and physical comfort. It's our third suite of the day, and again we closely follow the identical cleaning script we performed earlier. From my vantage point, housekeeping is like being caught in a revolving door. I am ready to mix things up to combat boredom, but Kichelle is not. I acquiesce, and we do it again.

Despite the many challenges associated with cleaning public areas and residential suites, Kichelle seems satisfied. The evaluative inspections conducted by micromanaging supervisors are what trouble her. Kichelle worked for several outside cleaning companies contracted by CU before becoming a CU employee. She uses these life experiences to offer a comparative analysis related to the changing nature of the department and staff supervision:

> January 1998 is when it started getting bad. At that time they hired supervisors and they started walking around. They [supervisors] harassed us and checked on us. If we are doing our work, leave us alone. Most people know their job and do it. Okay, there are some people who mess it up for all of us. Supervisors should go check on them.
>
> Now we have daily spot [unannounced] inspections, in addition to the regularly scheduled inspections. Supervisors walk their buildings two or three times a day. One time, I can see, but three times seems a little much. It's all about making sure we do our work. We don't need daily inspections. They [residents] are happy with the work I do. . . . I do my work well, and I know what I'm doing.

Despite the persistence of these frustrations, she knows that few alternatives exist.

> I pretty much like my job. I was thinking about leaving and getting another job, but the economy is bad. You know, people get laid off. Here you don't get laid off, so I might as well stay. They also have good benefits. I just stay here and do my work. If I think something is wrong I tell them, but I give them respect. I want them to give me respect. . . . This is simple work, but

they make it hard on us. I talked to my mom about them [supervisors] and about the job. She says, "Pray for them and go about your business." So I pray for them and go about my business.

Grime Scenes

These day-in-the-life stories of three custodians reveal insights about the custodians as well as both universities, which are the foci of the rest of the chapter.

Mixing Business With Pleasure

The gap remains wide between custodians' written job descriptions and their actual work. Like most custodians, Samuel, Ajla, and Kichelle understand their formal job responsibility, which is cleaning. Each day they diligently perform this duty. Yet custodians expand their work responsibilities to include the establishment of meaningful relationships with students and administrators. Ghidina (1992) discussed the importance of social relationships:

> Social relations are often reported to be an important aspect of all kinds of work. Not only may relations with others provide a source of satisfaction and pride in the work that is otherwise unfulfilling, social relations may also be relied upon for worker esteem and identification because it is through them that more glorifying definitions of work are created and sustained. (p. 76)

Samuel, Ajla, and Kichelle, like the research participants in Ghidina's study, value human relations. Getting to know the Other is as important as their daily cleaning routines. Samuel knows the name of everyone who works in Dudley Hall. He establishes relationships with individuals who respond favorably to his get-acquainted overtures. Ajla regularly interacts with faculty who teach in the living-learning center and cooks Bosnian meals for residents. Kichelle knows and cares about her residents and makes it a point to acknowledge and affirm them daily.

Reaching out to faculty, administrators, and students helps custodians become more successful in and satisfied with their work. Samuel works one or two hours each day without pay to ensure that his work does not interfere with others'. His birthday gifts and daily check-ins with support staff members symbolize his genuine care for others. Ajla learned from her daughter that it takes a village to support collegians. She applies this knowledge to her work, for example, by encouraging students to enroll in morning classes.

Kichelle's authentic relationships with residents minimize the need for her to use the department's Post-it Notes system to reprimand messy students. Even Kichelle's interest in forging a relationship with me enhanced the quality of my work.

Although managers, supervisors, and department directors appreciate and benefit from these relationships, campus-wide initiatives that provide opportunities for different subcultures to interact are infrequent (aside from the ubiquitous residence hall staff's meet-the-custodian gathering at the start of each academic year or the departmental holiday parties that often include custodians). Custodians envision their business as ensuring that the business of students, faculty, and staff succeeds. Conversely, neither the departments nor the institutions envision their business as forging relationships with and systematically supporting custodians.

Minding Your Own Business

Custodians value relationships with their constituents more so than relationships with supervisors. Paules (1991) found that waitress work does not lend itself easily to close supervision. Waitresses sought ways to sustain and expand their autonomy whenever possible.

> In spite of this extensive system of regulations, waitresses enjoy considerable autonomy, or freedom from external constraint (Katz, 1968) in their work lives. They control many of the decisions relating to the management of their stations and partially they regulate the tempo of their work and volume of business they do; they compromise dress code; and they eat and rest when it suits them—all without interference from management or coworkers. (p. 78)

Custodians, like waitresses, prefer independence and are fiercely protective of their autonomy. Custodians prefer for supervisors to make explicit their expectations and allow them the space to get the job done independently, with minimal management interference. Samuel respects his current supervisor because she provides him the freedom to complete his work. Ajla begins each workday independently and autonomously until her supervisor arrives a few hours later. Kichelle knows what she needs to do and insists on independence to complete her work. These cleaners desire insularity and autonomy when interacting with management, but not with the individuals they serve.

Stressing for Success

Few custodians expected to be career cleaners, and once on the job they seldom exhibited a "lust for dust." Yet most custodians take their responsibilities seriously. They aspire to be model custodians and do their part to support students, faculty, and staff in their quests for success. Dropping out of college, working for a few years in the community, being honorably discharged from the navy, and still being void of specific career plans influenced Samuel to follow in his father's footsteps and become an HU custodian. He tries to provide his constituents the kind of support he did not receive during his short stint as a collegian. A civil war drove Ajla and her family from their homeland and motivated her to do whatever it took in the United States (become a custodian, start a business, work two jobs) to provide a better life for her family. Her commitment to her family coupled with the tragic death of her mother influence the maternal-like relationships Ajla forms with residents. These life-scarring experiences remind her that even the most awful work situations are manageable when compared to war and death. Kichelle recognizes the critical role that mentors, such as her sister, play in keeping her children out of harm's way. On the job, Kichelle acts as a positive role model for residents. Likewise, Kichelle's faith guides her as she mediates stressful conflicts and strives for mutual respect.

Samuel, Ajla, and Kichelle recognize that stress goes hand in hand with efforts to forge relationships, maintain spotless buildings, and support others. Samuel remains stressed about not being able to balance his custodial responsibilities with the farm duties he manages with his aging mother. Uncertainty about how to pay his hospital bill represents a daily burden and perpetual stressor for Samuel. Kichelle's decision to send her son to live with her sister and her desire to move to keep her son away from the mean streets of her current neighborhood are daily sources of stress. Likewise, working full-time as a custodian, owning and managing a cleaning business, and supporting her family are daily stressors for Ajla.

For many custodians, the predictable daily routines (those I deem mundane) are stress reducers. Initially, custodians' comfort with and unswerving commitment to doing virtually the same tasks in the same order, day after day and week after week, perplexed me. What I eventually came to understand was that mundane, predictable, and repetitive tasks at work were often a much-needed respite from stressful, unpredictable, chaotic, and sometimes cruel home environments.

Custodians do not simply import stress from home to work. Their work also induces stress. Samuel seldom misses a day of work and accepts every overtime opportunity afforded him. Despite being one of the higher-paid custodians at HU (due to his many years of service), he still lives paycheck to paycheck. His low salary is a constant source of stress. He postponed his surgery because he feared, even with health insurance, that he would not be able to afford the patient contribution. He worries about increases to his health care premium. He can't afford to own a computer, and his home has neither Internet nor cable television service. He instinctively gravitates toward sale items even when selecting a birthday cake for his mother. Assuming the role of family matriarch and primary wage earner for her family induces stress for Ajla. Kichelle's tensions with her supervisor about inspections are a constant source of stress while on the job.

Miller and Reissman (1961) noted, "We suspect that one of the central determinants in working-class life is the striving for stability and security. External and internal factors promote instability and insecurity. Chief among the external factors [are] unemployment and layoff" (p. 91). Custodians simultaneously express feelings of stability (having a job) and insecurity (the possibility of losing a job), juggling contentment and uneasiness. Kichelle's thoughts of applying for a new job or Samuel's retirement are sources of fear and include tinges of fatalism; their destiny rests with others. Still they press on, hoping that someone will recognize that their work matters a whole lot more than the credit they receive.

Day-in-the-life custodian stories reveal that custodians value hard work and exceeding expectations. They value human relationships, independence, and predictability. They value helping others and providing for family. They arrive for work with many home-life stressors, and work becomes a sanctuary from these woes. And work stress (e.g., micromanaging supervisors) induces more stress, fear, and feelings of fatalism that complicate their home life.

Custodian stories also reveal much about the values of CU and HU. These universities value hard work and exceeding expectations, as do the custodians. The universities privilege custodians' cleaning performance, paying less attention to the intangible and hidden contributions that custodians make each day to the campus community, such as cooking for residents or arriving early for work. The institutions privilege accountability over autonomy. Unlike custodians who invoke family metaphors to describe their work, management invokes a business metaphor rooted in a bottom-line ideology. These differences between workers and managers take center stage in the next chapter.

6

THE SUPERVISING LIFE

The Clean Team

> They say things like, "I can do it. I clean my home." Here it is totally differ-
> ent. You clean up after people. You can't tell them to pick that up or don't
> throw that on the floor. You can do that at home with your kids, but here
> you can't. There are different rules. . . . They say, "How hard can it be?"
> They may clean two or three bathrooms at home; here you do 15 or 16 a
> day. It's different. At home, you don't mop your floor every day. Here, you
> have to mop every day.
>
> —Peaches

Peaches, a burly African American supervisor wearing a long-sleeve black T-shirt
underneath a bright, oversized red polo shirt, grins broadly as she recounts
how to explain to naïve job candidates the unique aspects of campus custodial work. Peaches' chic motorcycle cap hides most of her shining snow-white
hair, which augments her hip-hop storytelling cadence. The work responsibilities and routines of a custodial supervisor differ from that of custodians. This
chapter focuses on Harrison University (HU) and Compton University (CU)
housekeeping supervisors. Despite obvious differences between the two universities, their custodial departments are structurally and hierarchically similar.
Custodians report to supervisors, supervisors report to departmental administrators, and administrators report to senior university personnel.

HU's housekeeping department includes 112 custodians, 7 supervisors,
and 3 departmental administrators. CU employs 73 custodians, 7 supervisors, and 2 departmental administrators. All 14 supervisors (7 HU and 7
CU) are former custodians who earned promotions. None of the 5 administrators (3 HU and 2 CU) were affiliated with the university before applying
for the administrator's position.

Today Peaches has key duty, a daily ritual that the six day-shift supervisors rotate. It's 7:30 a.m., and Peaches will soon be distributing key rings

to custodians as they arrive. At the conclusion of the shift she will retrieve and store the keys to fulfill the department's security policies. Ready to go, Peaches refocuses her attention on me.

> I look for a strong person. I can tell by the application. Usually, if they are older and job hunting, to me that says a lot—they are moving and not focused. If they have six to 10 years on the job, they are more responsible and stronger. I am not talking about body strength, but mental strength. . . . I look to see if they are nervous. If they are nervous, quiet, or timid, this place will eat them alive.

As custodians filter into the room, they instinctively approach the key counter. Devin asks Meredith when the cleaning supplies he ordered will be delivered to his hall. Anna finalizes custodians' work assignments for the day. Noticing my curiosity, she describes the scheduling responsibilities. "They call in by 7:00 a.m. if they're going to miss work. We make the final schedule by 8:00. We don't want to miss anything if someone is missing. We have to figure out how to cover all zones."

Anna caucuses with a floater (a custodian who fills in for absent staff) to explain his substitute custodian duties. Nearby, Meredith briefs two custodians about setting up a large multipurpose room that will be the site of a major campus-wide program later in the afternoon. Peaches locks the key cabinets and then moves to an adjoining room, which includes two tiny private offices for the director and assistant director and a larger bullpen area with barely enough space for the six supervisors' desks and the copy machine. These close quarters are ideal for fieldworkers, not supervisors.

Peaches plops down in her chair and raises her hands above her head in an exaggerated fashion as she frantically searches for a piece of paper on her messy desk. She needs to find it before checking in with the two night-crew custodians who work the 10:30 p.m. to 11:00 a.m. shift. Managing keys, scheduling work assignments, distributing inventory, maintaining attendance records, consulting with staff, and ensuring safety are just a few supervisory responsibilities on display this morning.

Anna is the lone supervisor remaining in the suite, now that the clocking in and the mass exodus rituals are complete. Anna briefs me on her agenda for the remainder of the morning as she strolls out the door:

> I walk around and check in with each person before 10:00 a.m. to see how the morning is. . . . I know about crises by midmorning. The housekeepers who are good I leave to last. They will call me to tell me problems. After 10:15, if it is an inspection day, I start them.

Alone, I appreciate the calm. This morning my goal is to remain in this suite, the epicenter of custodial activity, to observe and talk with the six day-shift supervisors who spend several hours each day in this space. Meredith and Lance, engrossed in conversation, reenter the suite. Sensing a sensitive conversation, I slither out. On the loading dock I encounter Mone, who is packing cleaning and paper products into his trashmobile as his radio blares Motown hits. We talk music and sports until Anna passes and asks me if I want to join her as she tours buildings. I accept the invitation.

Inspections, a contentious policy that divides custodians and supervisors, dominate our conversation. Based on the intensity of the dialogue, I understand that Anna perceives inspections as a critical supervisory responsibility. Her description conveys her knowledge of each supervisee and her capacity to adapt her supervision style to the context. She keeps a close eye on marginal staff; these supervisees keep a safe distance from Anna whenever possible. Anna identifies five supervisees whom she deems "the best of the best." She acknowledges their stellar credentials and follows with a discussion of the shortcomings that she does monitor, like allowing dirt to build up. She is unapologetic about her high expectations and supervision style:

> After inspections, I go and talk to housekeepers that day. I don't leave it until tomorrow. I want them to know right away. Really good housekeepers have no problems with inspections. They say, "Go wherever you want." Other housekeepers, they try to show you what they want you to see. The good ones know they do a good job, and they know nothing can hurt them because they know they did good. They achieve expectations, even if they don't exceed expectations.

Shoddy work is unacceptable. Anna recounts an instance where a custodian failed to tie the trash bag to the can, which resulted in soda splattering on the bag, in the can, and on the wall. Raising her voice, she poses a rhetorical question: "Why not do it right the first time?" Anna explains that her style takes time for others to appreciate, and other managers sometimes undermine the socialization process she favors.

> We had an old supervisor, from years ago, who was not very good. After you follow that person, it's a mess. He didn't challenge the housekeepers. It is not fair. When I followed him, the first year they hated me, but the second year they liked me more.

Finally, Anna tracks down and consults with her supervisee. I observe the conversation from afar. Anna situates herself about midpoint on the "high and mighty boss–friend" continuum. Her efficient style is more professional than nurturing. She seems like an invaluable and accessible resource person, not a warm and fuzzy conversationalist. Intrigued by this verbal exchange, once in the elevator I ask Anna to describe her supervision philosophy. She responds with a few stories:

> Problems always start with the supervisor, me. I start a conversation about what is the problem. For example, I found someone in a room with her legs on a table. She said she got tired because of working so hard. She was supposed to be in one of two places at 2:00, and she was not at either place. She was in a totally different place resting. She was lying. That activates all of my nerves; I am steaming. I am tired, and I walk everywhere. I tell her, "I am giving you a verbal warning for an unauthorized break." I say no more words.

A new supervisee had worked for three months but still failed to produce high-quality work. Obviously, still concerned with this person, Anna exclaims, "How can he not know what to do after three months?" I knew a fuller account of the incident was forthcoming. One morning Anna inspects a public restroom that this supervisee cleans, and deems it "filthy." She tracks down the custodian, who was hanging out with cooks in a dining hall kitchen. "I need to talk to you," she insists. In private, she criticizes his work. He refutes her appraisal, arguing that he had cleaned the bathroom earlier in the day. Immediately, Anna calls two supervisors to reinspect. She explains her strategy: "I knew he was not going to believe me if I did it alone." He fails the second inspection. His confrontational response to the feedback results in Anna sending him home. The next day she issues a written reprimand for "acting out, being loud, and not doing his job." She explains the gravity of the situation: "That is severe. Verbal is if you miss something; severe is when you say you did something and you did not and you are loud." Punching a hole in the drywall exiting the room sealed his fate; Lance fired him.

Back at the suite, I encounter Peaches and Joanne. It is hard to ascertain if it is their late-morning break or an early lunch. I pull up a seat and sit between them, then ask, "What is it like to be a supervisor?" Peaches responds,

> It is interesting being a supervisor. It has its ups and downs. I would like to be doing something else, like being a furniture supervisor. This is a bit laid-back. I like to do more physical stuff, like floors, furniture delivery, or something like that. I rehab houses. My boyfriend bought one. He taught me how to fix things up as we went along. Then we bought another house. . . . I figured out it was not that bad. . . . Now I can mud

and tape—it's so easy. I also do light plumbing, ceramic tiles, and dry-wall. I don't do electrical. I don't like to mess with it because of the fires. I started [rehabbing houses] and kind of like it.

Joanne, a 20-year supervisor and a cancer survivor, disagrees with Peaches's preference for supervisors engaging in more physical labor. Having fewer physical demands as a supervisor helps her to cope with mental fatigue and lingering physical ailments, yet she still describes herself as a "working supervisor":

Supervision is okay, but I would rather come in and do my eight hours and go home, to be frank with you. With my team here, I tell them, "You have 20 minutes of my time." I ask them, "What do you want me to do?" I am the boss, but they are doing the work. The boss needs to do things every once in a while, so I appreciate what they do. . . . So, I do 20 minutes of work with them each day—like dusting or cleaning suites. That's just me.

Custodians prefer working supervisors rather than supervisors who won't work in the trenches. Custodians also appreciate supervisors who advocate on their behalf, like Joanne. As she explains,

I get along with most staff. I trained many of them. I tell them that they should learn things like waxing or floor care so that if you leave the university and start you own business you will have skills to have your own company and make more money. I can wax, buff, work on all kinds of floors, even wood floors. Jerry, my old boss, had a side job, and he pulled me in. We worked at eight hardware stores. We would clean with a crew of three and train people who were going to do the floors in those stores. I did this as my night job.

Strength, self-sufficiency, and independence are essential qualities for supervisors. Peaches chimes in to pay tribute to her most influential mentor, her mother:

My mother was an only child. She was born and raised here. My mother has been dead about 10 years. She was a strong woman who always focused on family. She would tell me to work and get my own job. "Don't rely on men," she would say. She stressed that with my sister and me—we should be backbones.

A wide variance of competencies within the custodial ranks is unavoidable. Despite clear expectations and close supervision, some custodians fail to meet departmental expectations. Coaching struggling employees to ensure that they remain employed is a primary responsibility of supervisors. Peaches shares a secret seldom conveyed to custodians: "It takes a lot to get fired. Lance will let a lot of things go by if you have good attendance. He wants to get 60% to 70% [effort] from you. If he can get that, you're here to stay." She draws on her 16 years of supervisory experience to accentuate the importance of attendance. Getting 60% out of a custodian who shows up each day is better than getting 100% out of a custodian who is frequently absent. I think to myself, *I guess Woody Allen was correct: "Eighty percent of success in life is showing up."*

Some supervisors want a name badge that says "Supervisor," not "Housekeeper." Joanne makes clear that she is not one of them. She lists dos and don'ts for supervisors: "Be a people person. . . . Don't act like you're better than others; it's a no-no. . . . Respect them." Peaches adds to the list: "You gotta be proud to be a custodian and speak your mind." She shudders as she mimics a popular grievance of coworkers: "We're only housekeepers." She raises her voice to ask, "What does that mean?"

> I am so tired of hearing that we are "just" housekeepers. Some people are ashamed of being a housekeeper. I don't get it. We are the backbone of the department. If it were not for housekeeping a lot of things would go down badly. We do stuff for housing and maintenance—stuff they don't have the common sense to do. We back them up. When they do programs and need help, we kick right in. We also let them know when they messed up on something or forgot about something. We know that we have to get it done—even if they don't.

For Peaches, working hard, being "real," and having common sense are the unique contributions that she provides the department and CU. She expands on this idea: "Educated folk lack common sense. They got degrees and credentials but no street knowledge and common sense. If they have to fall back, they can't even do housekeeping." I look quizzically at Peaches; she responds by shaking her head and continuing with her argument. "They commit suicide because they can't accept that they used to make $35 an hour and now make much less. They can't deal with that." She goes on, "If you hear housekeeper stories, you know they can deal with that. They can make $200,000 a year and lose it all, and they can fall back. They know how to do it, because they are already strong and have common sense." More gospel according to Peaches:

> Some people are educated, but have no street smarts. I see that a lot in students; I try to talk to them about it. I say, "You have to have common sense

along with your book smarts. If you don't, this world will eat you up. The reason a lot of stuff happens to you all is because you're naïve."

The sermon reaches a crescendo as Peaches recounts an incident where a student asked, "How do you use a broom?" Stunned by the question, she looked at the student and asked, "Are you very rich?" The student replied, "Yes," and then admitted that she had never had to clean. Peaches responded, "You are living by yourself on your mama's and papa's money. What happens if one day your papa is killed and your mama takes the insurance money? What do you do if you don't have a dime?" Alarmed, the student replies, "I don't know. I never did anything without money." Peaches says, "Just because your mama is rich, you still need to know what to do with the broom. You push it."

Peaches, Joanne, and Anna have risen through the custodial ranks. Telling it like it is to their subordinates is their supervisory trademark, regardless of how others perceive them, yet they are more reluctant to challenge their bosses. Peaches summed up how many supervisors cope with the administrators' many demands:

> Some people will stand there and hold a conversation with you. They're okay. And sometimes I get that look from people. You know, you're the janitor, why are you speaking to me? They act like because you are a housekeeper, you are no good, dirty, or not a real person. I guess it goes with being a housekeeper. You gotta be strong. You have to make it. You can't sit there and cry. You have to get off your butt and succeed. I have to succeed. I have a job and I am proud of it. I am not living in a box somewhere. If you don't want to smile at me, *don't*.

The Buffer

Worker-management tensions are common and escalate over time. Hazel, a floor-buffing custodian, recounted an example:

> Last summer we were waxing hallways. I said to Sal, "Are you getting hot?" He said, "Yeah." I was sweating. I told him the university doesn't turn the air [conditioner] off until 9:30. So we thought it was broke down. After taking turns waxing for a while, we went downstairs and ran into Karen, the girl who used to work here. She came here to get her [wax] stripper shoes. She said, "Hazel, what do you think about them turning off the air at 4:30?" I said, "What? I thought we had a breakdown." She said, "No, no, no. They turned the air off on us." I said, "Why?" "Money," Karen replied. I said, "How are we supposed to do floors here?" I guess that was our problem. We

had footprints in the wax, because the floors wouldn't dry. Supposedly they saved $900,000 doing it. When you walk in, the heat hits you in the face. I can hardly breathe, and it gives me a headache. The air-conditioning guy said it was not good to turn off and on the air-conditioner each day, but you know, you have to do what they [bosses] say.

For HU supervisors, the most challenging aspect of their job is acting as a buffer between custodians like Hazel and senior physical plant administrators. Being hierarchically sandwiched between these two subcultures is a regular and uncomfortable occurrence. Supervisors, all former custodians, recognize the invisible hardships and tough working conditions that the custodial staff regularly encounter. Supervisors are also keenly aware of universities' urgency to cut costs. Turning off the air-conditioning and inconveniencing only a few custodians seems like a responsible cost-cutting measure (unless, of course, you are a custodian). Ben, a 50-something supervisor who is nearing retirement, knows better.

HU supervisors' work responsibilities closely resemble those of the CU employees such as Peaches, Anna, Joanne, and Meredith. Supervisors like Ben manage schedules; maintain record-keeping systems; assign work tasks; control inventory and distribute supplies; train custodians and inspect their work; and maintain health, safety, and sanitation standards. His unique contribution to this research is his willingness to talk about tensions with senior administrators.

Ben accepted a custodian position in 2001, after working 28 years (15 years as a machine operator and 13 as a supervisor) in a factory that was on the verge of closing. Other supervisors at the factory regularly criticized Ben for being too close to supervisees. Despite these criticisms, Ben was unyielding. He recounts stories that validate his management philosophy. He initiated disciplinary action against a worker who manufactured a low-quality product. At the conclusion of the meeting, the worker apologized: "Ben, I'm sorry I let you down." Ben distills his theory of supervision to a single sentence: "You can read all of the books on management and leadership you want, but it's all about the people."

After a stint as an HU custodian, the department promoted Ben to supervisor. From the outset, custodians gravitated toward Ben due to his supervisory style—but for vastly different reasons. Some custodians respect his hands-off style of supervision, which provided supervisees the freedom to figure out and do their jobs. Ben's fluid expectations (when compared to other supervisors) appeal to other custodians, who sheepishly confess that they didn't have to work very hard to please him. Despite differences, custodians agree that Ben understands the job and is an advocate.

HU's fiscal woes resulted in reducing the number of custodians. Ben's boss expected the remaining staff in his buildings to increase their daily workload to compensate for the cutbacks. Ben, understanding that understaffing is a chronic problem, did not simply and instinctively jump on the "do more with less" bandwagon. Instead, he expresses concerns about staff reductions to his bosses and then coconstructs a plan of action with his supervisees to implement these changes.

> Say if we lose two people, they [administrators] expect the other staff to pick up the work. I tell my boss, "We can't pound them and tell them we have to do everything starting today." I ask them [supervisees], "What is the easiest way to get things done?" I say, "Can you guys do this?" I could be hard-core and have inspections every night, but that's not my style. But I can get there, where they [administrators] want me to be.

"Probably the single most important thing you can do to begin building a positive relationship with departmental staff is to get to know them. Talk to them. Find out if there's anything you can do to make their own lives easier" (H. Kreuter, 2011, para. 4). Ben heeds this advice.

Sweet (2001) concluded, "Bureaucracy promotes hierarchy, and does create goals that separate workers from management" (p. 79). Ben understands the debilitating aspects of bureaucracies and unobtrusively subverts hierarchies, crude efficiency initiatives such as staff reductions, and rigid divisions of labor. As a buffer, he minimizes friction between workers and managers. This is no easy task, since distrust between workers and management is at a near-epidemic level.

Recently the HU student newspaper published an article about a new Department of Physical Facilities policy that consolidated the day and evening work shifts of custodians. The article included quotes from custodians criticizing the new policy. The critics insisted that the journalist use pseudonyms to mask their identities. Ben's interpretation of this incident focused on lack of trust and leadership. "That says a lot. If you have good leadership, they [physical plant workers] won't be afraid to include their names."

Ben does not fear talking *about* fear. His candor is a stark contrast to many of his colleagues who talk *around* fear, by leaving proverbial breadcrumbs to allow me to independently discover problems (without having to talk explicitly about them). Ben matter-of-factly criticizes colleagues who worry too much about themselves and are too eager to please upper management. He argues that senior supervisors are the least likely people to challenge authority because they need to ensure that they remain employed until retirement. A recent termination of a veteran supervisor ensures that most supervisors will toe the line. Ben acts as a subversive rebel who knows there are few rewards for heroic actions. He deftly shields custodians from senior administrators and vice versa.

Nagle's (2013) findings from her ethnographic study of sanitation workers in New York City suggested that decision makers are seldom drawn from the ranks of those who do the work and seldom know what it is like in the streets collecting garbage. Ben offers an example that affirms this point. During a recent meeting of supervisors, Ben's boss reports on a dramatic surge in custodian accidents. Senior administrators are understandably alarmed and adamant about reversing this trend. Ben and other supervisors skillfully educate their boss about the potential correlation between the department's new early-morning shift and the increase in injuries. Because workers began work at 4:30 a.m. (rather than 4:00 p.m.), they often work outside in the dark, a contributing factor to some injuries. Inside their buildings, custodians hurry to complete the bulk of cleaning tasks during the first half of their shift, in order to not disturb administrators and faculty working in the buildings after 8:00 a.m. The uneven rhythm of custodians' work routines increases the probability of injury. Being a gentle educator to those with more power is a tricky endeavor.

Supervisors also act as intermediaries to communicate to rank-and-file workers senior administrators' ideological and policy shifts. Customer service was HU's ideology in the 1990s. Conventional wisdom embedded in this paradigm suggests that if custodians tend to customers (faculty, administrators, or students), the bottom line will take care of itself. A more contemporary institutional ideology centers on becoming "lean." A primary goal in this paradigm is to replace unnecessary or expensive services with bare-bones services to decrease costs. A supervisor's duty is to communicate this dramatic paradigmatic shift to custodians, without making the shift appear dramatic.

Balancing the interests of the university with the interests of custodians is another thorny task for supervisors. Ben, supporting a custodian involved in a custody battle, approved her request to start and end work later, because the custodian had taken out a restraining order against her estranged spouse and had to ensure that her child boarded a school bus before leaving home for work. Ben's immediate supervisors supported his decision, but the Department of Human Resources staff was unhappy about Ben opening up a proverbial Pandora's box related to work schedules.

Unions criticize supervisors when they occasionally assume the role of working supervisors. Ben explains, "We have to be careful what we do as managers, like working with them [custodians], so that they do not file grievances saying we are doing their work." Avoiding union conflicts and supporting supervisees is like walking on a wire.

Promotions are rare for custodians. Dozens of qualified applicants apply for custodial supervisor vacancies when they become available, usually one vacancy every two years. The odds for securing these coveted jobs are slim. Remaining in a seemingly dead-end job creates challenges for both supervisors and custodians.

Worker-Manager Strife

Variance among supervisors at HU and CU is unmistakable and an asset. Custodians appreciate the diverse ways each supervisor tells it like it is. Residents reap the benefit of Anna's quest to eliminate dirt buildup. Joanne practices what she preaches and gets her hands dirty, even though she does not have to. Peaches models ways for staff to use (rather than repress) street knowledge and common sense in their work. Ben's role as a conduit connects upper administrators with custodians, subcultures that seldom interact with each other. Since there is a wide variance of custodians, it makes sense to have supervisors with diverse management styles.

Each CU and HU supervisor had worked as a custodian; they effectively resolved their work challenges and ultimately got promoted. They know the grind, the injustices, and workers' resistance strategies. Supervisors also know that most custodians prefer high structure, flounder in ambiguous situations, and relish predictability, while resisting change. And they understand senior university management—the powerbrokers. Tuchman (2009) noted, "In many ways, being a member of a university's administration resembles being a corporate manager. In both spheres, professional managers follow many of the same rules. They include such behaviors as loyalty to one's boss, discretion about one's work, being attuned to practical decision-making, and not talking out of turn at meetings (Jackall 1988)" (p. 75). Custodial supervisors know what Tuchman knows: custodial administrators' loyalty is first and foremost to their bosses.

As organizations grow, interpersonal relationships and work responsibilities become more complicated. Whyte (1949) chronicled the evolution of a small restaurant. At first there was little division of labor; owners, cooks, and dishwashers worked together. Over time, the restaurant grew in size and complexity, yet the business and relationships remained flexible and fluid. Formal and elaborate procedures were virtually nonexistent. Bosses, employees, and customers still knew each other. Business growth eventually made it necessary to create formalized divisions of labor—waiters, cooks, dishwashers, managers, and owners—aimed at coordination and efficiency. Expansion of the eatery magnified existing management, labor, and customer service problems, while creating new ones. The expansion of the hierarchy added new levels of authority that separate decision makers from workers. As a result, administration is more complex.

The unprecedented growth and evolution of higher education in the twentieth century mirrors the growth and evolution schemas that Whyte (1949) noted in his study. Like restaurant managers who are saddled with the responsibility of administering the restaurant as well as acting as a conduit connecting owners, workers, and patrons, custodial supervisors spend an inordinate amount of their time acting both as buffers and conduits to try to keep separate and interconnect senior administrators with rank-and-file staff and service recipients. These conduit and buffer roles burden supervisors. Technically, supervisors are part of the company's managerial team, but a closer examination of their actual roles on the manager-worker continuum reveals that they are closer to workers than to senior managers. Criticized by workers and senior administrators both, they are caught in an administrative squeeze.

> The effects of centralization and routinization are most commonly associated with rank-and-file workers, and the assembly-line worker in the automobile factory is typically held up as the classic victim of deskilling. Yet, the foreman is also [a] victim of centralization; indeed, the deskilling of labor necessarily implies the deskilling of the supervisor who is condemned to monitor those who monitor the machines. (Paules, 1991, pp. 53–54)

Supervisors, often critiqued by supervisors and supervisees, become highly responsible yet deskilled employees trying to broker deals between detached high-level managers and vulnerable and disgruntled workers, while also trying to keep them apart. Like the custodians they supervise, supervisors find that trusting others (and vice versa) is risky. Fear of being unemployed is a worry, even during times of relative economic calm. "The share of working-age Americans holding jobs is now lower than at any time in the last three decades, and 76% of them are living paycheck to paycheck. No one has any job security. The last thing they want to do is make a fuss and risk losing the little they have" (Reich, 2014, paras. 6–7). Manager-labor disputes, an unstable economy, and job insecurity are commonplace. Less common and obvious is the harm that supervisors incur when serving both as buffer and conduit. The buffer role makes these low-level supervisors lightning rods for criticism, controversy, or negative comments that shield powerbrokers from harm. Powerbrokers pressure supervisors to protect the university.

Supervisors, in turn, expect custodians to do the same. Powerbrokers deflect the attention of their underlings away from the real epicenters of power and toward the supervisors. These dynamics fuel discontent and fear across custodial departments. Custodians fear that managers will, for example, use inspections to justify poor performance appraisals, which would harm them. Managers fear hostile reactions from subordinates and senior management. Managers and workers approach accountability efforts with passive acceptance and defeatism—feelings of powerlessness against fate. Accountability measures and formal and informal auditing seem normal, natural, and logical in tough economic times. But they are not. Instead, they deflect attention away from the dangers of these hegemonic expectations. The winners and losers are obvious.

7

FEAR THE WORST

Primal Fear

Loitering in a custodial break room at Harrison University (HU), I overhear two supervisors preparing a snow-removal plan for a storm due to arrive in a few hours. Apparently, during the previous storm, a vice president—who is the ultimate supervisor of custodians and an advocate of outsourcing—slipped and fell on a patch of ice outside of his office building. He called the Department of Physical Facilities (DPF) to alert staff of this safety hazard.

An aspect of this new strategy is to dispatch a four-person snow-removal crew to the vicinity of the VP's office. The crew will clear snow and ice and then remain on site for the entire shift to ensure that sidewalks and parking lots remain clear. Supervisors appear resigned to carrying out an order from departmental administrators that they deem is an overreaction to "the fall."

Four months later, on the Compton University (CU) campus, six custodians and I arrive at an on-campus residential apartment building two days after graduation. Since residents clean their apartments during the academic year, custodians must eradicate a year's worth of dirt and grime in a span of four or five hours to prepare these spaces for summer school students and conference attendees. We haul cleaning supplies, brooms, and vacuum cleaners up three flights of stairs for this ceiling-to-floor cleaning ritual. Housekeepers negotiate their division of labor and then begin to remove shower curtains, replace mattress pads, discard abandoned items, wash windows, sanitize bathrooms, vacuum air vents, and haul trash.

While touring one seemingly decimated apartment, I inquire as to why one bedroom door is locked. A supervisor explains that a student-athlete who is competing in a local tennis tournament has permission to remain in the suite. As a result, the crew will return to clean the space again. She elaborates, "That's how it is done here. . . . We take care of students. . . . Like this [locked room], it's more work. . . . It's crazy, but there's nothing we can do."

* * *

Prior to undertaking this research, I would have predicted that HU custodial supervisors would have been more concerned about removing dangerous ice and snow throughout the entire campus and less obsessive about pleasing their boss. And I would have predicted that CU supervisors would question authority and advocate for the relocation of a resident to another locale to ensure his safety and make housekeepers' work a little easier. During my fieldwork I crossed paths with custodians as well as supervisors who encountered routine work challenges and possessed the requisite wisdom to resolve the matters; however, their ultimate actions, rooted in fear, seemed counterintuitive and defied common sense. The importance that custodians and supervisors placed on placating a boss and providing unconditional customer service by demurring to students surprised me. In these two instances, the two goals undermine two other highly coveted values of the academy: being efficient and cutting costs.

In these unstable economic times, why are administrators seemingly inefficient and not so thrifty? The short answer is fear, which is the same answer to the opposite question: "Why are administrators hyperfixated on efficiency and cutting costs?" This chapter focuses on fear, which is central to the lives of custodians and supervisors.

Fear permeates all levels of custodial organizations. Senior university administrators pressure custodial departmental administrators to follow their orders or face the consequences. Custodial administrators expect supervisors to follow their mandates. Supervisors demand that custodians follow orders, period. This trickle-down chain of command reveals much about custodians and how universities do business.

Initially I attributed these organizational dynamics to outdated managerial practices coupled with inevitable worker–management tensions, such as miscommunication, inexperienced supervisors, or disgruntled veteran custodians. A more in-depth analysis revealed that these organizational ideologies and structures are contemporary and represent a dramatically different paradigmatic approach to doing business. This new philosophy advocates that universities operate more like a business or corporation than a nonprofit educational organization. A central tenet of this corporate ideology is fear. Chomsky's (2014) insights about this ideological shift shed light on the connections between corporatization and fear:

> When universities become corporatized, as has been happening quite systematically over the last generation as part of the general neoliberal assault on the population, their business model means that what matters is the bottom line. The effective owners are the trustees (or the legislature, in the case of state universities), and they want to keep costs down and make sure that labor is docile and obedient. (para. 2)

In this same essay, Chomsky also took exception with the chair of the Federal Reserve Bank whose glowing economic assessment report to Congress in 1997 suggested that imposing *greater* worker insecurity was a driver of economic success. Alan Greenspan, the chair, argued, "If workers are more insecure, that's very 'healthy' for the society, because if workers are insecure they won't ask for wages, they won't go on strike, they won't call for benefits; they'll serve the masters gladly and passively" (para. 2).

As Chomsky noted, fear and insecurity are profitable. A senior HU administrator's proposal to alter staffing criteria illuminates the relationship between cutting costs and inducing feelings of insecurity and fear:

> The mode of operation in the old days at Harrison was to take them through their career as a custodian. As they get to the end of that career— guess what, they can't do the same amount of work, so the areas they work get smaller, until they are dealing with some pretty small areas. That's what they can take care of. This is not a very efficient way to do business. Then you have someone whose area is getting bigger because they are making up for someone whose area is getting smaller.
>
> That is an institutional cultural aspect that needs to change and is changing. You have underlying questions: What is the university's underlying responsibility to people? What is the people side of that? Everyone knows you can't do the same thing when you are 60 as when you were 20. How do you handle that? As a director, you have to make certain that your operation makes business sense. How can you do that and juggle the human aspect of it? It is very difficult. It really is.

The answers to these questions become apparent when examining HU's custodial policies. The short answers to the question, "Who are the university's highest priorities?" are (a) tuition-paying collegians who demand first-rate service and (b) governing boards who demand efficient and less expensive campus operations that do not tarnish the university's brand of providing a high-quality education. The most efficient way to achieve this aim is to find ways to "compassionately purge" older workers from the payroll and replace them with cheaper labor. Older, highly competent, and loyal custodians recognize this ideological shift and the subsequent implications for them. Fear is a natural response to proposals such as this one. One custodial supervisor notes workers' response to this shift:

> The people they hire are not proud or pleasant. They are here to do their job and go away. Does anyone care if they come back? If you leave, they just replace you. . . . No one is being taught to take my place. My responsibility was to teach the next generation to step up. That is all gone. . . . It

started about 10 years ago. Little by little, it has been chipped away at over time. Years ago, everyone had a common goal. We would sit down and talk about it. We used to have more structure and goals. That does not happen anymore. The personalization is gone. Pride is gone in your job and what you did and what you shared. Everyone looked forward to coming to work because you enjoyed the people you work with. That is pretty much gone. Little by little you have to accept it. You can't fight it. You have to deal with it.

This managerial shift has a profound influence on policies, practices, and morale. Feelings of fear, which historically have been expressed by custodians, are now omnipresent and proliferating. Custodians are fearful of losing their jobs or keeping their jobs and struggling with expanded job responsibilities. Even acting to minimize fear (contemplating unionization) induces fear. This collective resistance to resisting ensures that the status quo will prevail.

Entangled with fears are feelings of fatalism. Supervisors and custodians convey that they feel powerless to control their destinies. Inadequate access to those in power and a legacy of self-reliance, which is currently under siege, are two contributors to these feelings of helplessness.

To speak of the "corporatization of the university" is not to speak narrowly or metaphorically. It is to speak broadly and liberally. While the university will never look or work exactly like a for-profit firm, it will continue to transform itself into something that does not resemble what most scholars and citizens think of as a nonprofit educational institution. (Ruben, 2000, p. 210)

Although custodians' interpretations of these ideological changes are not as eloquent and cogent as Ruben's, they know that the university is changing, and their instincts suggest that they should be fearful of change that will likely harm them. This managerial shift influences the quality of life for custodians.

Fear Factors

Fear is a near-universal feeling for custodians, evident in every phase of their career. Samplings of strands of fear and feelings of fatalism follow.

Disorientation

In 2013 HU's DPF hired Jonathan, a 22-year-old Caucasian to clean its largest academic building. He works the 4:30 a.m. to 1:00 p.m. shift Monday through Friday. Coping with his probationary custodian status is as exhausting as the manual-labor aspects of the job. Earning a paycheck, learning new skills, and modeling his Christian beliefs deflect Jonathan's attention away from long-term job security worries.

> I don't clean toilets for the love of other humans. I do it because I am paid. I think about how this experience pertains to me. Doing service for someone who does not appreciate it reminds me of Jesus, who died for some people who never appreciated him. I don't like cleaning toilets and picking up garbage. I humble myself to do these things. Some egotism will be broken. If we let little things each day humble us, ultimately we become better people.

Recent so-called efficiency initiatives have resulted in fewer custodians in Jonathan's building. As a result, he works alone, has more responsibilities than his predecessor, and receives sporadic direct supervision. A veteran custodian compared HU's current employee orientation practices with those of the past:

> We used to give people a week or two on-the-job training with a trainer. Now, you get thrown right into the mix. . . . In 1992, master custodians did training. I was one of them. Everyone who was new, we trained. We showed them the ropes. . . . When training ended, they were ready to work.

Nowadays the experienced custodians informally orient new staff, if time permits. Work annoyances breed negativity during informal orientation and mentoring interactions, which is predictable when morale is low and workloads are high.

As Jonathan and I wash blackboards and empty trash, he offers imaginative solutions to perennial custodial problems, such as cleaning hard-to-reach ceiling vents or removing gum from carpet. Unfortunately, being a creative problem solver is not part of a probationary staff member's job description. When interacting with his supervisor, Jonathan acquiesces to the role of apprentice, not consultant or innovator. He has already assimilated HU's brand of being businesslike: working hard, following orders, and keeping a low profile. "Who we are arises from how others address us over time" (Charon, 2002, p. 61). This is true for Jonathan and other new custodial staff.

HU socializes custodians to perform externally defined subculture scripts such as following orders (despite the absence of a formal orientation program). These scripts define and perpetuate custodians' narrow campus roles and affirm their low status. Fear and feelings of fatalism tamp down aspirations to challenge these conventional custodial scripts. Jonathan is happy with his job, confident in his abilities, and tireless. Yet he realizes that his fate, related to surviving probation, is largely beyond his control and in the hands of custodial supervisors and the DPF staff with whom he spends very little time. This can be disconcerting and disorienting.

You're Not Hired

> I'm 47 years old. I went to grade school and I went to high school, but I didn't complete high school. . . . I try to go back and get my GED; I got very close, but I got intimidated and quit. I have been here 16 years. I used to do home health care for about seven years. I kind of got fed up with that. After I left that job, I applied for unemployment. Then I applied for housekeeping. Two or three days later I got a referral. I came here and I've been here ever since.

Zoe has been a CU housekeeper since 1997 and enjoys her current job much better than her previous one. Zoe, an African American woman, works long hours and earns a modest salary, requiring her to work a second job. Her lack of formal education has limited career advancement, so she resumed her GED quest to be more marketable in case she applies for other jobs.

> I would leave here and go to class. I usually had about two hours between work and school to do my homework. The classes were about two hours. I went to class for about two months, but as the test got closer, I got intimidated and gave up. I've been out of school for a lot of years and going back and trying to pick all this up is hard. So many of the people were almost the same age as my kids. Between home, my job, and this, it was just too much. I would rather be doing something else than cleaning, but if I don't have the education, there is not much I can do. . . . I know I am old, but I don't think I'm too old to learn.

Zoe aspires to become a CU custodial supervisor. She interviewed for supervisor vacancies three different times and was never promoted. Although annual performance evaluations provide Zoe feedback about her performance as a custodian, she is not privy to feedback available from the interviews to inform her about her supervisory capacities. Zoe perceives that soliciting feedback to improve is a risk. Instead she sucks it up and simply accepts the decisions.

I ask Zoe if she met with her supervisor to debrief the job interviews and discuss future aspirations. She replies, "I don't want to cause any problems. I just want to do my job. . . . It won't do any good." Zoe's polite cynicism with a tinge of fatalism suggests that she knows that the university will not allow her supervisor to reveal the reasons she did not get a promotion. Litigation fears limit supervisors from providing specific feedback about candidates' interview performances. Green (2008), noted, "Some hiring managers will never give rejected candidates feedback, for fear of saying something that will open them up to a lawsuit. There's nothing you can do about these people; they are muzzled by fear" (para. 6). Likewise, Heathfield (2014) asserted,

> Most attorneys recommend that employers provide little feedback to job candidates. They are concerned that feedback can be used or misconstrued by the applicant to demonstrate discrimination in the hiring process. Since you fear the cost, time and staff attention that a lawsuit would require, many believe it is safest to avoid providing feedback at all. (para. 5)

Offering candidates constructive feedback is both appropriate and risky. When these two values collide in corporate-influenced environments, *minimizing risk* trumps the act of educating. Although I suspect Zoe's supervisor would meet with her to discuss interview experiences, candor and full disclosure would be unlikely (based on the advice of university attorneys). In this new educational milieu, soliciting feedback to enhance learning is a perilous act—which sounds like a hazardous way to do business.

Fade to Black

> I take out trash and work in all the public areas—like meeting rooms. I don't do dorms. The last thing students want to see in the morning in their suite—especially girls—is a huge-ass Black man. You know what I'm saying. I'd be knocking on their door calling out, "Housekeeping," at 8 in the morning. I don't want to do that. Especially since I am new and they don't know me. . . . The Black students, especially the guys, look away from me. I hold a door open; they don't say anything. . . . Sometimes they will ask for help with things. I was helping with their bags up the steps. The next time, they look down and pass. I fade to black that quickly.

Each day community members remind Calvin he is an African American male; sometimes they penalize him for being who he is. Although some collegians may assume Calvin is an uneducated custodian, unworthy of even a superficial greeting, I know otherwise. He keenly understands the politics of race, gender, class, and staying employed. He recognizes that stereotypes about African American men persist in higher education and that he is mostly powerless to confront injustices.

For Calvin, cleaning public spaces in residence halls such as building entryways is safer than cleaning residential floors housing women, but it is certainly not easier. Working in high-traffic areas results in nonstop opportunities for supervisors to monitor or evaluate his performance. He also has few opportunities to have sustained interactions with corridor residents, which is a favorite part of most custodians' work.

Calvin, relegated to cleaning public spaces, subtly reinforces stereotypes such as "Black men don't like to work and therefore need to be in public view so that they can be more easily monitored" or "Black men are sexually virile and lust after White women and therefore should not clean women's residential floors." Calvin understands yet disagrees with the policies of not assigning a young African American man to clean women's residence hall suites.

When working in public spaces, Calvin is not immune to stereotypical absurdities and microaggressions (subtle acts that remind him of his marginalized status as an African American male custodian). Calvin's description of the privileged African American students who shun him is an example of these debilitating encounters. I do not know what is in the hearts of CU supervisors who assigned Calvin to work in public spaces or the collegiate men who ignore him. Yet I know that his identities and work are entangled, and as a result, it makes his tough job even tougher.

When cleaning with Calvin I too encountered microaggressions and insults, which bothered me, yet I knew my feelings were temporary. When my fieldwork ended, microaggressions and acts of disrespect would also cease. Calvin did not have this privilege. To cope he develops strategies to resist acts of aggression, such as not placing himself in situations where others who believe these stereotypes could jeopardize his job and reputation. Although Calvin seldom fears the fools whom he encounters, the thought of losing his job because of others' ignorance is scary.

Calvin's "You have to suck it up" and "You gotta do what you gotta do" response to these threats is a form of fatalism. And it deflects attention away from the realization that equal access to all custodian opportunities eludes him because of his ethnicity and gender. Denton (2014) clarified the dynamics embedded in these stereotypes and microaggressions:

> Identities are neither fixed nor biological—they are the product of social contingencies, including struggles for resources and power. This often results in dominant groups (i.e., those groups in or with power) assigning greater moral worth or superior characteristics to members of their own groups and lesser status to members of subordinate groups (i.e., those with less power) as a strategy for "securing its position of dominance in the system" and, consequentially, justifying their possession of greater resources (Weber, 1998, p. 20). (p. 5)

Calvin's strand of fear (losing his job if he loses his cool) and fatalism (he can't change the hearts and minds of individuals or refute stereotypes of African American men) increases the probability that the status quo will prevail.

Big Brother Is Watching

> I [custodial supervisor] don't hear many complaints from staff about inspections. Every really good housekeeper has no problem with inspections. They say, "Go wherever you want." The not-so-good housekeepers, they show you what they want you to see. The good ones know nothing can hurt them because they know they did well.

This supervisor's comment is a striking contrast to a custodian's comment:

> We [CU custodians] all complain all of the time about inspections. We actually get inspected once a week—way more than we are supposed to. . . . Students think we do pretty good. Sometimes the kids call the office and say Miss _____ did a good job. They [supervisors] don't say too much when those calls come in. . . . Some people mess it up for all of us. And they have to go check them. . . . If there are no complaints what's the point. I don't get why they keep hassling us.

Worker-manager disputes such as this one are common. What is noteworthy and less obvious are the influences of corporate managerialism on accountability, which has redefined and worsened worker-management interactions.

Critics of higher education perceive universities as insufficiently accountable to constituents and governing boards. Hiring experts and external consultants to propose harsh accountability measures is a common approach to quell critics. Creating a more elaborate and intrusive auditing culture that involves intense oversight and surveillance is a popular "solution." For example, smartphones issued to custodians have the capacity to monitor their every movement while on the job. This policy raises custodians' fears that "Big Brother is watching" and will act on what is overseen. These contested manager-worker conversations deflect attention away from the more powerful and stealth architects of assessment and accountability initiatives.

Stuart Hall noted that dominant cultures exert "'total social control' over subordinate groups, not by coercion or by the direct imposition of ruling ideas, 'but by winning and shaping consent so that the power of the dominant classes appears both legitimate and natural'" (as cited in Hebdige, 1979, pp. 15–16). Selective traditions, which ratify and legitimate the dominant culture, sustain these communities. A brief hegemonic analysis of these custodial dynamics suggests that those in power shape the discourse so that being more efficient, accountable, and intrusive is a legitimate, natural, and rational response to ensure a healthy university. Less obvious are answers to questions such as, Whose interests are privileged and whose are ignored?

In this age of accountability, those with power determine what is good and how to do good, and hyperaccountability fuels discontent. Custodians fear that managers will use inspections to justify subpar performance appraisals. Administrators fear hostile reactions from subordinates and senior university administrators. Supervisors and workers both approach accountability efforts with passive acceptance and defeatism.

Critics of my interpretation might argue that these dysfunctional dynamics have been around for decades and have nothing to do with the gravitational pull of the university toward corporate managerialism. In the CU context, a culture of inspection has been in place since the mid-1990s, long before this corporate managerialism came into vogue. What has changed over the past few years is the formality and intensity of these inspections, rooted in the need to ratchet up accountability. In addition to weekly inspections, the department instituted surprise inspections. New evaluation procedures and forms are more formal, quantifiable, nonnegotiable, and more closely linked to salary increases.

> Being "business-like" has affected today's public research universities. . . .
> The new emphasis on business has introduced new sorts of administrators
> who have different kinds of relationships with the professoriate. Increasingly, they try to *govern* them rather than to govern *with* them. As a result,
> the process of auditing has become ever more important. . . . Indeed these
> administrative actions appear to be encouraging an accountability regime.
> (Tuchman, 2009, p. 21)

Governing them, rather than governing with them, whether referring to faculty or custodians, raises fears and worsens feelings of powerlessness against the inevitable.

Institutional Dementia

> I was looking for work at age 18. I just graduated high school. I started
> July 1, 1974. . . . I was living with my grandparents at the time. I definitely needed income. I was taught to be a hard worker, be accountable, be
> responsible, and do what you say you are going to do. And if you can't do
> these things you need to take a good long look at yourself. In 1974, HU
> was like a new world for me. . . . I heard that the president thought the
> wages here were comparable with other jobs in the region. Comparable
> to what? They [new custodians] are still starting off at $9.35 an hour. And
> health care premiums continue to rise. . . . It's not much higher than minimum wage. The university mismanages its budget, and custodians have to
> pay the price.

George's optimism as a new employee in 1974 was unbounded. In 2013, as a retiree, his time away allowed him to reflect on his 39-year custodial career and HU's changing nature. Although George did not explicitly use a corporate lexicon when telling stories about his work experiences, he implicitly suggests that HU's corporate-influenced practices have harmed the university. When positing his recommendations for change, he did not advocate going back to the good old days. He did not privilege custodians' interests over the interests of other campus stakeholders. He did not advocate for huge salary increases for custodians that would wreak havoc on university budgets. Instead, he advocates for others to respect custodians.

According to George, a new breed of university leaders pays insufficient attention to institutional history and ignores the wisdom of elders, which George deems disrespectful. Corporate-influenced practices jeopardize institutional memory—the collective experiences and know-how held by long-standing members of the community. In this new campus order, for example, senior administrators create incentives to entice senior custodians to retire in order to reduce labor costs by hiring cheaper and less experienced workers. Although short-term gains of profits are obvious, long-term losses in the experience and wisdom of elders, as well as a growing inattentiveness to the past, are shortsighted and costly. George's critique of the institution he loves is not about resisting change, but ensuring that the change is moral. He advocates (a) soliciting broad input from diverse constituents, (b) being respectful, (c) not disproportionally burdening the less powerful, (d) not conflating criticism with disloyalty, and (e) protecting institutional memory.

For George, the fear is that this new breed of administrators lacks the humility and long-term vision to seek advice from common folk and veteran staff. He expresses tinges of fatalism when talking about ways to alter the debilitating status quo.

The retirement of George's generation of custodians is not simply a loss of hardworking, loyal, and proud university community members. These retirements increase the probability of institutional dementia, which is something to remember.

Caste-Away Fears

Custodians' fear is unique. It is unlike more common varieties of fear, such as a melodramatic fear of death or panic attacks. Instead, it is a numbing, worrisome fear of being trapped with few viable options. One custodian described her fear using the familiar idiom, "waiting for the other shoe to drop." She expects a seemingly inevitable event over which she has no control. This fear transcends cleaning enclaves, including those such as (a) custodians and supervisors/administrators, (b) rookies and veterans, (c) superstars and slackers, (d) employees and retirees, (e) men and women, and (f) ethnic minorities and majorities. Custodians fret that universities are discarding their pasts like yesterday's trash while worrying about the future. Stakeholders put different and often competing spins on this fear. A current CU custodial manager offered one perspective, which suggests that the proverbial glass for custodians is half full:

> About seven or eight years ago the entry-level people paid nothing for health care. Their premiums now are pretty small, but going from nothing to paying is going to be an issue. HU has laid off folks a few times over the past seven years. There has been a strong feeling at HU with the staff group who lived in the region all their lives. They looked at HU the way people in Detroit looked at GM [General Motors]. HU is a great place to work and a great place for your kids to get an education. The only thing that has remained unchanged is the tuition waiver, and everything else has changed. A lot of people view it as a negative change. People who see the broader view realize it is not a change you have to manage. Everyone is seeing health care benefits rise. Sometimes it is difficult for people to see that.

This manager suggests that custodians are not looking at the bigger picture. The academy is not the problem. He posits that workers everywhere struggle, so custodians should temper their complaints and accept the new normal. A retired HU administrator offered a different analysis:

> The management philosophy of the current administration promotes unreasonable fear and distrust. The fear is that there is one big grand plan, which would never happen at any university. They [custodians] believe there is this big plan that has to do with hurting them financially—losing jobs and benefits. They fear being consolidated with other areas. Those are the big issues for the rank and file. Are they going to get rid of administrative assistants and move to a pool? Admins think that they don't need me. Wherever you go, all areas, there is a sense that the central administration is up to something. I think they are oblivious. They [custodians] don't have any contact with senior folks who could dispel these myths. When I hear crazy things, I would tell them I doubted the accuracy of the rumor, but I assured them I would check it out and get back to them. I would follow up and tell them the myth was not going to happen. That does not happen much these days.

This former administrator views the senior administrators as more culpable than the custodians for the current state of affairs. He posits that times are tough for custodians, but work does not have to be a drag, and fear is legitimate and expected. This individual recognizes that conspiracy theorists are alive and well, and perception is reality. Although fears are seldom palpable, they exist. Corporate managerialism coupled with existing campus caste systems are major sources of fear. He explains, "The [custodians] are very honest. They want you to tell them the truth. Don't lie to them. They come from that generation: integrity. If I shake hands, it means something. Now if you shake the VP's hand, it wouldn't mean the same thing. People are not what he is about." Indeed, it is all about the people.

Some educators hail American higher education as the great equalizer. Others challenge this optimistic view and instead argue that higher education creates castes that contribute to, rather than heal, social inequalities (Stuber, 2011). In the world of custodians, the latter view more closely resembles their experiences. The metaphor of the university as a bastion of wealth and privilege that perpetuates inequalities is slowly replacing the metaphor of the university as a beacon of egalitarian hope.

"The caste system in higher education—based on sifting and sorting of campus subcultures—is alive and well, according to a report issued by the Center for the Future of Higher Education" (Eisenberg, 2012a). This report revealed a caste system within faculty ranks, with part-time faculty members as second-class professors. Similarly, data from this study reveal that others view custodians as second-class citizens.

> At its most basic, class is one way societies sort themselves out. Even societies built on the idea of eliminating class have stark differences in rank. Classes are groups of people of similar economic and social position; people who, for that reason, may share political attitudes, lifestyles, consumption patterns, cultural interests, and opportunities to get ahead. Put ten people in a room, and a pecking order soon emerges. (Scott & Leonhardt, 2005, p. 8)

Higher education castes have existed and will continue to prosper. A unique finding of this study is that the corporate managerialism that has transformed higher education has disproportionally harmed custodians, widening the gap between them and other more powerful enclaves, which exacerbates fears. During HU's 2009 budget crisis, senior administrators protected all faculty positions from cuts; service workers had the highest percentage of positions eliminated. At CU, the shift of the custodial unit from an independent corporation to a CU department necessitated that the former "ma and pa"–like department staff alter its policies to adhere to existing CU policies. CU did not evaluate the Octagon Cleaning Company's personnel practices to ascertain whether any of its policies could benefit the larger university. In both of these examples, which reflect the norm, the caste of senior administrators rules.

HU and CU custodians both recognize and accept that as universities reorganize, implement new ideologies, and wrestle with budget crises, their caste's influence, status, salaries, and benefits will not likely improve. They, too, recognize what Williams (2001) concluded: "Despite cries of budget crises, one rarely hears of cuts in administration" (p. 21). Custodians, despite others' perceptions that they are uneducated, astutely realize that in tough economic times, not all castes experience similar pains.

In 2014, median CEO pay was approximately 257 times the average worker's salary (Associated Press, 2014). Income disparity of this magnitude in America is both numbing and normalized. Disparities such as these are becoming more commonplace in the ivory tower. Academia is not quite as removed from the real world as it pretends to be. In 2012, the Ohio State University president earned an annual salary of $6.1 million (Associated Press, 2014), which is approximately $2,932 per hour. In 2012 the annual starting salary for a newly hired OSU custodian was $10.28 per hour, or an annual salary of $21,382. Income variances and trends such as this one illuminate cavernous caste differences and the selective application of cost-cutting measures.

One HU and one CU custodian acknowledge caste differences, but identify allies who do not use class differences as a weapon and instead support custodians:

> I expected to be looked down upon as a janitor, but the people in my building know my first name. . . . I like the friendliness of people, the fact that they will take time to talk socially, like the graduate students and the secretaries. I will ask professors about plant problems, and they will take the time to look it up in the library. They will get stuff for me from other greenhouses. . . . The professors have encouraged me to take classes.—HU custodian

> Everyone has perceptions of who you are. Not everyone is going to accept you. Let's just face it. . . . Lots of people think you belong underneath their shoes. Let's be honest about that. There are a lot of people who want to get to know who you really are. They realize you are a human and you are their equal, and they realize you have a soul. Once they do that, you are already halfway home. Then, everyone can go on and do their business. —CU custodian

Another custodian from HU offers an example of microaggressions initiated by a member of a more powerful caste, aimed at keeping custodians in their place:

I talked to a faculty member about lizards and how you can cut out three fourths of their liver and they will regenerate. You know, at one time we had that ability as humans but we lost it. She said, "How do you know that?" I tell her I read! I don't spend every waking moment sweeping and mopping. She was amazed I read.—HU custodian

Custodians generally accept the proverbial hand they have been dealt and have spent decades learning how to manage their work with the hope of not losing ground. With the implementation of businesslike practices, those in power have changed how universities do business, which reinforces custodians' fearful perceptions that they are indeed losing ground and being left behind.

8

FAMILY MATTERS

Family Feuds

> Back then there was a reason to be dedicated and loyal. They used to preach to us about the Harrison family. They treated people, everyone—custodians, professors, and students—as family. Now we're supposed to refer to faculty as customers instead of the people you are taking care of. . . . We were all part of the family and here for the same reasons—to make sure the kids are educated. It was like we were a puzzle and we each were a piece. Now we have been torn apart. Now, they say we are running a business here.—HU custodian

Despite differences and tensions involving custodians (i.e., labor) and supervisors (i.e., management) as well as shared feelings of fear, both subcultures used the term *family* to describe past and present work environments. "Family" was the most frequent word uttered by research participants during fieldwork, formal interviews, and casual conversations. Participants both romanticized and critiqued this concept. Four conceptualizations of family reveal insights about custodians' lives beyond work and, more important, how institutional values influence custodians' job satisfaction and interactions with each other and the larger campus community. The first two discourses were more prevalent at Compton University (CU), while the final two were more common at Harrison University (HU).

The CU Family

When conversing with CU custodians, they frequently emphasized the importance of *family*. Upon closer examination of this popular term, two distinct conceptualizations emerged. The next two sections introduce and delineate these distinct family discourses.

A Family Affair

"One's 25, 24, 23, 21, 20, 19, and 17." Learning that Diane, a 44-year-old African American CU custodian, has seven children momentarily disorients me. She married at age 18 and had her first child at 19. She had five children with her first husband and two with her current spouse. Diane is keenly aware that her reproduction revelation surprises most. "I tell people I have seven kids and they say, '*What the #$%&?!!*' or 'Huhhh.'" She quickly credits her Creator, saying "It was the grace of God that made me able to have and raise seven kids." I think to myself, *Even with the grace of God, how can she possibly have the time and energy to raise seven children and work as a campus custodian, cleaning up after collegians?* Although I don't verbalize this question, Diane answers it:

> I've been doing this the past 12 years. I'm a boring person. I go to work. I go home. I go back to work. And I go home. I take care of my kids, and that's it. My husband works nights. We kind of split it up. It was harder for me when my kids were teenagers. When they're young, you know where they're at. When they're teenagers, they are out and doing whatever it is they do.

Diane wakes at 4:00 a.m. before beginning her commute to work at 6:00 a.m. She prefers working the morning shift because it allows her to get home to spend time with her children after school, and before undertaking the two additional daily responsibilities: cooking and cleaning. Diane explains her family's division of labor. "My first husband was a very good cook. My second husband as far as cooking goes, oh no. Nowadays, I do most of the cooking and cleaning at home. The kids, they have their chores." Diane reluctantly talks about struggles. "At first it was hard because I didn't even have any shoes for them. I was by myself. I sacrificed, but I got them shoes. The family made do until we could do better. You have to do what you have to do to take care of your business."

On as many weekends as possible, the family travels "to the country," where Diane's husband's sister lives. She insists the children get out of the city once in a while and experience something different, like horses, cows, and country food. Each summer, two of Diane's children, especially those she did not want idle in the city, spent summers in the country. She explains, "The neighborhood where I live, it's not a bad neighborhood, but it's not a good one." Diane assumed an active role in educating her children; she did not outsource the responsibility to local schools.

> If you teach your kids—not to say they're always going to follow the value of life, like respecting others, and being positive and happy—it's good.

My daughter wrote a paper last year before she graduated. She talked about all the things we did as a family when she was little. She wrote about the rope on the tree with the tire. She talked about how she swung on the swing. And she talked about how we made our first garden. We did all that. And we still do the garden. . . . She talked about a lot of stuff she remembered. . . . I tried to teach them the value of things. You know, we didn't have a lot. If you show them a lot of love and affection, they tend to be good kids. I got to admit it wasn't all peaches and cream. I had two—they gave me the blues. But in the end, they turned out pretty good.

Diane started a lawn care company, The Seven Wonders, so that her children could earn some money. Family members cut lawns for churches, apartment buildings, and even private residences. Diane explains her business model: "Like the elderly, we would not charge them; we would just do things for them. We made a little money from the churches and apartment buildings." Diane's life priorities and philosophy reemerged when talking about work:

You never bite the hand that feeds you. It has been a blessing to have this job. If it wasn't for this job I wouldn't be able to survive. The university is a good place to work. When you're working with different personalities, it makes it a little bit hard. What I do is focus on what I need to do. You do what you got to do. That's it. You never bite the hand that feeds you. Every job had some good and some bad. I have my likes and dislikes.

Diane knows most of the people on her shift. She spends time with them during work hours but does not socialize with them after work. She explains, "That's family and church time." She prioritizes all that matters in life: "I love my kids, I love my family, I love my husband, but first I love God. He's first. Then my kids come next." Diane reflects on the past as she contemplates the future:

If you lived in the neighborhood where I live, and you've seen the things I've seen, you have to have faith and be positive. And you have to keep moving. You can't look back. I'm grateful that God gave me the strength to live. There have been good times and bad times. He gave me the strength to stand. I am just grateful. I can't say anything more. If it wasn't for him giving me my job, I would not be able to do the things that I did. A lot of people don't believe, but I believe God is the key to everything.

Diane concludes our conversation with the confession, "I always wanted to write a book. I have great stories, but I don't know how to put them together. Now I go to school on Tuesdays and Thursdays. It's a GED class. I'm doing it for my kids." For Diane and her family, they continue to make do.

Diane's story represents the custodians' first discourse about family. Family, in this custodial context, aligns with contemporary conceptualizations (influenced by increases in the number of divorces, remarriages, adoptions, same-sex marriages, and single parents) that represent a more inclusive discourse when compared to conventional perspectives based on blood or marriage. Family in this context implies that members live or have lived together; keep each other safe; and offer unconditional love, acceptance, care, and support, emotionally and financially. The family doesn't fail its members and vice versa.

In this discourse, family and work domains are separate and unequal. Custodians such as Diane experience annoyances, injustices, and fears at work, but temper their reactions because, as Diane notes, it is dangerous to "bite the hand that feeds you" and because energy is better spent on family. In essence, a bad job that supports one's family is better than no job. Family is the epicenter of life, and work is the primary means of providing for and supporting family. For custodians like Diane, family is not an important thing. It's everything.

All in the Family

Sixty or so custodians, having finished their shifts, pour out of the break room at 4:31 p.m. So, too, do the frenetic vibes. Six custodians working the evening shift remain. Serenity reigns as they assemble around a table, quietly conversing, awaiting the shift supervisor to distribute daily assignments. The one Croatian and five Bosnians casually converse in their native language. I listen attentively, trying to identify their themes. My inability to translate the conversations gleans minimal insights—something about soccer and food.

Hamza, a lanky and soft-spoken housekeeping supervisor, inserts a quarter into the coffee vending machine and pushes the cappuccino button. He waits patiently for the coffee to brew, then graciously offers it to me, "For you, Professor." Hamza, a low-talker, insists on calling me "professor" despite my repeated requests for him to call me "Peter." To each custodian he distributes an index card containing a work assignment. The conversation resumes as each custodian glances at his or her card and passes it to me for my review. Elif, as she does each day, will clean the health center and housing department suite. Suki and Stafani will scrub tile floors. Max, Malik, and Eki will set up a multipurpose room before sanitizing residence hall stairwells.

With deployment orders in hand, I expect this tight-knit entourage to commence work. Instead, Hamza allows our informal interactions to continue, to allow the staff and me to extend our interactions. Hamza retrieves a slab of homemade smoked meat from a brown lunch sack tucked in his jacket. He uses a pocketknife to remove the vacuum-sealed wrapping and then cuts a coin-shaped chunk from the stick and offers it to me. I sample the snack, which tastes as good as its smoky aroma. Max reveals that Hamza was a chef in Bosnia and deems him one of the best meat smokers in the city. My curiosity in the art of smoking meats prompts Hamza to explain the art of smoking and storing meats. Malik displays a photograph on his phone of a do-it-yourself outdoor smoker. It appears primitive but is obviously functional.

The patience that Hamza exhibits while describing the intricacies of curing meat mirrors the patience he exhibits each day as a supervisor. Having devoured enough food to qualify for dinner, Hamza retrieves a second sealed beef stick from his coat pocket and offers it to me to take home. I smile to convey my appreciation.

I use this social time to verify my understanding of the department's family tree. Almost everyone has a relative who works as a CU custodian. Hamza and his spouse both work in the department; Eki is Malik's brother-in-law. Malik's sister works the day shift. So, too, do Elif's mother and aunt as well as Stafani's sister-in-law. Suki and Max alone appear to be relative-less. It is no accident that multiple members from multiple Bosnian and Serbian families have jobs in the department, since helping family and friends to locate work is part of their DNA. With a little help from my friends, in 10 minutes I create a flowchart that visually represents these interrelationships.

Cultural differences between the day and evening shifts are obvious. Day-shift staff members have predictable daily routines; the evening shift's duties are unpredictable. "Intense" best describes the day-shift ethos; work begins promptly. "Relaxed" best describes the evening-shift philosophy. These veterans understand the tasks at hand and what it takes to complete them. Despite discrete and unpredictable work assignments, often spread across the entire campus, the evening crew collaborates whenever possible to get jobs done.

I follow Max, Eki, and Malik to a large multipurpose room on the main floor. The mission is to arrange tables, chairs, and a podium for a program scheduled for the next morning. Max studies the setup diagram and then instructs his coworkers about his plan of action. A few students are spread across the room. The four of us assemble tables and arrange chairs, being careful to not disturb the students until absolutely necessary. As this 30-minute task concludes, a food-service worker enters and momentarily converses with Malik. A few minutes later, we rendezvous in a nearby private dining room, the site of a recent Mexican dinner buffet. The kitchen workers invite us to sample the leftovers before they dismantle the buffet and discard the food. Within moments our plates are overflowing with burritos, tacos, chips, beans, and rice. This impromptu 15-minute break is unexpected and nutritious. Dining hall workers supporting custodians, and vice versa, is a regular occurrence. These networks are strong and stealthy.

Onward to one of the oldest residence halls on campus, which is slated to be demolished in 2015 (and not a day too soon, in my opinion). The dark and dingy concrete stairwell resembles a bomb shelter. The 1970s-style steel and rubber treads on each step are badly worn and beyond repair. I fear that these deplorable conditions distract residents from noticing the custodians' cleaning efforts. The aged building has no electrical outlets in the stairwells. Eki carries a scrubber and extension cord up to the third floor in this elevator-less building in search of an accessible outlet. While waiting for Eki to handle the technical details, Max talks about the elusiveness of his American dream:

> They tell you when you come here everything is going to be good. Over there was war. We lost family. We did not have enough food to eat. Then someone offers you to come to America—dream job and dream every-thing. You think people will give you car, money, and apartment. It took me three months to get job. Hamza was working for a man who owned apartment where I live; Hamza also worked here. I asked him about job. He says, "No job now." He talks to people; still, no job. I think this is no good for me. I think about going back to my country. I have family to take care of. One time I go see Hamza. He says he has job for me, but he is not sure I will like. I tell him, "Okay, give me any job. I need job, any job." He says, "Okay—cleaning bathrooms." I say, "I don't care. I am ready for anything. I need job." He says, "Okay, come in and interview with Lance." I got the job. "Really?" We came here, but we had better there. People lie; they say it is good here. I came here and thought someone was going to help me—only these people [pointing to Malik and Eki] help.

It is no surprise that Max remains loyal to Hamza, since he helped Max to secure employment. As peers provide moral support to cope with culture shock and fears that seemingly never end, bonds continue to strengthen, blurring the boundaries between family and coworkers.

Malik fills buckets with water and retrieves mops from a nearby custodian closet. Unlike the efficient precision routines I observed when the trio set up the multipurpose room, this task is more complicated and chaotic. I untangle the extension cord snaked around the bucket and scrubber. Regardless of where I stand, I am in the way. Matters get worse when students ascend the stairwell. They manage this obstacle course better than I do, as I struggle to mop residual water from each step as Eki talks about his close, family-like relationships with coworkers:

> We have good people at work. Nobody hates each other. If you have a broken car, I drive you for a week. Don't worry about it. I take you home. I come tomorrow to help you with something else. We pretty much help each other. If you need help on the house—I come fix for free.
>
> For job, you don't have option; you work with whoever they say. Big boss does not want problems. We work in same building but when we drink coffee every day, those people over there stay separate—African people, Bosnian people. Everyone is good, but I stay closer to Bosnian people.

In slightly less than 45 minutes, one stairwell is clean. Our foursome moves equipment into a closet and walks outside for a break. I assume we are headed toward the housekeeping suite, but at the last moment we veer off toward a church parking lot, a few hundred yards away. Hamza is waiting with a cigarette dangling from his mouth. I correctly posit that since CU bans smoking on campus, this off-campus space is a safe haven for smokers. As an asthmatic, standing in a dark parking lot in below-freezing weather watching people satisfy their nicotine cravings and converse in a language I don't understand is hardly my idea of a good time. Still, I witness in these interactions a level of staff cohesiveness I seldom encounter.

These custodians socialize outside of work and help each other out with home and auto repairs. I learn that they also help each other out by transferring money from their personal bank accounts to the accounts of people who are applying for home loans, to ensure that loan applications are approved with minimal fees. These acts of solidarity and kindness are usually reserved for family, not friends. En route back to the residence hall to continue cleaning stairwells, Max talks about Bosnian family-like norms to which he adheres when interacting with friends and coworkers:

> I worked in Germany. If you get cigarette, they want one cent. We are different—Bosnian people. If you have no cigarette today, no problem. I give you one. Everybody is different in Italy and Germany. We help each other pretty much. It doesn't cost money to help people. We don't do like Americans. If we go eat with [American] friends, people pay their own. If I say, "Let's go eat," I pay for it; they [friends] don't expect me to pay. I pay because I called you. If he called me to get coffee, he is going to pay for coffee. He is not going to ask me to go with him for coffee and let me pay. They don't pay for each other and say they are best friends. I say, "No."

Back at the residence hall I join the trio to clean another stairwell, which is also a disorganized adventure. Afterward I walk to a nearby building to drop in on Elif, who is cleaning the health center. She greets me at the door to allow me entry into the locked facility. We tour the empty suite as she describes her responsibilities:

> I do the health center and housing every night. I work by myself. I clean lots of offices. In this building there are doctor and exam rooms and offices. I cleaned both. Some of my friends drop by during breaks. The health staff goes home around 6:30.

Elif explains that if the weather is mild she will travel back to the main office to take breaks and eat dinner with peers. On cold days, like today, she seldom ventures outside, except for work-related matters. Elif dusts around papers on office desks and medical apparatus in examination rooms, keenly aware of what items to clean and avoid, as she talks about life after the war:

> Before we got here we were in camp. We were in two different camps before we came here. For me the camp wasn't bad because I was young. Young people just hung out. We talked and stuff, and it was fun. For my mom when she was in the camp it wasn't fun. She was always worried whether we would have food. And then winter came. In the camp if you go into a house there's nothing in the house.

After surviving a war and refugee camps, supporting family and friends in the United States is instinctual. As Elif notes, "I don't know. You do it. You don't think about it."

The last stop of the evening is visiting Stafani and Suki. I find them on the third floor of a residence hall, cleaning a tile floor near the elevator. The noise level of the scrubber prohibits conversation, so I wait as they conclude their grime removal routine. Intense anger that often characterizes interactions between Serbians and Bosnians is not obvious as I watch Stafani interact with Suki, playfully bossing him around. Stafani explains, "The war was hard on everyone. It is hard to understand then and now. We just try to get by." Both appear to enjoy each other's company and cleaning floors. Stafani likes working the evening shift, because of the ever-changing responsibilities. Suki's English is adequate, but he asks Stafani to translate so that he can speak in his native tongue. She complies as Suki describes several family hardships, beyond the war, that provide me invaluable insights about his family-like commitments to coworkers.

After fleeing Bosnia and relocating to Germany, Suki married. He and his spouse's first child died because of medical complications. Afterward he returned to Bosnia and later immigrated to the United States in 2000. In

Oregon he worked in a factory that manufactured ceramic tiles while he learned to speak English. He then moved to Connecticut. Something to do with a vaccination resulted in the death of his second child. Then he and his spouse moved to the Midwest, where he currently resides. His current Bosnian coworkers helped him to get this job and have continued to help him move on with his life. I notice a smile on Suki's face as he talks directly to Stafani, which suggests that he is conveying some good news. Stafani returns the smiles as she translates. Suki is the proud father of a child who is both healthy and happy, which brings a smile to my face. For Stafani and Suki, their career options besides custodial work are limited. They know it is too late to further their education. Neither aspires to be a supervisor, so professionally, this work is it. The family atmosphere offsets job woes and fears about the future.

A few hours later the shift reassembles in the break room before clocking out. Hamza confirms the rumors that the assistant director of custodial operations is getting married this coming weekend. Immediately, the shift workers hatch a plan for a Bosnian celebratory feast for the next evening. A textbook example of teamwork ensues as the custodians negotiate the delicacies each will prepare. In about 15 hours the feast will commence. I am certain the team will celebrate *and* get their work done as well.

These evening-shift stories represent custodians' second discourse about family. Family in this context extends the first discourse to include a "work family." These unique on-the-job kinships refute the adage that blood is thicker than water. Hamza acts as supervisor and a fatherly leader of the evening crew. He assumes numerous roles: boss, job recruiter, career adviser, problem solver, and chef, blurring the traditional work-home and manager-worker dichotomies. The challenging life experiences of Max, Elif, Eki, Suki, Stafani, and Malik influence and blur distinctions between home and work as well as family and coworkers.

In this discourse, family and work domains are intertwined and equal. Custodians experience numerous annoyances at work and find support from coworkers on the job and at home. Family-like coworkers go a long way toward making a too tough job a bit easier.

The HU Family

Unlike the CU family discourses, the HU custodian family discourses focused less on individual workers and more on management systems and the larger university. These two discourses recognize that HU is changing, and not for the better, in the custodians' opinion. One discourse seeks to recapture the family-like organizational structure that is being eclipsed by one that is more businesslike; the other discourse is also critical of this businesslike emphasis but favors forward-thinking progressive politics, rather than trying to recapture a romanticized family discourse that never existed.

Family Ties

> I started as a cook. Then I had hand surgery—carpal tunnel and I couldn't do [food preparation] anymore. They moved me to housekeeping until I retired in 2000. They didn't have to do that, but they did. They treated me like I was family.

Fifteen years after her retirement, Margaret, during our first interview, assures me that she has no life experiences worthy of inclusion in a book. Despite disagreeing with her claim, I smile, but I don't refute it. As Margaret rummages through the two shoeboxes of memorabilia she brought with her, she sighs and confesses, "I can't remember their names and room numbers, but I have lots of good memories." She plucks a photograph from the box that appears to dislodge a long-lost memory.

> I tried to lead them [residents] the best way I knew how. This boy, he called me "Mom." He would say, "Mom, how do I look today, because I have to give a speech?" I looked down at his shoes and said, "I don't think they are going to see anything but your white buckskin shoes and it is January. If you have some other shoes, you should wear those." He came back and said, "Thanks." I miss the kids, but not the hard work.

Margaret has no children, but she assumed the role of surrogate mother with several HU collegians.

> Before I came to HU I had six boys rent rooms in my house. I spoiled them rotten. Before they went home for Christmas, I always cooked them a dinner. I made them homemade ice cream. I cleaned their rooms. One of the boys came back from Thanksgiving vacation, and the next morning the police knocked on my door. I thought there must be trouble. His father had passed away after he returned to school. I tried to comfort him.

While she was employed as a custodian at HU, students were at the epicenter of Margaret's life. Annually, the Tuesday evening of fall exam week, she and her spouse would visit her residence hall armed with batches of cookies and jugs of cider. She and the residents would socialize and sing Christmas carols together. Margaret digs through her boxes to locate additional photographs to further enhance this vicarious experience for me. She exudes humility and pride as she conveys how she gently and modestly educated and supported students.

> Once I made a homemade chocolate cake from scratch. A week later this girl came to me and said, "Margaret, I went to the grocery and I asked them where the scratch cake was." I started laughing as she explained, "They didn't have any scratch cakes." She didn't know what I was talking about. "Scratch" means it is a homemade cake—you take your sugar, flour, and cocoa and you make your own cake. There's no box.

Margaret's broad smile conveys that she is becoming a bit more comfortable with our conversation and the quality of her stories. She retrieves a 1980s wall calendar from an envelope and holds it up for me to see. On each page, the upper half includes a large photograph and the bottom half includes a 30-day calendar. She hands it to me and declares, "You are not going to believe this, but I'm Miss October." My puzzled facial expression prompts Margaret to elaborate.

In 1994 HU's Association for Women Students published a calendar titled "A Kaleidoscope of Achievement" that included 12 HU women whose campus leadership achievements were noteworthy. Alongside each of the 12 monthly photographs was a brief biography and a life philosophy statement. This calendar was an alternative to the Women of Harrison calendar, published by a fraternity, that showcased bikini-clad HU women. The Kaleidoscope of Achievement calendar intended to affirm women and challenge gender stereotypes by focusing on achievement rather than appearance. Margaret provides a backstory: "They came to me and said, 'We don't like the calendar that the men made; we want to do our own and we want you in it.' I said, 'Are you kidding me?' That's how I got to be Miss October." She flips open the calendar to October, displaying a photograph of her standing on a ladder, polishing a brass chandelier. I read aloud a paragraph from the biographical statement adjacent to the photograph:

> Although Margaret's general activities include the upkeep and cleaning of Ness Hall, the extra things she does set her apart. Whether she is giving students ironing lessons, advice about a problem, or a hug on a hard day, she always seems to be giving. Known to many in the quad as "Mom," Margaret prides herself on knowing the names of all the students within her hall. . . . Margaret's work at Harrison reflects the ways she lives her life. No matter where she is, she always seems to be giving generously.

Margaret blushes as she retrieves a news clipping from her shoebox. She hands it to me and explains, "This one shows I made national news." Margaret then reminisces about a few more of her moments of fame:

I thought I was in trouble once. When I got there [the housing office], Mr. Winston said, "Nothing's wrong, just go and sit down." I found out I was getting a Favorite Residence Hall Workers of the Year award that included a gift card to the campus bookstore. Another time, Mr. Winston, he [was] in charge of everything in housing, came by my building to give me a letter a parent wrote about me.

Winston read the letter to Margaret. The author recommended that Margaret get a raise. She tells me that she did not get the raise but that they read the letter at the Christmas banquet for managers. "I guess I was the talk of the town," was her appraisal. Margaret explains her philosophy of work: "People would complain about their jobs. I would say, 'Be thankful you have a job. A lot of people don't have work. You have a good job; be thankful.'" During the 2012 alumni reunion weekend, Margaret's former residents sponsored a reception to honor her. Afterward, the vice president of student affairs, who attended the reception, accepted my invitation to write and submit his interpretation of the event to include in this book:

Margaret took pride in her work. In a [residence] hall of honors students destined mostly for prestigious work, she modeled the dignity of work. That was a powerful lesson for students. She took pride that the building was immaculate; she took pride in contributing to the community. She never said that she thought the work (part of her work included cleaning bathrooms on hot days) was demeaning, but instead took pride in making the hall a better place. That affected students. Students saw her as a person who saw in her work meaning and value and who took pride in that value. . . . What I valued is how she modeled for the students a pride in work well done; she was an important "lesson" for them. (personal communication, November, 2013, Richards)

Harkening for the "good old days" when the university acted more like a family than a business represents this third discourse about family. This discourse laments the metaphorical shift from the university as family to the university as a business. A shared aspiration for custodians is to recapture and ultimately sustain these ideals that historically guided institutional values.

Margaret's stories illuminate the kinds of custodial and institutional values of yesteryear that many custodians believe are vanishing and should be sustained. Margaret baked cookies for residents and interacted with them after hours with approval from the university. Nowadays it is common for universities to prohibit such activity to minimize legal risks, such as students becoming ill from eating the cookies. Margaret's supervisors encouraged interactions with residents as well as cleaning. Outsourcing custodian services to cut costs, which is a common measure in the corporate university, would decrease opportunities for in-depth and sustained custodian-student interaction.

During Margaret's era the housekeeping department regularly sponsored celebratory events to recognize exemplary work by staff. However, expensive galas, team-building events, and socials are rare in these current austere times.

Prior to Margaret's retirement, custodians seldom followed a formal chain of command, which nowadays is a nonnegotiable expectation. This shift lessens opportunities for senior managers to interact formally and informally with workers. An HU custodian described what this managerial shift looks like:

> Management is different from when I started. It seems like they don't care about you anymore. When I first came here, Fred [the director of physical facilities] sent me a card on my birthday. He would come around and wish us a "Merry Christmas." He would come around and talk to us. He would even ask if you had any problems. He always had lots of meetings, but found time for us. Nice guy and very well groomed. There are no more Freds left. That all went away. Now, they don't care about you. Now it's a business.

Custodians who embrace this discourse accept the winds of change. They remain sensitive to rising costs and fewer institutional revenue streams but believe that managing the university like it is a family is a better option than pretending it is a for-profit corporation.

Modern Family

> We used to have events in August before school started—a dinner. Everyone brought something, and the managers would get the meat. People brought their favorite dishes. We would meet in the gyms and have a get-together and talk. We had games, like horseshoes. In August we would have it in the park. We did different things, and it was a time to get away and not work. There would be water fights. If you did that now, you would get in trouble. Back then, even the managers would get in on them—throw cups of water at each other—and it was a fun time. At Christmas we would have another dinner—like pizza or subs, or whatever. People would come, and everyone liked it. Now it is a different type of people they hire. People now do not want to be social.—Retired HU custodian supervisor

Another family discourse, like the "university as family" proponents in discourse three, opposes efforts that attempt to corporatize the university. These individuals support many of the values that characterize the previous movement but reject the agenda to return to the good old days. The metaphor of the university as a political organization best characterizes this discourse. Proponents of this outlook publicly criticize practices promoted by corporatization advocates. Instead of yearning for and romanticizing the past, they want to think strategically and politically about the future.

Wilding's (2014) "7 Signs Your Workplace Is Toxic" succinctly identified concerns that proponents of this discourse have about the changing nature of higher education:

> How can you identify if you're trapped in a hostile workplace? Here are seven telling signs you may be working in a toxic office environment: (1) "You're told to feel 'lucky you have a job.'" . . . (2) "Poor communication" . . . (3) "Everyone has a bad attitude." . . . (4) "There's always office drama." . . . (5) "Dysfunction reigns." . . . (6) "You have a tyrannical boss." . . . (7) "You feel in your gut something is off." (para. 3)

Two HU custodians bemoan autocratic management practices and their loss of influence in departmental decision making. One custodian notes, "We used to have an employee committee when we were hiring. We would interview them and we would give input. That doesn't happen anymore." A second HU custodian expresses concerns about management's disregard of workers' input:

> [The department administrator] thinks he knows everything. He doesn't. We tried to tell him. It didn't do any good. We tried to tell him that we also were security in the building at night. He said, "You haven't even been trained for that." I tried to tell him that we know faces that belong here. Yeah, well, we haven't been trained for that, but we still know them. I gave him a look, and then he gave me a look back. I thought he wanted to throw something at me. We don't have no education. But we know things.

Implicit in these two critiques are managerial assumptions about custodians. First, custodians should be happy they are employed, and thus not complain. Second, it is unnecessary for management to communicate rationale for policy changes to custodians. Managers make policy, and custodians adhere to the policies. Assumptions such as these contribute to unrest, drama, dysfunction, and workers' perceptions of the tyrannical bosses that Wilding (2007) noted. At the heart of these practices are business-influenced ideals: efficiency, cutting costs, accountability, and minimizing risk. A retired senior administrator provides an example of how these practices breed discontent:

One summer day about 400 mattresses came in on four semis. You have to carry them up four flights of stairs [in a residence hall], and you have to take the old ones out. You have one person per mattress carrying them up and down. The team gets the semi emptied, and a manager brought them a few cases of beer and pop. Everyone appreciated it. No one got drunk. Later, the manager got admonished. His boss told him, "You can't bring alcohol on campus." It's a bottle of beer, not the end of the world.

The beer, a small gesture of appreciation, resulted in the HR department reprimanding the supervisor, yet this same manager also supervises events where the president serves alcohol to donors as an act of appreciation. Recognizing these double standards breeds unrest. Nita, HU's only African American custodian, elaborates on the risks involved in embracing this discourse of criticism:

When I got here it was family oriented. Everybody cared, and if you needed help you could ask. Now it is like everybody is out for themselves. When my mom passed away, people surrounded me. They cared. They would ask, "What can I do to help you get through?" Now people are afraid to get involved. They are afraid of the consequences. Before, someone had your back; now those people are afraid to speak up to support you because they are afraid to lose their jobs. I pick and choose what I say, but I get my point across. That is how it should be run. You should be able to say what you want to say without getting in trouble for it.

Custodians who embrace this discourse accept the winds of change but don't retreat from family feuds. They understand that college costs continue to increase while revenue streams continue to decrease. They believe that it is important to respect and learn from the past, but to return to it would be unwise. Instead, they believe that taking risks, acting as critics, and demanding input in decision making—all political acts—benefit the university and all of its stakeholders.

Family Therapy

Examining and disseminating information about the everyday lives of custodians reveals campus-wide struggles associated with negotiating competing institutional values or principles.

Individuals who subscribed to each discourse use the metaphor of family differently. Some custodians posit that working is simply a means to an end, which is earning a sufficient wage to support family. Some custodians believe that forging family-like relationships with coworkers enhances their home as well as their work lives. Some custodians state that a shift from managing the university as if it were a family toward managing the university as if it were a corporation is a bad idea; their "solution" is to return to the good old days. Finally, some custodians posit that managing the university as if it were a corporation is ill conceived but so, too, is the "solution" of returning to the past. Instead they favor making explicit the politics of family and seeking solutions that focus on shared power and governance.

Each discourse represents a *community of interest*. These relatively autonomous groups, based on common ideals, give the members voice and identity. During meals and breaks, they congregate together, usually based on gender and ethnicity. In the community room at the start and end of each day, Bosnian women occupy several tables, as do African American women. Younger African American men sit on the cushioned benches around the perimeter of the room. These segregated enclaves are not much different from those I notice while cleaning in the dining halls, where collegians of color stake out their own tables, as do White students.

Communities of interest have merit, yet these autonomous and discrete groupings make it difficult to engage in dialogue about the public interest (Carlson, 1994). For example, Diane seldom interacts with evening-shift workers about their conceptualization of family, which differs from her own.

Communities of difference and diversity, rooted in democratic multicultural ideals, provide space for communities of interest to form and prosper, while a common, public culture is constantly and consciously being constructed and reconstructed through dialogue across and about difference. There are few examples of instances where these communities of interest substantively interact. CU's annual Staff Day celebration is an exception and the quintessential example of a *community of difference*; it invites communities of interest members to express a sense of solidarity and interact with the Other.

Staff Day invites each staff member to partake in a work-free day of celebration. The daylong event begins with the presentation of service awards that recognize nearly all staff communities of interest, including custodians. The free formal luncheon provides opportunities for communities of interest to interact with coworkers or members of other campus enclaves. During the afternoon the university sponsors a variety of tournaments and recreational activities and also sponsors a canned food donation drive to fight hunger in the city.

Staff have the option of participating in athletic tournaments, including golf, softball, and volleyball. Recreational and social events include bike rides, tennis, a group run, swimming, and bingo. Educational programs include a campus-wide diversity symposium, art museum tours, and historical campus walking tours. The day concludes with a formal awards ceremony, where the chancellor acts as the master of ceremonies. This closing program includes the awarding of trophies and prize drawings, as well as an ice cream social. Each staff member has the freedom to structure his or her day to accommodate preferences.

This program is an example of Carlson's (1994) multicultural democratic community because it (a) maximizes public participation, providing room for divergent perspectives and is sensitive to the concerns of all; (b) stands for something in the way of moral or ethical vision for the reconstruction of community (e.g., recognizing the important contribution of unsung campus heroes); (c) ruptures the borders that separate individuals into separate camps or neat categories; and (d) builds alliances.

Diane has the option of inviting her family to visit campus and partake in the festivities. The evening crew can spend an entire day together or use the event to connect with peers working the day shift. Staff Day organizers structure the campus-wide event so that it has a human scale with intimate walking tours and bingo tables around which coworkers can congregate. It aims to invite discrete campus enclaves to cross-pollinate. This therapy session, with an additional goal of healing and wellness, has both a nostalgic and progressive feel to it.

Although programs such as this one are an ideal way to recognize staff, provide opportunities to interact with the Other, and discuss differences, it is one of CU's most expensive events. In these austere times when the bottom line matters, can programs such as these survive?

PART THREE

CORPORATE MANAGERIALISM AND CIVIC DISENGAGEMENT

9

THE CORPORATE CREEP

Business as [Un]Usual

Dear President _____,

    I recently received the 25 Years of Service Award gift on March 10, 2014. I have been a loyal and hardworking employee since 1989. I appreciate the university's special recognition for people who remain at Harrison for a long time.

    This year those who had 25 years of service received a Harrison coaster set (with only two coasters). While I appreciate the gift, as a person with not much money and a low-paying salary, I hope you will consider changing the gift so that it is more practical. In the past the gift has been a pen and pencil set in a nice wooden box, with Harrison University written on top of it. That kind of gift I would have liked getting, since I could really use it. For staff like me, I hope you will think about picking more practical gifts, if you keep giving them to us.

    I realize there is nothing that can be done this year to change the situation, but I hope you will consider my suggestion for the future.

    I am sorry to have to write this letter, but you said at a lunch about three years ago at your house to about 10 other employees, "If you ever have a problem, my door is open." That is why I am writing. Thank you for taking time to read this letter.

Sincerely,
Samuel

Samuel mails this handwritten letter to the president's home a week after the reception honoring employees for their service to the university. For several years he has been eyeing the pen and pencil sets on the desks of several long-time administrators. He wanted to receive the gift and intended to display it on his desk in his custodial closet. Needless to say, the actual gift disappoints him.

133

Approximately a week after mailing the letter, Samuel, while mopping a floor, looks up and notices the president approaching. He smiles, hands Samuel an engraved wooden box that contains a pen and a pencil, thanks him for his many years of service, and shakes his hand. Flustered, Samuel expresses his gratitude, then offers to return the coaster set, which the president doesn't accept. Word spreads throughout the building about this impromptu meeting. A senior administrator, another quarter-century employee, retrieves his own coaster gift stashed in his desk and gives it to Samuel. By the time he calls me a few hours later to describe his unusual day, Samuel had already conversed and shook hands (three times) with the president, rearranged his desk to display his new pen and pencil set and four coasters, and finished mopping the floor. It was a memorable morning indeed.

I recount this story in this chapter about corporate influences on Harrison University (HU) and Compton University (CU) because it was (a) *unusual*—I expected to regularly encounter uplifting stories, but seldom did; (b) *profound*—I learned invaluable insights about Samuel, the president, and HU; (c) *sad*—I bemoaned the realization that some custodians have insufficient disposable income to purchase even inexpensive nonessential items for themselves; (d) *unbelievable*—I realized Samuel wanted to display his institutional loyalty by displaying engraved "Harrison University" paraphernalia on his desk, but could not afford to; (e) *disorienting*—I expected the university (after reading the letter) to purchase for Samuel his preferred gift, but I did not expect the president to deliver it; and (f) *revealing*—I scrutinized and symbolically interpreted business-as-usual practices, such as purchasing a gift that emblematically conveys the university's appreciation for staff and unintentionally conveys how little the university knows about some of its employees.

Samuel is both innocent and strategic. He heeds the president's recommendation to contact him if concerns arise. Samuel writes a letter to provide feedback and then mails it to the president's home, not office, which bypasses aides who traditionally buffer the president from trivial matters, such as anniversary gifts. I wonder: If Samuel had mailed the letter directly to the president's office, would the response have been the same?

The HU president is both kind and strategic. He could have read Samuel's letter, deemed the gift sufficient, and instructed an aide to reply, simply acknowledging receipt of the correspondence. Delivering in person an additional gift is a private act of kindness and respect, and this admirable, low-profile act of kindness is also strategic. Most savvy presidents know that this kind of feel-good story will spread across campus like wildfire, symbolically conveying core institutional values, such as leaders who care, and affirming the university's brand, which occurred in this instance. Despite the unavoidable political dimensions of the encounter, good things resulted.

Three issues evident in Samuel and the president's excellent adventure mirror three trends that both intrigued and perplexed me during my fieldwork. The rise of corporate managerialism at CU and HU has (a) negatively influenced the quality of life for custodians; (b) contributed to custodians disengaging civically from campus life, despite their desire for greater involvement; and (c) complicated custodians' efforts to make use of education-related benefits afforded to them as campus employees. Most honorees after receiving a not-so-practical gift, such as a coaster set, would toss the gift in a desk drawer (as did the senior administrator in Samuel's building) and chalk up the ill-conceived gift to a well-intentioned but clueless bureaucrat who selects a gift on behalf of the president. Disappointed honorees would not likely engage civically and provide feedback to and educate the president and his staff. The incident would affirm conventional wisdom that benefits and perks are on the decline and more difficult to redeem. Samuel, an exception, challenged by-products of corporate managerialism (e.g., the boss is always right) by engaging civically in writing to the president and educating him. Samuel challenged conventional wisdom that custodians should simply accept and be appreciative of the actions of those in power. I use Samuel's story to illuminate CU's and HU's *corporate creep*. This chapter introduces and examines corporate managerialism. Chapter 10 addresses two by-products of corporate managerialism: squandered educational opportunities and civic disengagement.

How's Business? Not So Good

Inside Higher Ed (2014) commissioned a survey of college and university chief business officers. Results revealed the following:

- Fewer than 25% of business officers strongly agree they are confident about the sustainability of their institution's financial model over the next five years.
- Sixty-six percent of survey respondents believe media reports suggesting that higher education is in the midst of a financial crisis are correct.
- Business officers agree that senior administrators are realistic about the financial challenges confronting their institutions, but give trustees (67%) and faculty members (35%) lower marks on this survey item.

These findings suggest that administrators responsible for managing administrative and financial operations generally agree that higher education remains mired in a fiscal crisis, strategic plans intending to quell the crisis are mostly inadequate, and the greater campus community does not fully understand the magnitude or origins of these crises.

Although HU and CU custodians seldom cross paths with these kinds of administrators or are seldom privy to university budgets and strategic plans, they correctly intuit that business is unusual these days. CU custodians recognize that something is amiss when their university—which has the reputation for being financially secure, with one of the largest endowments in the country—is looking to downsize and streamline services. CU hires a new vice chancellor, who in turn hires external consultants to identify ways to make services more efficient and cost-effective and proposes a campus-wide organizational overhaul. A senior administrator discusses these uncommon occurrences:

> One of the primary reasons we changed was that we had a new vice chancellor. . . . He was trying to understand what we were doing. . . . He could not figure out why they [custodians] were not university employees. I explained that it was a decision that the person in his job a few people ago made. At the time we were worried about things like unionization.
>
> We were the original Octagon Corporation. There was also a[n] [Octagon] housing company as well. The university started to buy up property [near campus], and it didn't have anyone to run these buildings and decided to do it in-house. It used the Octagon model for the operation of this. So there was a second Octagon out there and it caused some confusion. Some people in the same office were CU employees and some were Octagon. They were doing the same job. . . . Some mechanics worked for CU, some didn't. So the university decided to make them all employees. . . . It was not about saving money; it was more about fixing things. It costs more to have CU rather than Octagon employees. . . . From my vantage point it made all custodians CU employees, which is something I wanted.

CU's rationale for initiating the expensive consolidation was less about saving money and more about increasing efficiency, minimizing legal liabilities, centralizing services, increasing employee oversight, and implementing consistent personnel policies. The consolidation pleases most custodians and disappoints those who prefer working in a "ma and pa"–like business rather than a more impersonal university. HU custodians, like their counterparts at CU, have limited insider knowledge about strategic plans or university budgets, yet they are keenly aware that HU's financial struggles persist and major change is inevitable.

A cursory examination of the CU and HU custodial contexts might lead one to erroneously conclude that while universities are changing, custodial services are not. For HU custodians over the past few decades, their work responsibilities and campus status seemingly have remained unchanged, yet a closer examination reveals several dramatic shifts. In the past, the HU senior administrators perceived custodians as valued albeit not-so-powerful members of the campus community. Historically, administrators recognized and appreciated these unique and important contributions to the university community. As HU has embraced corporate managerialism, power brokers deem veteran custodians as expensive and thus expendable employees. An unsolicited e-mail from Lucy, a custodian at HU, provides glimpses into this ideological shift:

> (a) Each department (custodial, automotive, grounds) always did their own hiring until last August. HR [human resources] took it over deciding if/when someone would fill an empty position. (b) The recycling center is being discontinued because the local dump can do it cheaper. (c) They are prepping the faculty to get minimal services in the future. . . . They will have to take their garbage and recycling to designated areas in the buildings. (d) Custodial and grounds workers have to write down every extra job beyond their regular duties, "to account for our time to ensure we are not wasting time." Slackers will be identified and targeted for dismissal. (e) The vice president is comparing the time and cost of each job to see which is really cheaper, HU employees or a cleaning company.

At CU for nearly 18 years, the inspection model has been *the* way of doing business, which seems to refute the claim that corporate managerialism is on the rise. But a closer examination of CU custodial operations reveals subtle changes, such as the escalation and formalization of inspections by supervisors and the escalation and formalization of personnel mandates initiated by the centralized Office of Human Resources. Kelley's (1997) assessment of higher education, published almost 20 years ago, aptly describes the current state of affairs at HU and CU:

> During the past decade we've witnessed massive downsizing of staff and even faculty, while enrollments have remained steady or have increased. The circumstances translate into layoffs, wage freezes, speedups, and the increased use of part-time and temporary labor without benefits or union protection. (p. 146)

Getting Down to Business

"From its medieval origin as a corporation of scholars or students, the university is evolving into the contemporary entrepreneurial university" (Etzkowitz, Webster, & Healey, 1998, p. 1). Ruben (2000) offered a caveat about this shift: "While the university will never look or work exactly like a for-profit firm, it will continue to transform itself into something that does not resemble what most scholars and citizens think of as a nonprofit educational institution" (p. 210). As public support for higher education shrinks, state and federal funding decline, and federal research grant funding evaporates, concentrating on the bottom line is understandable.

From the vantage point of university trustees and presidents, sustaining the status quo is untenable. A prevalent response is to accelerate the transformation of nonprofit educational universities so that they more closely resemble for-profit corporations. Modeling service industry practices, universities adopt accountability and efficiency practices (Rosow & Kriger, 2010). In theory, the goals are to increase revenues and cut costs without damaging the reputation of the university or ostracizing key constituents. In practice, universities eliminate or reduce nonessential services with the hope that as few people as possible notice. Giroux (2005) explicated what is at stake as this ideological shift progresses and why all higher education stakeholders should care: "If colleges and universities are to define themselves as centers of teaching and learning vital to the democratic life of the nation and globe, they must acknowledge the real danger of becoming mere adjuncts to big business, or corporate entities in themselves" (p. 2).

Senior administrators more often seek counsel from consulting firms with expertise in these kinds of transformations than from local experts such as faculty and staff who are intimately familiar with the institutional culture. External consultants generally advise presidents to act more like chief executive officers rather than academic leaders, create hierarchical authority structures that facilitate rapid and decisive change, and rely less on inefficient shared-governance models.

Consultants also advocate for the formation of partnerships to increase revenues. For example, The Ohio State University (OSU) signed an exclusive vendor contract for beverage distribution with Coca-Cola. The alliance netted the university more than $32 million. Administrators skirted the question, "Did other beverage distributors compete for the contract?" Instead, a spokesperson addressed a positive outcome resulting from this lucrative and not-so-transparent agreement: "By entering into an exclusive vendor contract, it increases guaranteed revenues, which is aimed toward aiding in the student experience and creates stability" (Essig, 2013, para. 6).

Institutional powerbrokers who redefine their job responsibilities, consolidate decision making, and pursue lucrative corporate partnerships solve some institutional problems but create new ones. Deals such as OSU made disenfranchise some campus stakeholders, such as campus eateries that want to provide customers soft-drink choices. Centralized decision makers' entrepreneurial initiatives can easily eclipse other institutional priorities, such as academic primacy. Universities beholden to corporations that provide generous financial support experience weakened institutional independence and autonomy. Eisenberg (2012b) expanded upon these concerns:

> Moreover, many colleges have become big businesses, reflecting corporate values: management efficiency, top-down decision making, a wide divide between top salaries and those of the lowest-paid workers, and trustees who care little about academic matters but a great deal about finances and fund raising. Like corporate executives who want to cut budgets and maximize profits, college administrators say there is no money in their budgets to raise the wages of their low-income employees. Yet they find plenty of money for athletics, new buildings, and additional highly paid administrators. (paras. 5 and 6)

Despite stark ideological differences between proponents and opponents of the transformation of universities to more closely resemble for-profit corporations, they both agree that public and private universities must increase revenues and cut costs. They disagree about how to accomplish these aims. Proponents view this shift as a technical and rational task, while opponents view change as a moral one. Mark Burstein (2015), president of Lawrence University, elaborated on the importance of treating change as a moral act: "Strategies from the business world can help us streamline our institutions, but we must take care that the tools we borrow not jeopardize the values of the academy. If business concepts dominate our thinking about the future, we will have lost our way" (p. 14).

A Corporate Managerialism Business Model

Corporatization discourses in the academy encompass a broad array of issues: governance, curriculum, alliances, intellectual property rights, branding, leadership, ethics, decision making, profits, corporate sponsorship, outsourcing, and privatization. Corporatization discourses involving custodians participating in this study are narrower, focusing almost exclusively on labor-management relationships. I use the term *corporate managerialism* to describe custodians' unique discourses about this topic.

For custodians, the corporate managerialism often promoted by custodial and university senior administrators is replacing a *customer service* management ideology that many custodians favor. N. Kreuter (2014) offered an overview of this latter philosophy:

> We see the manifestation of the "always right student-customer" everywhere in academe: in grade inflation (who's going to pay top dollar for Cs and Ds?) in the resort-ification of campuses (come check out our 90-foot climbing wall and palm-shaded socializing pool); in the hesitance to hold students accountable for their behavior (pick your high-profile college athlete crime example, or laughable university honor code). (para. 11)

Despite critique of this antieducational, "give the people what they want" approach to management, the idea of treating constituents as customers appeals to custodians. It is a popular metaphor they use to conceptualize and organize their work. Custodians struggle to navigate the clash between their customer service agenda and their supervisors' corporate managerialism plan, which values consumers but privileges fiscal stability over customer satisfaction. Implementing these two ideologies is a complex and fear-inducing undertaking.

Analysis of the lexicons and idioms of custodial administrators and custodians reveals differences. Administrators' corporate managerial lexicon includes terms like *downsizing, outsourcing,* and *subcontracting.* Managerial idioms include *tightening one's belt, biting the bullet, pulling one's weight, swallowing a bitter pill,* and *facing the music.* These terms convey that, in tough economic times, it's custodians, not their universities, who must sacrifice. When administrators talk about the need to tighten one's belt or pull one's weight, the onus for change rests not with these administrators but with those who report to them. Ginsberg (2011) documented this trend:

> Every year, hosts of administrators and staffers are added to the college and university payrolls, even as schools claim to be battling budget crises that are forcing them to reduce the size of their full-time faculties. As a result, universities are filled with armies of functionaries—the vice presidents, provosts, associate provost, vice provost, assistant provost, deans, deanlets, deanlings, each commanding staffers and assistants—who, more and more, direct the operations of every school. (p. 2)

Workers' customer service lexicon includes terms such as *caring, being responsive, quality management, cooperating, solving problems,* and *assisting others;* idioms include *striving for excellence, ensuring the customer is satisfied,* and *aiming to serve*. All together, these terms convey that the customers' interests are of paramount importance.

Although custodians integrate supervisors' corporate managerialism expectations with their brand of customer service, it is always business before pleasure or pleasing others. The business of corporate managerialism centers on three principles: centralizing power, minimizing labor costs, and increasing accountability.

Centralizing Power

> In the present environment conflicts between administrators and professors may be more acute, for many who study higher education believe that now central administrators can only achieve meaningful change if the faculty cede some power . . . or, as others imply, . . . administrators simply centralize power. (Tuchman, 2009, p. 7)

Centralizing power is the first of three principles of corporate managerialism. Lustig (2010) described tensions centering on centralizing power:

> American colleges and universities increasingly impose corporate methods of governance within their domains. They seek large-scale bureaucracy instead of collegial organization, uniform roles as opposed to diverse practices for different purposes, and a centralization of authority in place of the traditional decentralization. . . . This adoption of a corporate form of governance undermines the long-term efforts of faculty, as previously noted, to establish shared governance. (pp. 17–18)

Aronowitz (1995) noted that crucial campus decisions traditionally negotiated through shared governance structures such as the faculty senate began to vanish, replaced by centralized governance structures—that is, senior administrators. Ten years later, Giroux (2005) affirmed the continuance of this trend, whereby power resides with the few, and shared governance in academia is rapidly becoming an antiquated ideal:

> As corporate culture and values shape university life, academic labor is increasingly being transformed in the image of the new multinational conglomerate workforce. . . . The modern university once was governed by faculty, with the faculty senate naming the university president. That era of faculty control is long gone, with presidents being named by boards of trustees, and governing through hand-picked (and well-paid) bureaucrats rather than through faculty committees. (Giroux, 2005, para. 13)

Powerbrokers believe that governing is their responsibility and that campus stakeholders in most instances should keep their noses out of the governing business. Schrecker (2010) described characteristics of a new breed of administrators who favor efficient and authoritarian forms of governance:

> In any event, as these new—and often highly paid—administrators surveyed the institutions they had been brought into to save, they concluded that they would need much more authority to carry out their jobs. . . . Flexibility became their mantra, presumably because they felt it was impossible to make those "tough choices" without it. Moreover, because they were unused to academic norms, many seemed unaware that it might be possible to combine that flexibility with the university's decentralized and democratic form of decision-making. (p. 180)

The leadership and decision-making shifts that Aronowitz (1995), Giroux (2005), Lustig (2010), and Schrecker (2010) described trickle down and influence CU and HU custodians' work. Soon after the Octagon Cleaning Company (OCC) merged with CU, custodial supervisors' power and influence decreased as the centralized decision-making responsibilities of HR staff members increased. At HU, custodians' opportunities to participate in advisory and interview committees have been steadily declining over the past decade. Custodial roles at CU and HU continue to narrow, transforming them into "mere workers."

Insular decision makers diminish the benefits of centralized decision-making. As Samuel's story suggests, the gap between a university president and a custodian is wide. A retired HU administrator acknowledged this insularity by comparing the current chief financial officer (CFO) to previous CFOs. He estimates that the current CFO knows only approximately a dozen divisional staff, while his two predecessors each knew over 50 division staff.

> He does not want to meet and see staff or go to events where they are cleaning out residence halls. He does not go to special events. . . . In fairness to him, people [like him] are so busy having to get things done regarding planning because there is a greater level of bureaucracy in these jobs these days. It's hard to get out. . . . Still, staff thinks that management does not listen to them. It hurts.

At CU, custodial administrators struggle to cope as they merge effective practices and policies they devised as an independent corporation with CU's nonnegotiable campus-wide policies. These growing pains are uncomfortable as local governing capacities erode.

Eckel and Kezar (2003) advocated for the involvement of diverse campus factions in major campus-wide initiatives aimed at reform. The ever-growing imbalance of power makes attaining this aspiration unlikely. For custodians, their desire is not to involve themselves in macro campus politics but instead to have opportunities to influence decisions related to their work.

Minimizing Labor Costs

Minimizing labor costs—by keeping wages as low as possible and staffs lean—is the second characteristic of corporate managerialism. Eisenberg (2012b) documented burdens that low wages have on custodians: "More than 700,000 employees at American colleges—gardeners, security guards, cleaning crews, janitors, food-service personnel, etc.—do not earn a living wage, the bare-bones amount sufficient to provide a minimally decent standard of living for their families" (para. 1). CU's student sit-in and hunger strike protesting the low wages of service workers as well as HU service workers' strike affirm Eisenberg's assertions that low-paying service jobs are pervasive and contentious in higher education. Conventional wisdom for corporate managerial administrators is that being an underpaid custodian is better than being unemployed. Custodians disagree.

Downsizing labor while concurrently increasing the number of managers is another cost-containing strategy. With fewer workers and stagnant wages, tension between labor and management is predictable.

CU and HU differ in approaches to minimizing labor costs, although market forces influence both. Because numerous cleaning departments coexist on the CU campus, the Department of Housing (DOH) monitors competitors' compensation packages and intentionally offers packages that are slightly better. This strategy yields healthy applicant pools and high staff retention. Although the DOH prides itself on offering one of the best compensation packages in the city, some employees are still dangerously close to falling off the living wage fault line. This approach to minimizing labor costs is mostly satisfying to both labor and management. From CU custodians' perspective, not being the lowest-paid custodians on campus offsets other wage-related concerns.

HU's approach to containing custodial wages is highly contested. The goal is to hire the least expensive entry-level staff available. There are several reasons why HU has successfully implemented this plan over the past few years. First, the two independent in-house custodial operations (Department of Physical Facilities [DPF] and Auxiliary Services) offer similar salary packages to custodians. Because interdepartmental competition does not exist, salaries for all custodians remain low. With high unemployment in the region, it is an employer's market. HU has the luxury of minimizing starting salaries, which hover around the state's minimum wage, and still filling custodial vacancies. A retired HU supervisor made explicit the values undergirding this approach to management: "They don't value experience; they just want to save money." A retired HU custodian reacted to HU's wage-containment strategy:

> I heard that the president thought the wages here were compatible with others in the region. Compatible to what? Here I am two years post-retired, and they are still starting off at $9.35 an hour. What is that compatible to? It's not much higher than minimum wage.

HU is in the middle of implementing a new hiring program intended to significantly decrease labor costs. The plan redefines custodial work as a *job* rather than a *career*. The goal is to hire "promotable custodians"—entry-level custodians who will work for a few years to gain invaluable training and experience, then reenter the job market. The idea is that a short-term stint as an HU custodian will make them more competitive in the job market. Administrators promote this plan as a win-win situation. Custodians get training and a better job down the road, and HU decreases the number of career custodians by replacing them with entry-level custodians earning entry-level wages.

From the vantage point of custodians, the *promotable custodian initiative* advantages the university and disadvantages custodians, because custodians prefer long-term job security rather than a short-term, low-paying job that provides training and promises for advancement in a different work setting. This initiative guarantees that custodians will return to the job market, which historically has been unkind to them. Even first-rate custodians who aspire to become HU supervisors know that "being promotable" does not mean one will be promoted. At HU, becoming a supervisor is a long shot, because there are far more aspiring supervisors than vacancies.

Administrators suggest this promotable custodian program is analogous to an organizational blood transfusion that replaces old with new blood to ensure a healthy university. Custodians who neither have a desire to be promoted nor seek employment outside of the university predict that this plan will cause institutional hemorrhaging and stir up bad blood.

> Outsourcing campus services has become common and, administrators plead, necessary. Why keep a feudal army of custodians to shovel snow when a commercial service will do it better and faster? (Matthews, 1997, p. 230)

From an institutional perspective, outsourcing jobs is efficient and economical. Outsourcing typically involves a university or department contracting with an external corporation, with the aim of cutting costs and improving services. Institutions disseminate a simple request for proposal and accept the lowest bid, despite having the option during negotiations to require contractors to provide employees with a livable wage and benefits. The external agency oversees processes and personnel. Contractors hire current employees and often reduce their work hours so that they are ineligible for benefits. Arrangements such as these advantage universities and contractors and expose custodians to risk. A senior custodial administrator reveals conditions under which outsourcing is advantageous for universities:

> The university is not here to provide us a job; it is here to teach students. We support that mission, but we need to do it as effectively and efficiently as we can. The university needs to be putting less money into our part of it [cleaning] and more money into things that directly relate to teaching kids. I think most folks understand this. But the more you try to operate efficiently, the more difficult it is to keep a handle on the human side.

For CU custodians, outsourcing is not a concern. In the 1990s, CU's DOH outsourced custodial services, and the results were disastrous. This experience, coupled with the recent decision to make all OCC employees CU employees, renders the outsourcing of custodial services unlikely in the near future. CU custodians remain unconcerned about outsourcing, despite the flurry of efficiency studies under way.

Outsourcing is, in contrast, a highly contentious issue for HU custodians. They are acutely aware that HU recently outsourced its motor pool, recycling center, and health center operations. These cutbacks, coupled with a vice president's advocacy for outsourcing, fuel gossip and fear. HU custodians recognized that if HU must choose between saving money or saving jobs, it will opt for the former.

When campus-wide reductions are necessary, personnel cuts are difficult to avoid, because HR costs are one of the largest budget expenditures. Historically universities protect faculty from layoffs and minimize cuts to academic programs. Instead, senior administrators disproportionally reduce budgets of nonacademic units, such as custodial services. In circumstances such as this one, custodians are low-hanging fruit. Compared to other departmental personnel, eliminating custodial positions is politically and administratively easier.

Low membership in local unions coupled with high dues has hampered efforts for HU custodians to mobilize and collectively bargain to improve their employment status, packages, and salaries. Alternative mobilization strategies have yet to take root.

At CU, the DOH has not downsized its custodial staff during the past decade; having residence halls filled to capacity each year contributes to sustaining the status quo. HU has been far less fortunate. The contentious layoffs and downsizing initiatives that occurred in 2009 created political quagmires that persist today. HU continues to downsize and outsource, but the institution no longer lays off custodians who are in good standing. Instead, it consolidated custodians' work shifts. An HU senior administrator explains this downsizing strategy:

> There was [*sic*] once three separate departments we brought into one: grounds, special facilities, and custodial. There were three separate directors. Three years ago we brought those groups together. The base of that unit is all a single job description. Within that group of people, the entry-level staff, you have a lot of absences—even without FMLA [Family and Medical Leave Act] and people calling in at the last minute. We had 48,000 hours a year we don't have people here—comp or sick or child time. There are jobs linked to those 48,000 hours that have to be done. What we started to look at is ways to address this issue.

The department has three different shifts. In the past, if someone didn't report to work, the solution was for a custodian to do two jobs that day. To respond to high absenteeism the department consolidated its three shifts to a single shift (4:00 a.m.–12:00 p.m.). This policy provides the DPF greater latitude to achieve its downsizing goals by not filling every vacancy and using the entire workforce to clean spaces deemed a priority.

Increasing Accountability

Accountability, the third characteristic of corporate managerialism, again pits management against labor. Unlike downsizing and outsourcing, which primarily concern HU custodians, accountability tensions influence the quality of life for HU and CU custodians but in different ways.

Custodial administrators/supervisors perceive accountability measures as positive and necessary to ensure productivity, efficiency, and cost savings. For administrators, accountability procedures are straightforward, and the division of labor is crystal clear. Managers set clear, challenging, and attainable standards; assign tasks to workers; monitor progress; evaluate performance; and administer either rewards or punishments, depending on the work quality. Workers complete directives assigned to them or suffer the consequences.

Custodians perceive accountability measures as negative and unnecessary, contributing to conflict, mistrust, fear, and frustration. Workers assert that administrators and supervisors use accountability measures as a weapon to keep workers busy and down; a carrot and stick, dangling rewards and threatening punishments to induce certain behaviors; or ammunition for blame and punishment.

Although my observations of accountability-related interactions involving workers and managers at both CU and HU are not as stark and simplistic as this brief overview suggests, issues of power, trust, and respect are at the root of these differences.

The inspection, the DOH's primary accountability metric, is the single greatest concern for CU custodians. The work responsibilities and evaluation procedures for custodians are unambiguous and nonnegotiable. A summary of a job description (which includes evaluation metrics seen in Table 9.1) substantiates this claim.

This inspection form enriches understanding about a custodian's daily work duties as well as the department's personnel evaluation criteria. During formal inspections, custodians need to score between 95 and 100 to be deemed "outstanding," 90 to 94 to "achieve expectations," and 85 to 89 to be rated "satisfactory." Scores below 84 suggest that custodians "need improvement." In this example, the custodian can earn a maximum of 60 points for cleaning public areas, 30 points for cleaning student suites, and 10 points for maintaining housekeeping closets.

As someone unfamiliar with custodial supervision, the comprehensive and regimented list of expectations is an invaluable guide to orient new staff (and ethnographic fieldworkers). Yet, for experienced custodians, the formal and highly quantifiable point system seems excessive and adversarial. A CU supervisor discusses the origins of this particular system of accountability:

> Lance created this. If we are an A, he wants us to strive for an A+. We strive for higher. We are detail oriented. We do inspections every two weeks, which is during a pay period. You get inspected twice a month. Lots of housekeepers go in and do their regular cleaning. They don't do anything special. They just work every day—same thing every day. Most of the time they don't miss anything.

CU custodians concur with the claim that departmental expectations are and should remain high. Unlike this supervisor, custodians deem inspections a big deal.

> We don't need inspections. We've been talking about inspections for years. And they keep doing it. I don't know what's going on with that. I'm just going to do my job—good and thoroughly. I work from 8:00 to 4:30. This is simple work, but they make it hard on us.

TABLE 9.1
Compton University Custodian Inspection Rubric

Public Areas [60 points]
Entrance: Door, glass, carpet, floors, wooden panels, mats, lights, fixtures, baseboards.
Great Hall: Floor, fireplace, tables, chairs, cushions, pillars, windows, patio, closets, shelves, walls, ledges, rugs, lamps, vents, lights, fixtures.
Classrooms: Boards, doors, sinks, tables, chairs, floor, glass, trash cans/recycling, equipment, windows, vents, lights, fixtures, blinds.
Main Kitchen/First Floor Kitchenette/Fourth Floor Kitchenette: Stove, refrigerator, microwaves, range hood, floors, walls, cabinet, countertops, sink, door, trash/recycling vents, baseboards, lights, fixtures, dishwasher.
Computer Room: Doors, floors, tables, chairs, computers, glass, trash can/recycling, printers, vents, baseboards, walls, lights, fixtures, windows, blinds.
Hallways (first floor/lower level): Floors, baseboards, bench, walls, doors, drinking fountains, glass, ledges, vents, tracks, lights, fixtures, flyers, sanitizers, boards.
Restrooms: Doors, floors, sinks, mirrors, toilets, urinals, countertops, sanitary box, stall dividers, supplies, cleanser tub, trashcans, vents, lights, fixtures, flyers, baseboards.
Fourth Floor Lounge: Cushion chairs, couches, tables, lamps, floors, doors, glass, chairs, vents, walls, lights, fixtures, windows, baseboards.
Prayer Room: Floor, glass, shelves, vents, walls, baseboards, fixtures.
Student Suites [30 points]
Suite: Floors, corners, showers, sinks, toilets, shelves, mirrors, countertops, cabinets, doors, paper products, stall dividers, walls, baseboards, vents, shelves, pipes, shower curtain.
Housekeeping Closet [10 points]
Basement: Sink, chemical station, vacuum, floors, doors, cart, schedule, vents, baseboards, lights, fixtures, pipes, shelves, walls.

Another custodian augments this argument:

They will still come around and watch you. I don't like people standing over me. That's stressful. I don't say anything; I just keep my head down. Other people, they have arguments. I just do my work and that is all that matters. I get hassled a lot. I really do. They can't complain, because I am always working. . . . I never know what they are looking for. I call them and tell them that I am tired of being harassed. Lance and I have talked. I tell him that I don't think it is right what the supervisors do. They seem to target me. He says he will talk to them, but it gets worse.

Veteran custodians depict inspections as too formal and too frequent. Inspections accentuate power differences and symbolically communicate that management neither trusts nor respects workers. Custodians generally prefer respectful and collaborative supervisors, rather than nitpicking or authoritative inspectors.

I don't care about saying what I am saying. Right is right and wrong is wrong. You don't mistreat people. If the people do their job, leave them be. They should mind their own business. Who is looking at the supervisors? . . . Tell a person they are doing something right. It's not like that. They keep finding stuff. If there are no complaints, what is the problem? Every time they do an inspection, they find something new or focus on something new. After a while, you laugh. You can't get mad, because it has been going on for so long.

This example provides glimpses of corporate managerialism in action. The DOH bases inspections on authoritative appraisals, suggesting that supervisors, not workers, know what counts as "good." The power differential I observed during inspections is stark and makes clear who is in charge and who is not. Inspections ensure that mechanisms are in place for management to hold workers accountable, yet few mechanisms exist to assess the performance of supervisors/administrators or hold them accountable. Inspections represent a culture of surveillance, a not-so-sophisticated way of keeping a close watch on the Other. Justified in the name of efficiency and excellence, authorities keep a careful eye on custodians to monitor their choices, gather information about them, and keep them in line, which are foundational values of corporate managerialism.

On the HU campus, accountability systems have little to do with surveillance or inspections. Instead, the DPF concentrates its accountability efforts on maximizing productivity. For example, the DPF remains concerned about aging and longtime custodians who struggle to "pull their own weight." These workers represent a productivity threat to corporate managerial loyalists. A senior administrator elaborates on this issue:

Being a custodian is a highly physical job. Now we have far fewer folks doing that work. Juggling that now to make sure things are distributed evenly is hard. If you take Tom, who is 65 and not getting around too well, and put him on auto-scrubber all day, then Dick is going to say that that is not fair, since I have to do all of the physical work. Dick will say other people get to do the easy work. You have buildings where people will do that for their coworkers. But is that fair? They are willing to make those accommodations. If you put on an extra 100 pounds, do you get to drive the lawn mower all day?

This administrator's concern centers on work equity for custodians. Custodians counter that this administrator is less concerned with equity issues in the workplace and more concerned with nudging older, loyal, and higher-paid workers out of the workforce in order to replace them with less expensive workers. The department devalues veteran custodians' unique contributions, such as mentoring new staff, that these experienced workers make to the organization. This "What have you done for me lately?" approach to management discounts workers' long-standing contributions to the university and accounts for workers' collective uneasiness with accountability.

This accountability measure signals a shift in the department's operating philosophy. During previous administrations, competent, aging, and loyal workers with seniority earned the right to informally negotiate revised job responsibilities to accommodate declining work skills. In this management paradigm, experienced and dedicated workers were assets. The current management philosophy privileges the university's interests more than the workers'.

Centralizing power, minimizing labor costs, and increasing accountability have a debilitating influence on custodians by excluding them from key policy and decision making and inhibiting them from gaining a voice. Reinstilling site-based or local decision making and finding ways to include the voice of these groups in the deliberative process are necessary steps to enhancing community participation (Fields & Feinberg, 2001).

Going out of Business

I began this chapter with a story about Samuel's rendezvous with the HU president, a story that I deemed unusual, profound, sad, unbelievable, disorienting, and revealing. This chapter concludes with a discussion of six aspects of corporate managerialism in the context of custodial life at HU and CU.

Unusual

> Colleges and universities do not simply produce knowledge for students; they also play an influential role in shaping their identities, values, and sense of what it means to become citizens of the world. (Giroux, 2005, para. 5)

When talking about the influences of colleges and universities on society, it is common, as Giroux noted, to zoom in on the university's capacity to influence collegians, shaping their identities and values. Less common are discussions about the university's influence on other campus subcultures, such as custodians. Corporate managerialism influences custodians' senses of what it means to be a "good" campus citizen: placing the interests of the university ahead of all other interests (including one's own), respecting and refraining from questioning authority, sacrificing, and following orders. Stories describing custodians' fears and feelings of powerlessness raise an unusual question: What would a university look like if custodians had the capacity to define what it means for the powerbrokers to be good campus citizens?

Profound

> Listen rather than talk. . . . Walk around campus. . . . Talk with staff who do not have offices. . . . Show up with coffee and donuts when the early shift of facilities staff or custodians or food service folks arrive. . . . Talk to retired faculty and staff who best examplif[y] the values of the institution and then ask two or three of those who are named individually to have coffee. . . . Sidewalk conversations. . . Overcommunicate. . . . Give people the information that they need to make their own choices. (Pierce, 2009, para. 1)

Pierce offered this advice to administrators embarking on new leadership positions in the academy. Although highly practical and initially superficial, the advice is deep—and it is profoundly different from most experiences I observed at HU and CU. Seldom did I observe powerbrokers listening, walking around campus and informally interacting, soliciting feedback from retired custodians, overcommunicating, and giving custodians information they need to make their own choices. Custodians have suggestions about how to make their university efficient and productive that align with corporate managerialism ideals, yet powerbrokers seldom solicit this wisdom from them. What would happen if proponents of corporate managerialism heeded Pierce's advice?

Sad

> In a story, a challenge presents itself to the protagonist who then has a choice, and an outcome occurs. The outcome teaches a moral, but because the protagonist is a humanlike character, we are able to identify empathetically, and therefore we are able to feel, not just understand, what is going on. (Ganz, 2009, paras. 10–11)

In corporate managerial settings, collecting and retelling stories is inefficient and unusual—and thus "bad." Yet, as Ganz argued, stories humanize experiences, which is beneficial. Samuel's letter to the president recounted not simply what happened but how he felt. The president read Samuel's letter (rather than a summary of the letter prepared by an aide), which allowed him to vicariously experience Samuel's sincerity and disappointment—feelings that, I suspect, influenced his response. My story, contained in this chapter, recounts not simply what happened during the exchange involving Samuel and the president but also my feelings. These stories illustrate the power of stories and how they can enrich understanding and lead to mutually beneficial outcomes. The stories remind readers that even in environments steeped in corporate managerial ideals, there is space for and merit in storytelling that yields "productive" outcomes. How can feeling and understanding coexist in the corporate university?

Unbelievable

> The more students, faculty, and custodians worked together, talked together, argued and fought together, the more socially constructed barriers were challenged. This isn't to say that race and class prejudices and divisions did not remain salient; they were always with us. But by openly confronting them, we began the long process of reshaping their contours and meaning. (Dolgon, 2000, p. 356)

Two golden rules of corporate managerialism are: (a) Don't ostracize key constituents, and (b) Forge mutually beneficial partnerships. Corporate managerial advocates seldom followed these rules when interacting with custodians, which, from my vantage point, is unbelievable. Powerbrokers ostracize custodians, and interactions, when they occur, seldom resembled the kinds of relationship that Dolgon advocated. The consequences of ignoring these two golden rules are significant and result in fortifying, rather than dismantling, subculture boundaries. This is not in the interest of the organization and its stakeholders. What would happen if powerbrokers more broadly defined key constituents and forged partnerships with un-like-minded people, especially the less powerful?

Disorienting

> My argument is that if we do not prioritize the mission and establish a firm understanding of what a democratic education is, the university will implode under the weight of its own entrepreneurial instincts. (Gould, 2003, p. x)

Higher education aspires to be the great equalizer—a place dedicated to lifting up the less advantaged and improving their chances for success. The promise is that if students work hard and play by the rules, good results will take place. A common way to level the proverbial playing field for collegians is through democratic education (rooted in values of justice, respect, and trust). This pedagogy involves students in decision making, solicits multiple perspectives, facilitates dialogue across differences, and encourages students to become active participants in the control and organization of their education. While these equity ideas are mainstays in progressive college classrooms, the ideas are seldom applied to settings beyond the classroom and seldom involve any campus stakeholders besides collegians. What would happen if powerbrokers applied their entrepreneurial energies to finding ways to democratize work settings?

Revealing

> The treatment of low-wage workers on campus is an issue that flies below the public radar, is ignored by public-policy officials and college trustees, and is dismissed by college administrators as little more than a nuisance. The insouciance and apathy of faculty members throughout academe has permitted administrators to avoid taking any action to remedy these inequities. (Eisenberg, 2012b, p. 19)

Over the past two decades, students have used living wage protests to pressure university administrators to temper corporatization efforts. The protests have produced some noteworthy victories (increases to wages and benefits, and dialogues with workers and students) as well as considerable media attention. Still, low wages persist, with efforts to remedy these ills eclipsed by other matters. Custodians' low standing on campus, struggles to mobilize, and fear make it unlikely that they will be the epicenter of future grassroots activism.

Universities are hardly neutral, and they operate according to the ideologies of the dominant class. Carefully examining and mobilizing to challenge the influences of these ideals on various campus subcultures are rare and necessary approaches to take (Nelson, 1997).

10

SOILED EDUCATIONAL ASPIRATIONS AND CIVIC DISENGAGEMENT

Doing More Harm Than Good

> I moved from North Carolina to Ohio in 1985. When I got there I went to a community college and got a list of courses to take to get a degree in elementary education. . . . I was taking a lot of classes each semester. I did pretty well—mostly As and Bs and a couple of Cs. During my last semester, my dad died, so I missed two weeks of classes and my math final. It brought my grade down to a D, so I couldn't graduate. I went to watch my friends graduate. When they were calling the names [of graduates] they called my name. I thought it was a mistake and didn't think about it. A few weeks later I got two diplomas in the mail. I didn't know what to do, so I went to the school and gave them back. A few weeks later they mailed the same diplomas back to me. I went back again, and this time I talked to someone. I found out that I didn't need to take every course on my list. You're not going to believe this; I took so many classes that I earned two associate['s] degrees, in general studies and education. I didn't even need that math class to graduate.

Twenty-seven years after her community college graduation, Lucy, a Harrison University (HU) custodian, recounts this all-too-familiar collegiate tale: A stranger in a strange land void of academic networks and insider knowledge goes it alone. Disengaged from the curriculum and cocurriculum, Lucy encounters challenges and unsuccessfully navigates unfamiliar and bureaucratic labyrinths. She accepts the blame for setbacks and then quits college. Unlike Lucy's humorous unsuccessful dropout adventure, few stories about marginalized members in the academy have happy endings.

Lucy expresses similar feelings of confusion and marginalization when discussing her custodial job at HU. The ever-changing university exacerbates Lucy's feelings of vulnerability and marginalization.

> Academia is commonly referred to as the 'ivory tower,' the place where scholars and students stow themselves away to wrestle with abstract ideas. It stands in marked contrast to the 'real world,' the place where people concern themselves with things that are of practical importance. (Sweet, 2001, p. 1)

Lucy struggles to understand the "logic" and core values of HU, her ivory tower—how it works and why it works the way it does. This uneasiness tempers her enthusiasm for the job and HU.

This story introduces two additional perplexing trends I noted during my fieldwork. First, institutional infrastructures and policies, rooted in corporate managerialism, made it difficult for Compton University (CU) and HU custodians to benefit from their education benefits (e.g., tuition waiver). Unwieldy bureaucracies, inflexible work parameters, stagnant wages, and turbulent lives at home make it difficult for custodians to matriculate or participate in skill- and salary-building job enrichment opportunities.

Second, institutional policies and infrastructures did not prepare custodians to contribute to the university beyond their cleaning responsibilities, which deflated their desires for civic involvement. Cipolle (2010) noted,

> One of the primary missions of education is to prepare students for democratic and civic engagement. I believe as educators it is our responsibility to help students acquire the necessary information, skills, and desires to be engaged citizens who can meet not only today's social and economic challenges but who will also work to eradicate the root causes of inequality and injustice. (p. iv)

Although CU and HU are highly adept at preparing students for democratic and civic engagement—two cornerstones of the academy (National Task Force on Civic Learning and Democratic Engagement, 2012)—this agenda seldom extends to include custodians. This was especially true of custodians who wanted to make use of their tuition waiver to continue their formal education and earn a college degree or participate in job enrichment seminars to increase their hourly wage.

Higher education professes to be in the business of education and civic involvement, and American universities have historically prepared students for active citizenship and to produce knowledge that serves the needs of society (Bringle, Games, & Malloy, 1999). Yet custodians are seldom the beneficiaries of these interventions.

It was Horace Mann who wrote in 1848 that education "beyond all other devices of human origin, is the great equalizer of the conditions of men, the balance-wheel of the social machinery" (qtd. in Altenbaugh, 2003, p. 81). Although this quotation is almost 170 years old, the economic and inter-generational evidence is overwhelming that education continues to increase income, improve health, reduce most types of crime, and increase civic participation. Inequalities persist, and higher education strives to improve society and the individuals who inhabit it by fostering citizens' moral development, critical thinking, and practical skills (Bowen, 1977).

Newly hired CU custodians partake in a formal, high-quality, and terminal apprenticeship program that provides invaluable on-the-job training and supervision. Because custodians (at the time of this fieldwork) were employees of the Octagon Cleaning Company (OCC), they had no CU tuition benefits, which made earning a college degree improbable. (After CU dissolved the OCC and OCC staff became CU employees, they became eligible for modest tuition benefits.) Beyond a comprehensive new employee orientation, CU's Department of Housing had no formal ongoing professional development or job enrichment program for custodians.

HU, despite its seemingly perpetual economic instability, has left untouched its comprehensive tuition benefits—for workers and their families—and innovative job enrichment program. (Completion of professional development modules results in modest salary increases or onetime bonuses.) Yet a closer examination of custodians' struggles regarding access and use of these two benefits reveals barriers. Despite the generous tuition waiver program, HU custodians seldom pursue college degrees or enroll in college classes because they, for example, work a second job or assume child-care responsibilities—circumstances that interfere with educational aspirations.

HU's job enrichment program restrictions frustrate some custodians. For example, custodians' professional development seminars must directly relate to current job responsibilities. HU would approve a custodian enrolling in an enhanced floor-waxing seminar but would not approve a custodian enrolling in a financial-planning seminar, since financial planning is only tangentially related to custodians' work responsibilities. Influenced by corporate managerialism, these restrictions favor universities' interests while disadvantaging custodians.

Ehrlich (2000) defined *civic engagement* as "working to make a difference in the civic life of our communities and developing the combination of knowledge, skills, values, and motivation to make that difference" (p. vi). Ehrlich (cited in Tannenbaum, 2008) also noted,

> One of the most important roles institutions of higher education play in a democratic society is providing opportunities that help individuals recognize themselves as members of a larger social fabric, to consider social problems to be at least partly their own, to see civic dimensions of issues, to make and justify informed civic judgments, and to take action when appropriate. (p. xxi)

CU and HU seldom provided opportunities for custodians to cross subculture borders to work with other campus community members. If border-crossing interactions occurred, custodians initiated them. Ignoring custodians' worth and wisdom contributed to their disengagement from campus life. Custodians expressed a desire to clean and make a difference in the lives of others. Yet institutional infrastructures thwarted custodians' efforts to develop knowledge and skills to help them achieve this engagement goal or share their wisdom with the larger campus community.

Over 50 custodians are European refugees who possess keen firsthand insights about how to successfully navigate the "coming to America" experience. Despite custodians' collective wisdom about cultural assimilation, the university seldom tapped into these sources of wisdom by inviting these workers to share their stories with or offer advice to new international students studying in the United States. Having few opportunities to earn a college degree, refine existing or develop new skills, or cross borders to teach and learn from others further insulated CU custodians from the larger campus community.

Continuing education aimed at increasing democratic engagement and civic learning was the exception, not the rule, for custodians. Departmental administrators eschew local (i.e., grassroots) knowledge and seldom sponsor open forums inviting workers and managers to share concerns or knowledge. A nagging question persists: Why do institutions narrowly define who should partake as teachers and learners in civic engagement educational opportunities that focus on critical issues such as "liberty, equality, individual worth, open-mindedness, and the willingness to collaborate with people of differing views and background toward common solutions for the public good" (National Task Force on Civic Learning and Democratic Engagement, 2012, p. 3)?

With minimum power and authority, custodians resemble what David Mathews, president of the Kettering Foundation, called "sideline citizens" (London, 2010, p. iv) or democratic spectators. After CU dissolved the OCC and incorporated custodians into the university, custodial supervisors' influence on the selection of new employees diminished. They remained on the sidelines during critical departmental hiring decisions. Likewise, HU custodians assumed the role of spectators in departmental decision making.

Paradoxically, custodians accepted cleaning jobs at universities with the hope of "getting educated" to offset feelings of being left behind and losing ground, only to resurrect these feelings once on the job.

The Good, the Bad, and the Ugly

Four brief case studies illuminate this miseducation trend. Two stories are about custodians pursuing college degrees as part-time students and full-time employees, and two stories center on custodians who participated in departmental professional development seminars.

Good Will [Job] Hunting

On a warm and windy November afternoon in 2012, I track down Will in a stairwell in HU's College of Education. At age 32, Will looks and is too old to be a traditional-age college student and generally too young to be a career custodian. Chatting in this public space is feasible, since most afternoon classes have concluded. Today, Will's work routines are unusual; after walking the building to check for any major cleaning crises that need attention, he will participate in a mandatory staff development program for snow-removal personnel, sponsored by the Department of Physical Facilities (DPF). As Will and I inspect stairwells he talks about how HU's educational benefits lured him to the custodial life:

> [In high school] I was sitting in our small engines class, where you learn to take apart a small engine. My buddy told me he got a job working here at Harrison as a student worker. . . . He told me that when you work full-time, you get free tuition. I started to think—hey, I could afford to go to college if I do this. So I followed him over here one day and he connected me with the management people. . . . That was 1998; I was 17. . . . Back then, they let me work 20 hours a week, and when I was out of school for breaks or summer vacation I worked 40-hour shifts.

About 20 minutes before the start of the training session, we drive across campus to the locale. Not wanting to enter the building too early for the 5:00 p.m. workshop, we remain in the car and continue our conversation. I learn that a few weeks before Will graduated from high school, his supervisor informed him that HU could no longer employ him as a student worker, since he was no longer a high school student. Subsequently, Will applied for and accepted a custodian job.

During the 2001–2002 academic year, while working full-time, Will earned 13 academic credits by completing a botany class, a history class, and two composition seminars. Shortly thereafter he discontinued classes for five years to spend more time with his two children. When they enrolled in preschool, Will returned to the classroom with a sharper career focus:

> When I got here [2001] I knew I just wanted an education, but I didn't understand what liberal arts meant. In 2006 I finally realized what I wanted so I started on an associate['s] degree. Now [2012] I kind of wish I would not

have wasted my time with it, since some of it does not go toward my bachelor's degree. I have my associate['s] degree, and it is not really doing me much good. I have about another year or so until I complete my bachelor's degree.

Will commutes 22 miles to and from work. When working the second shift, he leaves home at 3:15 p.m., clocks in at 4:00, and works a few hours before clocking out and driving 15 miles to attend a three-hour seminar on a regional campus. After class, he drives back to HU's main campus, clocks in, and then finishes his eight-hour shift, usually returning home by 3:00 p.m. a.m. When working the graveyard shift, Will's schedule is equally intense. He starts work at 10:00 p.m. and departs at 6:00 a.m. After work, Will exercises at the recreation center, eats breakfast on campus, and then attends morning classes (two or three days per week). Around noon he drives home before returning to campus at 10:00 p.m.

Minutes before the start time of the training session, we approach an oversized garage that is serving as the meeting locale. The building resembles a small airport hangar and includes old cars, vans, and trucks. Oddly there are no chairs, tables, or podiums. Will and I lean against an aging truck, waiting for the session to begin. Will predicts what will transpire since this is the tenth time he has attended this annual event. The department requires all custodians who have snow-shoveling responsibilities or custodians who aspire to work on the campus-wide snow-removal team to complete this training module. Minimizing risks and lawsuits, I suspect, are at the root of this mandate. Will assesses this program: "It's okay. Being here is no worse than being back in my building cleaning."

Participants huddle together around the facilitator. The local physical therapist places his notes on the hood of a car, glances at his agenda, scans the audience, and then begins. Attendees appear respectful. The speaker educates attendees about human physiology and snow safety tips. "What should you wear when shoveling snow?" "Why layer clothes?" "How much heat escapes from your head if you don't wear a hat?" "What are the common injuries resulting from shoveling snow?" Each question elicits an immediate response. I imagine some attendees' midwestern politeness coupled with their discomfort with silence contributes to the high level of involvement. I wonder, *Why hire an outside consultant when at least a dozen of these attendees could do as good if not a better job facilitating this session?*

My body aches as I stand in this damp space, observing this 30-minute presentation. Just when I think the session is about to wrap up, the facilitator instructs attendees to move outside for a snow-shoveling demonstration and assessment. Attendees meander outside, eventually congregating around a mountain of gravel. The facilitator exaggerates his shoveling techniques to illustrate the proper way to position one's body to effortlessly and safely scoop and discard snow.

Will and I muscle our way into the middle of a line that is forming as I observe the surroundings. Each attendee approaches the mountain, selects a shovel, twice scoops and discards gravel, then listens to the expert's critique. As this seemingly endless and repetitive assessment gets longer, the feedback gets shorter. Eventually the critiques are one or two words: "Good." "Very good." "Bend." Approaching the mountain, I lament my decision to participate rather than observe. I survive the public evaluation, learning that I need to further bend my knees and keep the shovel closer to my body. Will and I step away from the crowd to converse without disturbing others. I expect Will to critique this all-too-familiar and not-so-educational training session. Instead, he discusses macro concerns about the department's leadership team:

> I applied for a manager job here. Of the three people they brought in for interviews—they were all internal—I was the only one with a college [associate's] degree, which is what the ad required. And they did not give me the position. I interviewed with managers, and they all picked me. They said to me that I had the education and I had what they needed. They seemed to have my back. When it went to the next level, the people above them—they gave the job to someone else. It is still about who you know more than the degree. It was a bummer. They let me work and go to school. They know why I am doing it. I have a degree in management. When it comes down to it, I don't get the management job in the department where I have worked for over 10 years.

Like many custodians, Will works hard to earn an honest wage. He makes personal and professional sacrifices each day to "get educated," which he hopes someday will provide him access to better and higher-paying jobs. Despite strong support and encouragement from local supervisors, few senior administrators in the DPF inquire about Will's progress toward graduation or how the knowledge he has gained in college classrooms could be applied to his job and benefit the department and the individuals the department serves. HU's fiscal investment in Will's education is significant, yet the university neither systematically monitors its investment nor purposefully acts to strengthen it. Oddly, corporate managerialism values return on investment, efficiency, and reducing costs, yet the university's quest to cut waste and improve accountability measures does not apply in this custodial context.

Despite an associate's degree in hand and a bachelor's degree nearly complete, Will remains a custodian. Symbolically the department illuminated the wide gap between its espoused and enacted value—hiring educated supervisory staff—when it ignored Will's many educational accomplishments and hired a supervisor who did not possess even a college degree, a job requirement listed on the job posting. Will's response to this hiring decision was to apply to become a supervisor in HU's Auxiliary Services custodial department. He did, and he got the job.

Good for You

Inside a makeshift office, a converted custodial closet, Nita, a 50-something African American woman, looks across her desk at me as we exchange introductory pleasantries. I am confident we will not be disturbed, since it took 10 minutes to locate the stadium elevators that granted me access to the football team's restricted offices and meeting rooms—spaces Nita cleans each day. Nita recounts how she learned about the job she has held for over three decades:

> I started part-time in 1982. I just had a baby. I needed a job to take care of my child. I worked part-time at the conference center. There was a housekeeping supervisor who knew my mom and dad. I was looking for a full-time job, so I could get benefits. I went to Mr. Fonda; he knew my parents. . . . I got hired on [full-time] in 1985. It's been a journey. I didn't think I would last this long, 30 years. . . . I have three kids. I put two of my kids through college [because of the tuition waiver].

Nita's father was a custodian in the student center for 15 years before becoming ill and retiring. Her mother worked in the residence halls as a food preparer. Both parents persuaded Nita that HU's insurance and tuition benefits made this dirty job desirable. Approximately two decades after Nita started work at HU, her oldest daughter earned an associate's degree in accounting and her younger daughter earned an associate's degree in business management. In 2006, after raising her family, Nita enrolled in the applied business associate's degree program. She reflects on her educational journey:

> I am [now] getting my BA in 2014. I have been doing it part-time. It's been six years. I go during the days, summers, and nights. I went when my kids got through school. My kids now have kids, so I have to help out there. I am a single mother. All three of my kids live around here. My son still lives with me. My two daughters are on their own and have kids of their own.

Nita intends to work in an office setting that will allow her to apply her business administration knowledge. She explains, "I'm tired of cleaning. It pays my bills. I am not ashamed of my job, but I know I can do better. That's why I went back to school. It has taken me this long. I want to do something else. I am determined to get to the end."

Nita's accomplishments are many and inspirational. As a single parent she worked hard, remained frugal, and sacrificed so that family members could have a shot at the good life. Nita labored for decades so that her three children had opportunities to graduate from college. Nita recognizes that she can do more with her life, yet she waited until her children were financially independent before pursuing her college degree on a part-time basis while working full-time as a custodian. HU's tuition waiver made these dreams a reality. Many of Nita's coworkers aspire to earn a college degree yet ultimately abandon this dream. One CU worker made explicit the insurmountable challenges that many custodians share.

> My husband worked first shift. He would be coming in the driveway as I was leaving, so the kids did not need a babysitter. The school bus would be following him. I would be around during the day. I would have supper done and it would be on the stove before I left. I would go to the car, give my husband a kiss, and go to work. We were all coming and going, and that is the way we kept our home and kept the kids going. That's the sacrifice I had to make.

Many family members of custodians (like Lucy) enroll in college using tuition benefits and then drop out of college due to their lack of familiarity with how universities operate. Despite the high costs associated with subsidizing college, HU does not maximize its investment assets by, for example, preemptively offering academic success seminars for custodians and their family members or mentoring custodians who enroll in college courses.

Looks Good on Paper

> Amusement park—liked it, but it was seasonal. . . . Grocery store cashier—liked it, and not sure why I quit. . . . Fast-food waitress—liked it, but quit because I moved away. . . . Nanny/babysitter—liked it, but kids got older. . . . Steak house waitress—loved it, but started at the time they were struggling to stay open. It was embarrassing. They did not have any money to purchase extra silverware, mugs, even food. . . . Day-care worker at my house—I hated it; parents never respected me. . . . Warehouse worker at a cosmetic distribution center—hard work and good money, but my year as a temp ran out. . . . Magazine warehouse worker—loved it but got laid off. . . . Activities assistant at a nursing home—liked it a lot. It was rewarding, but I quit because of the work they were pushing on me. I wish I had not quit.

As this story suggests, Elaine, a 30-something White woman, has sampled most jobs near her home. Being an HU custodian is the most stable and appealing job for her to date. Conscientious and curious, Elaine is the only interviewee who confessed to searching for me on Google before our initial face-to-face meeting. Shortly after we begin our conversation, Elaine inquires about the origins of my study and my motivations for pursuing it. A few days after our meeting, she pens the passage that opens this section because she forgot to mention it during our conversation.

Like many custodians, learning interests Elaine. She is a regular participant in HU's Job Enrichment Program (JEP), a voluntary educational initiative for custodians. JEP focuses on clarifying job expectations (e.g., sexual harassment policy), enhancing technical skills (e.g., computer technologies), and maximizing work performance. Custodians who complete JEP modules earn modest salary increases that they hope will lead to career advancement. Elaine describes the program's intricacies:

> The job enrichment program is great. . . . It is where you can learn more about your job, take a test, get a $500 bonus, and a little raise. You learn a lot from it. They have tons of topics. . . . My mind is going blank. I finished all three sections for one phase, and now I am waiting for my raise. It was hard, but I did it. One was on cleaning floors. There are so many different kinds of floors. There are different ways to clean and strip it . . . cleaning restrooms, walls, and windows. Everything you can think of—carpets. You have a book, you read it, and you take a test in a room. If you pass, you get a raise. . . . You take online or regular class. . . . You have to get 150 points. Every 50 points leads to a onetime bonus. When you get 150 points you get a 70-cent raise.

Despite Elaine's thirst for learning, her past academic missteps have lessened her educational aspirations.

> I can go back to school [making use of the tuition waiver], but I haven't done it. I enrolled here after high school and only lasted half of a semester. In high school, I got straight Cs. I did all of my homework but failed my tests. In college, your grades are based on quizzes and tests. I struggled and quit. I tried it, and it didn't work. College isn't for everyone.

Elaine, a first-generation college student, was unfamiliar with campus life, which exacerbated her academic insecurities. At the time she was unaware that she was entitled to free academic advising and academic support such as tutoring. Feeling alone and on her own, she simply dropped out. A decade later, Elaine appears more career-focused, yet apprehensions persist:

> Now that I am older, I know what I want to do. I love animals. But they don't have a vet-tech program here. If they had a program that I liked, I

might go back. Business classes don't interest me. My husband gets almost free schooling here, too. It is hard for him to go back to school.

Elaine values education and possesses many qualities and skills that are predictors of academic success. In 2008 she earned a $100 bookstore gift card for perfect attendance for an entire calendar year (since then, HU scaled back this incentive program to contain costs). The quality of her work is noteworthy. In 2011 Elaine received a Rising Star Award because of exemplary work. She smiles broadly as she describes the aftermath of her Rising Star Award: "I got a letter from a VP saying, 'Congratulations' and that I would get a $300 bonus in my next check. . . . I'm a better worker because of the occasional recognition."

As Elaine ponders her future, she is wiser but still clings to two assumptions: she can go only so far, and wherever she goes, she must go it alone. She aspires to work as an animal advocate, yet she remains reluctant to consult with academic advisers to identify ways to gain the necessary training to achieve this goal. Despite cleaning buildings where dozens of faculty and academic advisers work, she refuses to burden them with her life challenges. Few individuals whom she encounters inquire about her life. Elaine elaborates on her relationship with others: "Some staff are snobby. Only a handful know me. Most know my name. They tell me about their troubles. I know more about them than they know about me."

As HU recognizes, to ensure that students optimize their collegiate experiences and graduate, the university must provide academic opportunities and supportive academic infrastructures that encourage students to learn about and use available academic services. HU seldom applies these best practices to ensure the academic success of custodial staff. The university invests minimally in the academic infrastructures aimed at supporting custodians, making it difficult for them to recognize and use services to achieve their desired academic goals.

Custodians like Elaine encounter roadblocks when attempting to serve others. She volunteers three days a week at her local dog rescue shelter. As a member of HU's custodian caste, it is unlikely that Elaine will share her expertise with faculty, students, and staff. When an animal advocacy student organization searches for an organizational adviser, Elaine will not likely be on the organization's short list of viable candidates. Dynamics and norms such as these upend Elaine's desire and efforts to become more civically engaged and active in the life of the university and its students.

Elaine enjoys her job and relishes opportunities to participate in HU's JEP, which improves her skills and increases her annual salary. Yet her past educational missteps and struggles to engage with the larger university have contributed to her sustaining a self-imposed glass ceiling and sense of isolation.

Good Grief

For Samuel, simply enrolling in a finance and accounting professional development seminar to prepare for retirement is more difficult than mastering the retirement seminar content. Samuel wrote to HU's Department of Human Resources to request permission to enroll in this JEP seminar:

> To whom it may concern,
>   I would like to take the finance and accounting program because I think that this type of course would be the most helpful and useful to me in all aspects of life, compared to other courses that are listed. It would be interesting to learn more about the ways of finance and how to deal with certain situations that pertain to money since we need it for survival purposes. Please allow me to attempt this course and if I should complete this program successfully, maybe it will help me get a better position here at Harrison.
>   Sincerely,
>   Samuel _____

Eleven days later, the Department of Human Resources replied:

> Mr. Samuel _____,
>   We have received your preapproval request for the finance and accounting course. The Job Enrichment Administrators met, and upon the conclusion of our discussion related to your request, this course does not align with the required job skills listed in your classified job description, and is not approved to receive credit in the Job Enrichment Program. Thank you for taking the time to inquire.
>   Best regards,
>   _____, Job Enrichment Administrator

This administrative decision is reminiscent of Goffman's (1952) and Clark's work on what they termed *cooling out* (Clark, 2008). The human resources department assesses Samuel, determines his expectations were too high, and redirects him to what they consider more "appropriate" aspirations. Since enrolling in the finance and accounting course would benefit Samuel more than HU, the centralized human resources department board denies the petition. HU's interest trumps Samuel's interest, which is antithetical to the espoused belief that higher education is a public good. Determining the appropriateness of learning opportunities based on one's social status within the university hardly aligns with HU's espoused mission of equity and education for all. Samuel tries to gain practical knowledge about financial planning and retirement that will benefit both the university and him, but fails. His only recourse is to enroll in custodian courses that ensure modest salary increases. The decision to deny Samuel's petition does not save the university any money, since the retirement seminar occurred without Samuel's involvement and Samuel enrolled in another seminar in order to get a raise. HU's decision to educate staff based on social status contributes to Samuel's disappointment and disengagement from campus life. It also reveals the disconnect between the university's rhetoric and action.

Too Bad

Will, Nita, Elaine, and Samuel value education, and each forged a unique path to get educated and educate others. Despite institutional practices that minimized opportunities for them to participate in the university, they endured. In theory, educational benefits and professional development opportunities provide diverse pathways to a better life for custodians; in practice, pathways, often lead to dead ends.

CU and HU both regularly and successfully deploy numerous best practices that optimize learning for collegians; the application of these best practices to custodians' educational quests are irregular and seldom successful. Laissez-faire oversight of custodians' educational pursuits, inadequate academic support infrastructures, and centralized decision making create unintended and unnecessary educational obstacles that few custodians can circumvent.

The absence of support, stability, and autonomy disadvantages custodians and undermines the educational aspirations of these historically marginalized campus community members, denying them opportunities to contribute more broadly to their place of employment.

These case study analyses suggest that universities believe that an educated and engaged workforce is a luxury but not a necessity. Thwarting or downgrading custodians' educational goals is dehumanizing to a subculture that is already viewed by others as "way down low." These dynamics lead, at best, to ambivalence toward the university and, at worst, institutional resentment.

William P. Quigley, director of the Gillis Long Poverty Law Center and of the Loyola Law Clinic, noted, "Universities constantly hold themselves up as special assets to the community, and ask for special accommodations and special rules, things like zoning variances and exemptions from taxes" (Van Der Werf, 2001, p. A27). He further argued that universities' treatment of workers is an indicator of how well universities are fulfilling their mission. Corporate managerialism makes it more difficult for custodians to take advantage of educational opportunities to which they are entitled and contributes to custodians' reluctance to engage in campus life—beyond cleaning. Both by-products of corporate managerialism are antithetical to access and equity ideals that the academy commonly espouses—making universities not-so-special assets in society.

Colby, Beaumont, Ehrlich, and Corngold (2007), when discussing the nuances of civic learning and democratic engagement, defined *democracy* as "fundamentally a practice of shared responsibility for a common future. It is the always unfinished task of making social choices and working toward public goals that shapes our lives and the lives of others" (p. 25). Custodians have few opportunities to get involved and partake in campus governance.

What would it take to change this trend? Berger's (2015) discussion of democratic engagement of students helps answer this question. Advocating for change, he recommended that universities (a) infuse civic learning and democratic engagement practices throughout each and every university department, (b) dissolve functional divides across campus subcultures and create opportunities for genuine partnerships and shared governance aimed at "innovative and transformative" work, and (c) encourage all stakeholders to become more imaginative with the aim of inspiring change. He made explicit both the processes and outcomes of this transformative agenda:

> Universities would challenge students to free their imaginations and re-conceptualize institutions as human-created and open to change. Instead of adopting the mainstream social science view of the world (viewing public problems as byproducts of root causes and systems, and that the latter must be vanquished to make any meaningful progress) as we often do in service-learning work and alternative break service trips, students would learn how to work with campus and community stakeholders to determine which aspects of the problem *could* be transformed and embark on relationship-building and strategic planning in pursuit of that change. This approach would emphasize continually improving environments and cultures, thereby creating new opportunities and frontiers for positive change. (para. 8)

Enacting this ideal in the context of custodians would go a long way to rekindling custodians' educational aspirations and desires to civically engage while at work. As Berger (2015) further noted, "If universities are genuinely committed to democratic engagement, they must examine what messages their cultural practices and campus traditions transmit to students and other members of the university community regarding their agency" (para. 10).

Embedded in these case studies are custodian concerns about education, democracy, representation, participation, and authority (see Fields & Feinberg, 2001). Earning a college degree or participating in a professional development program provides custodians benefits such as political knowledge and communication skills to help them professionally and personally. More importantly, attending to these issues models ways for universities to not simply talk about the value of social justice but live it. Providing barrier-free educational opportunities and encouraging campus community members to be civically engaged are important steps toward transforming existing social inequalities and initiating meaningful social change. Promoting social justice necessitates that universities craft policies that contribute to equality, decrease discrimination, and most importantly reduce stark income inequalities. Modeling social justice aligns institutional actions with mission and balances the university's interest with the interest of its employees.

> Many commentators have also chronicled a widespread lack of trust in and respect for U.S. democratic processes and an overall decline in civic and political participation (Petnam, 2000). . . . This mounting political apathy bodes ill for the future of U.S. democracy unless the generations of young people come to see both the value of and necessity for civic engagement and political participation. (Colby, 2003, pp. 7–8)

This lack of trust has trickled down and contaminated democratic ideas that are the foundation of American higher education. Enacting Berger's ideas about engagement with socially just policies and procedures will go a long way toward combating apathy and reengaging individuals in civic-oriented initiatives. Colby, Ehrlich, Beaumont, and Stephens (2003) provided a moral compass to guide actions aimed at education and civic engagement:

> Few would dispute that colleges' educational and scholarly missions entail a core set of values, such as intellectual integrity, concern for truth, and academic freedom. By colleges' very nature it is also important for them to foster values such as mutual respect, open-mindedness, willingness to listen to them take seriously the ideas of others, procedural fairness, and public discussions of contested issues. . . . Recognition of the obligation to prepare citizens for participation in a democratic system implies that certain values, both moral and civic, are to be represented in these institutions' educational goals and practices. . . . These values include mutual respect and tolerance, concern for both the rights and welfare of individuals and the community, recognition that each individual is part of the larger social fiber, critical self-reflectiveness, and a commitment to civil and rational discourse and procedural impartiality (Galston, 1991; Gutmann, 1987; Macedo, 2000). (p. 13)

PART FOUR

EDUCATION AND POSSIBILITIES

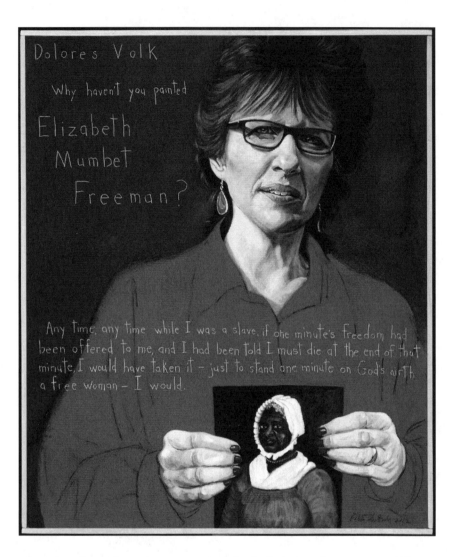

II

THE COURAGE TO BE
(IN TROUBLE)

Urine Trouble

> Once Vida was cleaning a bathroom in a guy's suite and a guy walked in. He whipped his pants down and starts peeing right next to her. She looks at him without flinching and said, "Would you do this in front of your mom?" He was shocked. He did not expect her to say anything. He said nothing. That never happened again. — Nikolina, Vida's (a Compton University [CU] custodian) daughter

"Who we are arises from how others address us over time" (Charon, 2002, p. 61). Corporate managerialism does little to foster civic engagement and educate workers. Instead it socializes custodians to perform particular externally defined subculture scripts—working hard; remembering the customer is always right; and acquiescing to the more powerful, even if they are disrespectful urinators. Dutifully following these scripts perpetuates custodians' narrow campus roles and reaffirms their low status. Fear and feelings of fatalism make it difficult to challenge these debilitating scripts. In the hierarchical world in which custodians work, to grin and bear it, or have to watch others bare it, represents a course of least resistance. Vida is an exception. Although her job title is *custodian*, she is also an activist–educator who quietly campaigns for social change and challenges what counts as "normal."

Typically, higher education civic engagement initiatives involve working with communities outside the university, such as service-learning excursions to address societal ills. Yet the findings from this study suggest that subcultures within universities are equally in need of civic revitalization. This chapter showcases three custodians who engaged civically by setting aside their pervasive fears and feelings of fatalism; respecting, yet challenging, corporate managerialism policies and practices; engaging in both teaching and learning; and modeling civic and democratic practices. They cleaned, but they also challenged conventional wisdom about (a) what custodians do (simply clean), (b) who possesses wisdom on college campuses (faculty), (c) where wisdom resides (inside the classroom), (d) what counts as teaching and learning (acquiring and regurgitating knowledge), (e) what civic engagement looks like (respecting the university's conceptualization of democracy), and (f) power protocols (consequences of confronting individuals with more power).

Troublemakers

The three stories and analysis in this chapter enrich understanding about custodians' stealthy, unique, and substantive contributions to their universities. More importantly, this section reveals ways that custodians thrive—to not simply survive in the corporate managerial environments in which they work but find ways to civically engage in campus-wide discourses that facilitate teaching and learning. Considered "troublemakers" by those in power, these individuals act in ways that offset negative by-products of corporate managerialism.

Don't Try to Put Yourself in a Housekeeper's Shoes

At the start of each academic year, Vida, a Compton University (CU) custodian, posts a letter on the bathroom mirrors of every residence hall suite she cleans. Her 2012 letter read,

> Welcome Students! My name is Vida. I'm originally from Croatia (part of former Yugoslavia). I have been living in the United States for fifteen years now. I'm married and have two children, a 23-year-old daughter and a 17-year-old son. My daughter just graduated from Compton in May 2012. She majored in romance languages and literature. This will be my 14th year working here. I put a lot of effort in making this place a comfortable home for learning and living. I know this is your first year at Compton—everything is new and difficult. I am here to help you feel more at home, so don't hesitate to come up and talk to me. I'll do my best to help. I wish you a successful and clean year! —Your housekeeper, Vida

Vida's letter conveys her desire to form substantive interpersonal relationships with residents, enact the core values of the Department of Housing, maintain a clean residence hall, and educate residents. Vida's daughter, Nikolina—who earned a four-year academic scholarship to CU and graduated in 2012—provides insights into the origins of her mother's courage and resolve to undertake such an ambitious agenda.

Nikolina, in her admission essay to CU, recounted a life-changing family incident that occurred in 1995. While her father was away from home and enmeshed in the Yugoslavian civil war, he called Vida to urge family members to flee their home because "Croatian nationalists known as 'the bad guys' were coming." Amid gunshots, explosions, and cries for help, Vida and her two children began their exodus to escape extermination. Nikolina, in her essay, recounted traveling in cars and tractors, often ensnarled in traffic, while watching enemy tanks crush stalled vehicles as well as the people inside them. She elaborated on the horrors:

> After a while my mom started having a really hard time trying to keep me safe and holding my baby brother at the same time. While we were crawling, one of "the good guys" told a soldier to take my brother so "at least all the little children could be saved." My mom really had no other choice and was forced to do one of the hardest things she has ever done—hand my brother to a complete stranger in the hope that he would be safe. We tried to follow him for a couple of miles, but then he got on the wagon of a tractor and we lost sight of him.

A few days later Vida and her daughter located a safe haven. Nikolina's essay provided vivid details about her mother's frantic quest to reunite with her son:

> At last she located a hospital nearby that had a baby that fit my brother's description. As soon as she walked in the room, my brother made a sigh as if to say, "Where have you been all of this time?" Although the story does not end there, and while I know I will never get my innocence back, I can proudly say that I am a strong, grateful young woman with the greatest appreciation for life.

Qualities such as strength, gratitude, and appreciation of life apply to not only Nikolina but also her mother. Vida, after sharing Nikolina's essay with me, provides additional details:

> I must give him [away], our little guy, to save him. We didn't know if we would survive. He tried to take my baby out. . . . I tried to see them for about half a mile, but I lost sight. On the fourth day I found him. I still have that paper about my unknown child.

In 1997 Vida, her spouse, and two children arrived in the United States. Unlike many of her colleagues who provide me only chronological information about coming to America, Vida includes insight about the politics of war and refugees:

Serbia is not our country. We are Serbs, but it is not our country. Croatia is my country, but I can't go back. I am a Serb from Croatia. I am the bad guy. That is what politics says—that kind of stuff. I hope you know about what happened there. There are always sides—good sides and bad sides; the truth is something different.

Once settled in the United States, Vida spent a year at home caring for her children and learning English by, for example, watching the television show *Barney* with her son. She explains, "I still sing that song. I learned little by little. My husband was pretty good with English, but I knew only a few words from movies. Mostly bad words, like 'I love you.'" I appreciate her sense of humor, especially when revealing horrific life occurrences, a gentle reminder that escaping a war does not mean escaping pain.

Before the war, I was different. I was different before. I never was speechless before. After that, I am different. My memory is not good. I read an article about it in [the] United States, that if you are under stress for more than one week, you lose memory cells. You can't recover. That is maybe the reason why I changed. Religion [*sic*] conflicts never end. It's ridiculous. . . . I had a good job there. I was a secretary and gave receipts to tourists going in and out of hotel. I was a good student and a hippie who liked rock and roll. I always loved rock and roll. I like a little country music, but always rock and roll—Rolling Stones, Janis Joplin, and Jim Morrison. I was always serious and unserious in some places.

Vida accepted a job as a custodian at CU in 1998. Anna, an acquaintance who already worked at CU, informed her about the job vacancy. "She [Anna] saw me and remembered me in the airport [both arrived in the United States at the same time]. I didn't remember her—too much stress. It was pretty bad at that time."

Vida's spouse worked the night shift at a factory, despite his stellar educational credentials and previous role as a staff member for the United Nations in Croatia. Feelings of disappointment hang in the air as she describes her spouse's transition to America: "He worked in a factory to provide for our lives. He never did here what he did back there. He never had time to go to school. Now it's too late. There is a future here for our kids. That's why we came here. I did not want to be a housekeeper, but I am."

Residents view Vida as a custodian as well as a courageous, resilient, humble, and optimistic teacher. One resident succinctly described the kinds of relationships Vida establishes with residents:

She never thought while in school in Croatia that she would be a housekeeper. But she is really happy to be here safe with her children. That is important to her. . . . There is a sense of entitlement for many of us students; the housekeepers see this. It's impossible to avoid. Getting the housekeepers' perspectives—I know this sounds like classism—helped me. I appreciated hearing her perspective. . . . Vida is a good-spirited individual and works really hard. She is interested in doing what she can to support students. She taught me that happiness does not have to come from making a lot of money. She reminded me that being in the United States and safe is important. These things I had not considered.

Vida intertwines cleaning and teaching responsibilities as another resident revealed:

I dyed my hair blue during the semester. It turned the entire bathroom blue. It got all over the walls and the sink. Of course, Vida cleaned it up. I felt really bad, because I did not want her to spend time cleaning my mess. . . . I ran into her in the common room one morning on the way to class. She said, "I noticed that there is a lot of blue on your walls." I said, "Sorry about that." She launched into a conversation and taught me a life lesson. She said, "Everybody makes mistakes. If you don't try things, you will never know." I was not expecting that insight. I thought that was really true. . . . I don't know her well, but she had a life lesson to give me.

A full-time residence hall director also talked about Vida's unique contributions to the residential community and staff:

The staff was not doing a good job seeing that residents were putting their furniture back in their rooms [when they moved out at the end of the academic year]. The housekeepers have to rebuild the rooms for the summer, and their supervisors wanted all furniture back in the original locale. It was really hard on housekeepers. We did not know about this burden. Because we had a relationship, she felt comfortable bringing the concern to me and I brought the concern to Housing. We made sure we were more intentional to make sure we did not create unnecessary work for the housekeeping staff. Our relationship deepened.

Despite Vida's socialization that discourages custodians from crossing borders and interacting (and sometimes confronting) the other, she does what she believes is right, even if it means going off script. This was especially the case after a CU student wrote a letter to the campus newspaper accusing residence hall custodians of being thieves. An excerpt of the letter reads:

Does it bother anyone else that our stuff is being stolen from our rooms? . . . This leaves two culprits for the thefts on campus: students and housekeepers. . . . Try to put yourself in housekeepers' shoes. You work hard for not much money. You clean toilets for teenagers who all seem rich, look the other way when they see you, and have more expensive stuff in their small rooms than any entire family you know.

The rant continues but the message remains unchanged—housekeepers are envious thieves, hell-bent on stealing as retaliation for being treated poorly by students. Not surprisingly, several CU students and faculty write rejoinders, condemning the author. Yet Vida's letter to the editor, responding to the accusations, blends a persuasive argument with respect and humility:

> I can't remember the last time I read something so embarrassing regarding a group of people, in this case housekeepers. . . . You are probably bright enough to realize you can't judge a group of people like that. Before doing something like this, you should think hard about how many people you will hurt. Many times there will be an individual that will give the group a bad name. . . . I was once in a situation like yours. I talked like you. I thought things like, "I will never clean somebody else's home." Then something happened and I lost all of my material belongings. I was still happy, though, because my family was alive and safe. I got a chance to work and support my family as a housekeeper, and I don't feel ashamed. I make an honest living and can provide a good life for my family. I can never imagine an instance where I would steal anything. While I have not lived in a student's shoes, please don't try to put yourself in a housekeeper's shoes. It is not an easy job. In conclusion, please don't blame a group of people for an individual's shortcomings. I wish you happiness and good luck in all your endeavors.—Vida

Vida upends the student's effort to stereotype custodians, and she implicitly cautioned readers that they should not essentialize CU students based on this particular student's perspective. Oddly, Vida cautions students to not put themselves in the shoes of housekeepers, yet her letter provides readers a vicarious experience about what it is like being a custodian walking around in those shoes.

Why Haven't You Painted Elizabeth Mumbet Freeman?

In 2012, while conducting fieldwork on the CU campus hundreds of miles from Oxford, Ohio, Dolores, a night-shift custodian (who did not participate in this study) is cleaning the bathrooms in the campus building where I work on the Miami University campus.[1] One evening Dolores marvels at one particular art exhibit, displayed on the walls of a hallway, which includes large portraits of historic and contemporary American citizens—some iconic figures, some unsung heroes—all advocates for social justice who courageously acted for a common good. Emotionally moved by the exhibit, Dolores e-mails the artist to praise his work and offer a recommendation.

> Hello Mr. Shetterly,
>   I clean the restrooms on 3rd shift at Miami University in Oxford, Ohio. I was moved to McGuffey Hall a few weeks ago and have been fascinated by your paintings because they look like they could come right off of the canvas and talk to me. Every night when I am walking that hallway I think of one thing. Someone is missing. It's Elizabeth "Mumbet" Freeman. She would be a worthy subject for your series. . . . My husband says they should erect a monument of her right next to Thomas Jefferson (America's revered slave owner). I think it would be wonderful to see her portrait on that wall some day! What do you think? Here's more of her quote: "Well, Mr. Sedgwick, I was listening to the reading of the new law. I heard it said that all men are created equal and that every man has a right to freedom. Now I ain't no dumb critter! Won't the law give me my freedom? Isn't that what the law says, Mr. Sedgwick?"
>   —Dolores

Robert Shetterly replies to Dolores's e-mail, and a face-to-face meeting follows. Shetterly's research about Elizabeth Freeman reveals that she was the first female slave to be freed in North America (during the time of the Revolutionary War). Freeman attended a public reading of the Massachusetts Constitution and then asked a lawyer, Thomas Sedgwick, to represent her. A jury ruled in Freeman's favor and granted her freedom and compensation for lost wages during the years she worked as a slave. Shetterly concurs with Dolores's recommendation that Mumbet's story be told, and he intends to tell Dolores's story as well.[2] Months later he paints a portrait of Dolores holding a small watercolor painting of Freeman.

Robert Shetterly's decision to include Dolores in his portrait gallery of advocates for social justice, who courageously acted for a common good, both surprises and humbles Dolores. This 50-something, relatively new employee, who had spent the past 10 years as a library aide for a tiny school district, was the talk of the town and front-page news in her hometown and campus newspapers.

While Dolores's activist spirit astonishes neighbors and coworkers, her bold initiative is no surprise to her spouse and two sons. For the past decade, Dolores has spent most of her nonwork time pursuing legal remedies from federal defense and energy agencies for failing to inform her spouse that the energy plant where he worked as a chemist exposed him to dangerously high levels of uranium. The intentionally harmful and negligent act disabled her spouse, making it impossible for him to resume work. Dolores's spouse and two sons offer a succinct and perfect assessment of the Mumbet campaign: "Well, that's Dolores."

On March 28, 2013, Miami University unveils the Dolores and Mumbet portrait during a reception attended by university dignitaries as well as Dolores's family and friends. During the formal program Robert Shetterly explains why he painted the portrait:

> This [Dolores's] e-mail was different. It was different for a couple reasons. One, the story was so incredible and so important. It wasn't just a great story it was an important story. The second thing that was amazing was who was telling the story. She was telling me about a slave in Massachusetts in the 18th century. Here we have Dolores in Ohio, being paid, but doing similar kind of work. She is cleaning toilets. That moved me; it was coming from a person who was doing that kind of work. And that she was so concerned about untold stories, which was an injustice. . . . The story that she told was so interesting that I e-mailed her back and then started to do some research about it.

Later in the program, Dolores speaks passionately about the qualities she most admires in Mumbet. Probably unbeknownst to Dolores at the time was that she exhibited these identical qualities when she initially contacted Robert Shetterly and in her remarks during the dedication ceremony.

> I think she [Mumbet Freeman] is awesome. At first his [Robert Shetterly's] interest was different than mine. For me, I wanted him to know about this awesome and tenacious woman who realized when she heard the truth. . . . Initially Mumbet thought this is how society worked and stayed in her role. So when she heard the truth, something innately triggered something. She knew something was just not right. Other slaves heard the truth but just went back to being slaves. She did not do that. She took the risk to do something. She heard the truth and acted on it. She risked everything. From that she gained the freedom for her children and grandchildren.

Robert Shetterly follows with his remarks:

> I love what she stood for. She heard truth and acted on it. I wish we could all do that. We hear things from our government, from our schools, parents, and religions that things are a certain way. Throughout our life we determine and learn that things are not always just that way. We put our blinders on, but we just can't do that. You have to research, ask questions. That's what I did. When I heard about her I thought she belonged up there with those people [on the portraits].

A few times each workday as I pass the Mumbet and Dolores portrait, I pause for a moment and reflect on the meaning I have assigned to it. After becoming acquainted with Dolores, her passion to thoroughly research the history of Freeman as well as her intensity to educate others about this invisible and historical figure no longer surprise me. I read about the history of the Americans Who Tell the Truth initiative (www.americanswhotellthetruth .org), after which I realized that Robert Shetterly's decision to paint the Mumbet and Dolores portrait aligns with his personal and organizational aspirations. Dolores and Robert Shetterly's actions inspire me, but a lingering question tempers these feel-good feelings: Had it not been for Dolores's courage and passion to educate, would her wisdom remain unnoticed in the hallowed halls of academia?

Mr. Fear

Approximately a month before Lee's retirement, he prepares for an exit interview mandated by Harrison University's (HU) Department of Human Resources. As a custodian for nearly a quarter of a century, he readily acknowledges the many opportunities that the university has afforded him. He intends to reciprocate during the exit interview by sharing the wisdom he has gained while on the job. The interview did not go as expected.

> When you retire you have an exit interview. I thought they would ask me about my experiences. It was nothing like that. I met with them and they told me—Here is when you will get your last check, blah, blah, blah.
>
> I told Patton [Lee's supervisor] I was going over for the interview, and when I got back he jokingly asked me if I let them have it. I said, "No, they did not give me a chance to." I explained what they did, and he asked if I still wanted to tell people what I thought. I said, "Sure." He said, "Write me a memo." I said, "Okay, but I will be honest." He said, "Okay."

Lee heeds Patton's advice. Excerpts from his letter read as follows:

> First, I would like to apologize for how this is written. I worked on this over a three-week period and things are not necessarily in order. Sometimes I would write a sentence or two and then it might be several days until I picked it up again.
>
> With almost 24 years of experience here at Harrison University, I have seen a huge amount of changes, most of which were not good for the employees. When I started here, I took a cut in pay of almost $10,000 per year. I did this knowing that the benefits made up for it. Our benefits were excellent, but over the years our benefits have dwindled. From paying medical insurance premiums to paying for parking, from taking away Internet services at our residences, and to taking away the ability to use the mechanics' bay in the motor pool. And the list continues to the point that we are not sure what benefits we will lose or pay for tomorrow.

With the combination of loss of pay, loss of benefits, and cutbacks—morale is at an all-time low.

We are consistently asked to come up with ideas of ways to save money or increase productivity. My first suggestion would be to quit hiring outside consultants. So much money is wasted on getting someone's opinion that is not associated with the university. And occasionally we have hired other consultants when we didn't get the answers we were wanting. This university is full of bright students and teachers, not to mention the employees who could be used for suggestions. Also pay employees for their suggestions, not with a promise of a possibility of a Rising Star Award.

TRIM [a campus-wide cost-cutting initiative]—What a joke! This is the same old product with a different name. You can call it what you want, but it's the same old bovine excrement. Do more with less!! And the university paid good money for this. . . . What is this latest TRIM project that I heard about? Replace all the 32-watt bulbs with 28-watt bulbs at the library. And you are going to pay overtime to replace good bulbs. Why not replace them as they go bad? How much electricity do you save by eliminating 4 watts? How long will it take to recover all the overtime used and for the disposal of the fluorescent bulbs?

. . . The biggest asset this university has is the people. They [custodians] have more interaction with students and teachers than anyone else on campus. They work harder physically than anyone else on campus and for the least amount of pay. The employees are the heart of Harrison, so treat them as an asset not a liability. The first positive move I have seen in a long time is the satisfaction survey put out by the director of the Department of Physical Facilities. Whether it is a success or not depends on the honesty of the people. Either way, this is a step in the right direction by getting the people involved. . . . Don't get me wrong, I still believe Harrison University is a good place to work, but it is not a great place to work like it used to be.

The way I see it the real problem Harrison University has is that it is a
Mismanaged
Reckless
Feckless
Endangering
Aggravating
Regime.
This is only my opinion. Feel free to share this with anyone you choose, including Human Resources.

Sincerely,

Lee _____

[emphasis in original]

At first glance the list appears to be a laundry list of Lee's concerns about HU management. A closer examination reveals that the first letter of each word in the list (M R F E A R) spells the name (here a pseudonym) of the vice president of business and finance, Mr. Fear[3]—the senior administrator who is the ultimate supervisor of the Department of Physical Facilities and HU's strongest advocate for corporate managerialism.

If I generated a list of the top 50 disgruntled HU employees, Lee would not make the list. His quiet and affable personality obviously reached a breaking point as he prepared to retire. HU's centralized decision-making philosophy, which privileges the judgments of the most powerful members of the "company" while discounting local knowledge and the professional judgments of on-site workers, ignites Lee's ire and prompts him to share his concerns.

I suspect that HR staff members perceive extended-length exit interviews that allow workers to share their wisdom or offer recommendations as inefficient and cost-prohibitive. Implicit in that policy is the belief that those in power already possess sufficient knowledge to make informed decisions. Even tapping into local knowledge—especially from those members of the campus community who have worked for decades—does not warrant extending the exit interview. Discounting the valuable knowledge of employees reinforces the perception that HU senior administrators know it all. Policies such as this one disenfranchise custodians long after they exit the university. The university's reluctance to learn from others is good for neither Lee nor HU.

Trouble in Paradise

Vida, Dolores, and Lee ignore their caste designation; they reenvision and expand their social scripts to also include civic engagement and education. Vida's story exemplifies the power of human connection. Her letter to the campus newspaper recognizes the value of creating in-depth and sustained learning-centered relationships, even with those with whom she disagrees. Dolores's story exemplifies the benefits for custodians of stepping outside their prescribed roles and subculture boundaries and speaking out for what they believe. Dolores knows that she need possess neither academic nor artistic credentials to critique an artist. And she understands that risk taking is a prerequisite to deep learning. Lee's story is about one worker's last failed attempt to educate the university he loves about ways to accomplish its espoused goals, such as saving money. Despite Lee's vast knowledge—about custodial work, cutting wasteful spending, and increasing productivity—HU appears disinterested in learning from him. Lee's pent-up tirade is a result of the cumulative effect of the university disrespecting and ignoring custodians. His temporary transformation from mild-mannered custodian to "trouble-maker" is a far greater indictment on HU than on Lee.

When discussing Vida's letter with her coworkers, most custodians acknowledge that the student's letter upset them but confess they would not challenge the student, especially by writing a letter to a campus newspaper. Engaging in such activities might jeopardize their standing with students and get them in trouble. Lee's coworkers (who know about his letter) were inspired that a worker finally took the university to task and stood up for disrespected workers. Dolores acts as an advocate by championing the life story of the unknown Elizabeth Freeman. Yet few campus community members look at and advocate for invisible and courageous individuals like Dolores, Vida, and Lee.

Castes

Mumbet's status as a slave did not inhibit her from fighting to alter her slave script. Much of society, especially slave owners, deemed her a troublemaker. Dolores's e-mail, quoting Mumbet Freeman, to Robert Shetterly supports this claim: "Well, Mr. Sedgwick, I was listening to the reading of the new law. I heard it said that all men are created equal and that every man has a right to freedom. Now I ain't no dumb critter!" Dolores, too, is no dumb critter. She recognizes the wisdom and strength of Mumbet's actions and models them. Like Mumbet, she was troubled by the status quo to the point that she induces change and ensures social justice—even if it means the risk of getting in trouble.

In the letter to the editor Vida writes, "You are probably bright enough to realize you can't judge a group of people [custodians] like that. Before doing something like this, you should think hard about how many people you will hurt." Vida recognizes that stereotyping a subculture is troubling, dangerous, and harmful. She advises the student who accused custodians of stealing to think hard about how his actions harm others. Ironically, Lee reminds the HR staff that, "The biggest asset this university has is the people. . . . The employees are the heart of Harrison, so treat them as an asset not a liability." In all three instances, Vida, Dolores, and Lee cross borders and interact with individuals who possess more power. They disrupt the status quo, knowing their actions are worth the trouble.

Crossing Borders

It is fashionable these days, when "difference" is a hot topic in progressive circles, to talk about . . . "border crossing," but we often have no concrete examples of individuals who actually occupy different locations within structures, sharing ideas with one another, mapping out terrains of commonality, connection, and shared concern with teaching practices. (hooks, 1994, p. 30)

Genuine border crossings are rare in teaching. This is also true in higher education and custodial work. Advocates of corporate managerialism discourage border crossings. In Dolores's situation, offering advice to an accomplished artist is unthinkable, a campus norm that she unknowingly violates. Her desire to teach and learn coupled with her courage to act on her convictions eclipses supervisors' expectation to simply follow protocol. Lee's letter reflects a level of risk taking I seldom observed during my fieldwork. Vida also took risks when confronting the urinator and writing a letter to the campus newspaper. Her desire to educate superseded implicit norms that custodians clean and they do not challenge students in bathrooms or in newspapers. Robert Shetterly's response to Dolores affirms the urgency to challenge hegemonic norms and provides hope for risk-taking educators like Dolores, Vida, and Lee.

Crossing borders provides opportunities to deconstruct borderlands and is essential because borderlands are "sites for both critical analysis . . . [and] . . . a potential source of experimentation, creativity, and possibility" (Giroux 1992, p. 175). In *Borderlands/La Frontera*, Anzaldúa (1999) discussed the invisible yet powerful borders that isolate disparate groups from one another both physically and socially. Anzaldúa used the Mexico–United States border as a cultural, psychological, historical, and social border to explicate how it created an us-and-them dichotomy. This limited duality in turn brings with it inherent norms of performing those separate and unequal roles in society.

Anzaldúa argued that the physical border does much more than divide countries and cultures; it goes further, psychologically, sociologically, and historically, having detrimental effects on both the oppressed and their oppressors. The border makes a clear divide between the respectable and the depraved, the sheltered and the treacherous, the valuable and the worthless; it is meant to keep the unsightly undesirables from the sight and spaces of the elite and purposeful, the holders of "wisdom"—dynamics evident in the stories contained in this chapter.

In this study, borders between the archetypes of elite, professional academics and the working-class, laboring custodians persist and communicate a caste system that negates the ideals of diversity, civic engagement, equity, and knowledge sharing that universities espouse. These borders limit the potential for employees by enforcing unstated, yet influential, divides among classes, occupations, and spaces on campus.

Mestiza consciousness breaks down borders, transcends dualities, and heals the injuries made from splitting space and purpose.[4] A CU residence hall director's description of Vida's border-crossing efforts illustrates this elusive idea:

> [Vida] invited my partner and me to her house for dinner. She made a traditional Croatian dinner with more food than we could possibly eat. We

got the chance to meet Nikolina and her son. . . . That night I got to know Vida on a more personal level. She was so willing to share her story. She felt it was important for other people to know her story and understand where she and others like her came from. And where she is now.

Vida crossed subculture borders that blurred socioeconomic classes, occupations, and spaces (on- and off-campus), transcending dualities (work versus home, custodians versus residence hall staff). Efforts such as these heal the injuries, as Anzaldúa noted, from splitting space and purpose.

Many HU and CU custodians crossed borders and interacted with the other (and vice versa). Often individuals, not institutions or departments, initiated these border crossings. Sponsored events that brought together various castes—such as an annual residence hall department breakfast involving residence hall staff members and housekeepers, or annual meet-and-greet socials sponsored by academic departments that involve faculty and house-keepers—seldom include substantive dialogue about issues of difference or equity.

A recent newspaper headline read, "Millionaire WalMart CEO Says He's Just Another Associate" (Kaufman, 2014). This CEO argued, "I'm one of them," since he worked in a WalMart warehouse early in his career. This argument rang hollow to workers who posted responses to the CEO's claim ("He is at least part of the word ASSociate, so we will give him a 1/2 point"). Pretending power differences don't exist does more harm than good. Explicitly discussing power differences and explicitly discussing ways to empower the historically disenfranchised is formidable but fundamental to achieving the aim of enhancing consciousness.

Crossing borders and nurturing a *mestiza* consciousness is about neither pretending that we are all the same and that castes no longer exist nor crossing borders to simply get acquainted and socialize. It is about breaking down borders; interrogating the social, political, and economic forms of oppression; deconstructing caste scripts; confronting ambiguities and contradictions; and negotiating collective and courageous actions to respond to injustices.

Dolores, Vida, and Lee do not simply talk about the merits of crossing borders, becoming civically engaged, and educating others. They enact these ideals, which results in remedying past injustices, such as slavery, as well as contemporary injustices, such as marginalized, invisible, and maligned custodians. The consciousness-raising pedagogies that Vida, Dolores, and Lee embrace reconceptualize what it means to be an educator and how campus community members can get involved. They blur distinctions between teachers and learners and challenge the hegemonic assumptions that subjugated custodians accept narrowly defined scripts or jobs as natural or normal. Too often, this inhibits most custodians from imagining alternative roles (e.g., educator, advocate). Their actions challenge the foundations of corporate managerialism.

CU custodians, years after Vida's letter appeared in the student newspaper, still talk about her courage to write and disseminate the letter to the larger campus community. Miami University senior administrators continue to celebrate Dolores's actions, and HU custodians go on celebrating Lee's courage. Although these universities benefited from these individuals' courageous acts, the three universities seldom encouraged other custodians to challenge the status quo in similar ways.

The aim of crossing borders is to provide opportunities for dialogues and action rooted in difference. It is not about creating an imagined romanticized cohesive or monolithic community. As history has revealed, this type of campus community is neither realistic nor attainable. *Communities of interest* (subcultures), based on shared identities and norms, fill this community void and often provide support and safe space, especially to marginalized individuals and groups. A major limitation of subcultures, which are often insular enclaves, is the absence of public dialogue and civic action centering on the public interest. Crossing borders celebrates subcultures and subcultural differences and provides space for a public dialogue. Tierney (1993) briefly discussed the connection between border crossings, dialogues about difference, and enacting cultural democracy ideals:

> Our struggle is constantly to cross these borders and exist in tolerable discomfort with one another as we confront difference. The reason I mention discomfort is that by its very nature "difference" is discomforting; to engage in dialogue and action with individuals who may have conflicting ideas and constructions about the world is hard work. . . . Such work creates conditions for change and what I call *cultural democracy*. Cultural democracy involves the enactment of dialogue and action that are based on a framework of trying to understand and to honor cultural difference rather than of subjugating such difference to mere attributes of an individual's identity. (pp. 10–11)

The challenge in promoting this recommendation—crossing borders to achieve the aim of cultural democracy—is to celebrate differences rather than dismissing, suppressing, or ignoring them. In these borderlands, communities of interest remain intact as communities of difference interact. Discourse and action rupture the ideological borders that separate camps into neat categories and initiate public dialogue and public action across and about difference. Put simply, campus community members, as Giroux (1992) noted,

> must be encouraged to cross ideological and political borders as a way of furthering the limits of their own understanding in a setting that is pedagogically safe and socially nurturing rather than authoritarian and infused with suffocating smugness of certain political correctness. (p. 3)

Cultural democracy involves the enactment of dialogue and action based on trying to understand and honor cultural difference rather than subjugating difference to mere attributes of an individual's identity (Tierney, 1993).

Critical Consciousness

Numerous questions arise from these stories about Vida, Dolores, and Lee: Why does the academy ignore untapped sources of wisdom? Why does the ever-present gap between campus castes appear to be growing wider? Why are the risky and courageous acts of crossing subculture borders and educating the other unusual? Why does civic engagement by those on the margins, such as custodians, seem odd? Admittedly, there are no easy answers or simple solutions to these questions. Findings suggest that HU's and CU's gravitational pull toward corporate ideologies and practices discourages courageous acts, amplifies caste differences, and discourages subculture border crossing—three outcomes antithetical to American higher education's core values of teaching, learning, and equity. Dolores, Vida, and Lee invite participants to reconceptualize their world and devise ways of changing it.

Aspects of corporate managerialism—breeding civic disengagement and undermining potent teaching and learning opportunities—discussed in this and the previous chapter are not likely to be dismantled and replaced anytime soon. Crossing borders, deconstructing borderlands, and nurturing a mestiza consciousness are three modest ways to create opportunities to monitor and take continual corrective actions on negative by-products of the corporate university.

If universities aspire to enact the espoused values of teaching, learning, social justice, equity, inclusion, and valuing differences, then recognizing and working with all castes to alter these scripts are natural "next steps." Tending to and scrutinizing subculture scripts, paying particular attention to issues of power and authority, and crossing borders to learn from the other all rupture existing impermeable castes.

Cipolle (2010) presented a model that contains four essential elements of critical consciousness: (a) *self-awareness*—understanding one's privileges, values, roles, and responsibilities to society; (b) *awareness of others*—moving outside of one's comfort zone and interacting with the other; (c) *awareness of social issues*—such as living-wage and corporatization debates; and (d) *fostering an ethic of service and acting as a change agent.* The actions of Vida, Dolores, and Lee closely track each aspect of this model. They were self-aware; were aware of the other; understood the importance of social issues such as stereotyping, equality, and social justice; and displayed an ethic of service acting as agents of change.

Courageously altering scripts, crossing borders, and deconstructing borderlands provide opportunities to

- critically examine and appreciate ordinary interactions involving ordinary campus community members;
- learn more about one's self and the other;
- scrutinize the seminal higher education ideals of entrepreneurialism, efficiency, shared governance, civic engagement, equity, teaching, and learning that the academy cavalierly champions and seldom dissects;
- reconceptualize what it means to teach and learn both inside and outside of the classroom;
- challenge rigidity, dualities, hegemony, and exclusivity; and
- embrace ambiguity.

Border thinking creates a new mythos—a change in the way we perceive reality, the way we see ourselves, and the ways we behave. More importantly, crossing borders and nurturing a *mestiza* consciousness are necessary first steps to cleaning up higher education by making "the world visible in ways that implement the goals of social justice and radical progressive democracy" (Denzin & Giardina, 2010, p. 14).

> The cornerstone of a diverse society is positive relations between its different communities. Religious pluralists hold that people believing in different creeds and belonging to different communities need to learn to live together. It is therefore a sociological, not theological, pluralism. Religious pluralism is neither mere co-existence nor forced consensus. It is a form of proactive cooperation that affirms the identity of the constituent communities while emphasizing that the well-being of each, and all depends on the health of the whole. It is the belief that the common good is best served when each community has a chance to make its unique contribution. (Patel, 2007, pp. 5–6)

Although Patel's commentary focuses on ways to think differently about faith and religious differences, his ideas are relevant to secular, higher education castes and border crossers including custodians. Patel's recommendations could go a long way in lessening fears and elevating custodians' involvement in campus life. Castes need to do more than merely coexist; they need to cooperate as well as create space for each caste to affirm its beliefs and allow space for the other to present and affirm its beliefs. As Patel noted, the common good is best served when each subculture has a chance to make its unique contribution. In a corporate managerial milieu, the contributions need to be expanded beyond those in power making the rules and the less powerful following these rules. Patel and Meyer (2010) offered a vision of what this different kind of participation might look like, evident in the actions of Vida, Dolores, and Lee:

> Respect for individual identity means that participants in pluralism feel like they can bring their full identities to the table. That means they are allowed to believe that they are right and others are wrong, and they are allowed to think that their beliefs are true and others' are not; this is necessary and pragmatic. If we insist that one has to concede exclusive truth claims to begin interfaith dialogue, we run the risk of only bringing the most liberal of every religious tradition into conversation. But there need to be rules for how this conversation can play out. One way we often put this in the course of a dialogue is, "acknowledge that others' religious or non-religious perspectives are as precious to them as yours are to you." (p. 2)

Although the ideas of dialogue, respecting difference, pluralism, and respect of the other regularly take place in many of the rooms that custodians clean, putting these ideas into action is foreign to them. Venues do not exist for custodians that allow for the exchange of insights or perceptions. HU expects custodians to respect historical institutional norms and heed the wisdom of the more powerful, yet there are few opportunities for those in power to listen to and discuss custodians' historical insights and wisdom. Engaging in these kinds of dialogue can diffuse fears, foster genuine teaching and learning, and create more democratic engagement opportunities. Patel and Meyer (2009) noted,

> Taking a longer view, interfaith leadership and religious pluralism are not just about the mediating of potential religious conflict, but also about creating a stronger civic fabric in general. We draw here on the work of Robert Putnam, recognizing that religious communities, groups, and organizations have a particularly powerful sort of social capital. While Putnam warns that unengaged diversity leads to a decline in trust, community, and overall social capital, when that diversity is engaged by forming intentional networks across lines of difference, the long-term benefit is strong, stable, and engaged societies (Putnam, 2007). (p. 6)

Creating a stronger civic fabric keeps corporate managerialism in check and creates opportunities for dialogues across difference to occur. Repressing these values leads to the unengagement previously mentioned. Dialogues across castes and differences are about creating civility and civic engagement, which sounds inefficient and costly, yet is morally the right thing to do. Enacting these ideas could be a small step to strong, stable, and engaged campus enclaves, which would benefit the entire community and, most importantly, channel toward constructive means the pervasive fears that many campus enclaves experience.

Notes

1. Due to this unique and idiosyncratic event (easily identified using a simple Internet search), I do not mask the identity of the custodian (Dolores), the artist (Robert Shetterly), or the university (Miami).

2. Elizabeth Mumbet Freeman was born into slavery in upstate New York circa 1742. In 1781, while living in Massachusetts, she sued for her freedom. The court ruled in her favor, and she became the first African American woman to be set free under the Massachusetts state constitution.

3. To protect the name of the vice president, I changed his name and used a few synonyms to create the name "Mr. Fear" while remaining true to the essence of Lee's letter.

4. *Mestiza* consciousness, as described by Anzaldúa, is a consciousness of duality that embraces both ambiguity and contradiction. It is a response to Western thought that privileges binaries, in which one concept or identity is privileged over the other (e.g., male/female, Black/White). Anzaldúa challenges this Western ideology by intentionally rupturing identity categorizations.

12

A DOG'S LIFE

M uddy fields, dilapidated barns, and nearly melted snowbanks gar-
ner my attention traveling these rural back roads. Only railroad
crossings and tiny villages momentarily slow me down on this
early Saturday morning. Forty minutes into my trip my cell phone's naviga-
tional app locates the dead-end road I am looking for. I turn onto the gravel
lane and immediately notice a handmade "Dog Shelter" sign with an arrow
pointing in the direction I am traveling, which is good news. I hear dogs
barking and howling nonstop in the distance as I pass a rusty trailer park; I
doubt serenity is an option for the park residents.

I park on the grass near the animal shelter and exit my car. My flannel
shirt and wool sweater are sufficient attire for this glorious 45-degree January
morning. I shed my coat as Elaine approaches and greets me. We update each
other about our respective holidays. She spent time with family, relished the
weeklong mandatory vacation from her custodial job at Harrison University
(HU), and is glad to be back to work.

Elaine changed jobs since our last encounter. She relinquished her building custodial position to become a rover, someone who fills in for absent
staff. The new job is "okay," but her partner, a 30-year veteran, is not. His
low motivation and negativity frustrate Elaine, but better days may be on
the horizon. She is eyeing a crew-chief vacancy, but she remains tepid about
the opportunity since it does not include a raise. Elaine clarifies her mixed
feelings: "It's like babysitting for free. . . . It's not about money. I want the
responsibility but don't want to be taken advantage of." If the rumor that the
department intends to offer crew chiefs a $1.60-an-hour raise is true, Elaine's
interest in the job would increase, but overall happiness is more important
than money.

Inside the shelter the dampness coupled with the smell of wet dogs and
feces wreaks havoc on me, as my eyes water and I wheeze. I step outside, sensing a looming asthma attack. The stench sticks to my clothes, so I remove my
sweater and drape it on my car's trunk to air it out. Meanwhile Elaine returns

with two canine companions, Moe and Hunter, and hands me Moe's leash. Then she steps aside so that Moe and I can get acquainted. Elaine's attire—rubber boots, jeans, and a beat-up jacket—remind me that she is a veteran dog walker. I am not. My sneakers are no match for these muddy fields. When the melting piles of snow and puddles of water force Moe and me off the path and into the pastures, my sneakers immediately sink into the mud.

Today's turnout of eight walkers thrills Elaine, especially since there are only 25 dogs in the pound. This is the lowest occupancy rate since she began volunteering two years ago. She speculates that families adopting dogs as holiday gifts as well as the dogcatcher's weeklong vacation contribute to these unusual circumstances. As we follow a path, Elaine provides background information about the facility and occupants:

> If they adopt a dog, it's about $80. That's to spay or neuter it. We process over 400 dogs a year. We have about 35 kennels, but sometimes we double up dogs. At one time we had about 60 dogs. Usually it stays around 35 to 40. If we have 30 or less dogs, we're doing great. . . . I would love to find a way to get some of the community to understand what goes on here. There are about 400 or 500 dogs brought in each year. Last year there were 25 dogs that were put down.

Elaine is intimately familiar with most shelter operations and almost every animal. She names each dog and memorizes the medical vitals of the long-term residents. Her dedication is obvious. Today she arrived earlier than usual to open every window in the shelter to ensure that the animals enjoy the unseasonably mild day. She explains, "Dogs like the fresh air," and then describes one of her passions:

> I'm a dog person. We chose not to have kids. We have three dogs: a boxer and two mixed-breeds. It's hard not to take them home from the pound. . . . Every time I go to the pound I usually volunteer for about two hours. Saturday it's usually about four. It just depends if there's a lot of dogs that need attention, like if they need shots or baths. If no volunteers show up it takes longer.

The walking route is approximately half a mile. My agenda is straightforward: avoid dog poop, evade puddles, and chat—in that order. Elaine's agenda centers on educating me about the inner workings of this advocacy operation. Every Tuesday and Thursday she identifies new dogs, then spends the remainder of her visit walking them, conducting assessments, and administering shots. She spends Saturdays at the shelter or trying to find suitable homes for the dogs or new ways to comfort the animals. "I always give them fresh water. Even though they're not human they deserve to be cared for."

Adjacent to the shelter is a recreation space demarcated by a chain-link fence. Elaine removes the leashes from Moe and Hunter and lets them run free in the contained space. She explains the rules of recess: "It's critical to not mix male and female dogs in the pen." She keeps an eye on Moe and Hunter as she retrieves dog toys scattered about the yard and empties standing water from nearby drinking containers. I eavesdrop on the three men leaning on the fence conversing about the Holy Trinity of rural life: cars, guns, and sports. Elaine enters the fenced-in area and runs with Moe and Hunter, allowing them some extra exercise time. Then she puts leashes back on both dogs and returns them to their respective cages, reappearing moments later with Anderson and Lance.

This time we walk the route in reverse, starting at the fenced-in area and ending at the shelter entryway. Elaine kneels in the mud and talks to Lance to calm him. Her unique rapport with each dog intrigues me. As our trek continues she provides a shelter update. A woman intended to adopt a pregnant dog, but by the time the shelter completed the paperwork the dog had given birth to the puppies and the woman terminated the adoption process. She also offers background information for each volunteer: Mary is at the shelter all of the time, Lenny is a teacher, Adam is a former animal control officer, Jake has no car (and has no sense of responsibility), and Sharon and Mike are married.

This walk is less stressful because I relinquish control to Anderson. He gets his way by hanging out near a pile of junk, and I get my way by mostly remaining on the paths. Elaine reveals her most recent dispute with the dog-catcher, who accused her of feeding extra food to the dogs. This defiant act angered him because it resulted in additional cleaning chores. She smiles and says unapologetically, "Guilty." Elaine confesses that she regularly smuggles contraband into the shelter. A few weeks ago each dog received leftover ham from a holiday dinner. Today they will be recipients of several loaves of stale bread stashed in the back of Elaine's sports utility vehicle. The distribution criterion is straightforward: "Mamas and older dogs get the most; everyone else gets the same portion." She refocuses her attention on the dogcatcher.

> He would rather we were not here. He doesn't care what we do. If he had his way, he would keep dogs for three to five days. Then if they are still around he would shoot them. He's happy to get rid of them. . . . He thinks we are nuisances. If the dogcatcher told us we had to leave we would have to. These are the things I think about all the time. There's a little poodle that weighs about five pounds; he is always cold. I made him a little bed last Saturday. I went back on Tuesday and the dogcatcher had drenched the bed with water.

Our final walk is with Paige and Sky. Paige's claim to fame is that she snorts like a pig, and Sky has the most seniority in the pound. As we wander, Elaine explains the Saturday adoption program; I listen attentively while trying to ignore Paige's entertaining snorts.

> We do it about once a month. We usually take about eight dogs. Sometime before Saturday we go to the pound and get them bathed. Lots of times they stink. On Saturday morning, if there are enough people we try to get them all walked. Sometimes it is just a short walk just to get them outside. We load them up and haul them to a Tractor Supply store. It's about a half hour from the pound. We're usually outside, and we just hang out with the dogs all day. This is where you find out a lot about the dogs. Even if none of them are adopted, it's great to get them away from the pound for a day. We usually get at least one adoption every time we go. If one gets adopted, it makes it all worth it.

Our final task of the morning is an impromptu photo shoot. I retrieve my camera from my car as Elaine collects several dogs from the shelter. We carefully position each dog for each photo. Volunteers use the portraits in the county newspaper each week.

As I pack my gear, Elaine retrieves the stale bread stash from her car and systematically distributes the treats. She explains, "Even though these dogs have so many bad things happening to them, at least they have the volunteers." She sighs and continues, "It's hard to think about all the ones we saved, when you think about the ones that have to be put down. Even though it's a small number, it's still stressful and bad."

Having a Dog's Chance

This story provides a glimpse into the inner workings of an animal shelter and a campus custodian's nonwork life. Elaine encounters daily political predicaments yet seldom allows them to dampen her spirits or activist agenda. She is fearless, unafraid to metaphorically "step in shit" if necessary to advocate on animals' behalf.

Shelter dogs are an invisible animal subculture. Adoption days and the weekly rescue ads in newspapers are two ways that Elaine and other volunteers intentionally make this subculture visible to the public. Despite their numerous pathways to the shelter, Elaine knows these animals have done nothing wrong, despite the public's perception that they are abnormal and hence a problem. She understands that dogcatchers and volunteers are more culpable for shelter crises and drama than the dogs. Advocacy is her response.

Responsibilities such as walking or grooming dogs are moral issues, not mere perfunctory tasks on Elaine's to-do list. The humane treatment of animals is good. The decision to ignore the dogcatcher's mandate that volunteers do not feed animals reveals what Elaine deems as "right." The self-imposed rule that prohibits male and female dogs from being in the pen at the same time and the norm that mothers and older dogs get the most illegal food symbolically convey her concerns and values. Elaine's vision of good is different from that of her nemesis, the dogcatcher, who perceives animals as nuisances and burdens.

Elaine, a *tempered radical* (Meyerson, 2008), partakes in acts that advocate for alternative beliefs and norms. "Meyerson identified and described a spectrum of tempered radical strategies that include resisting quietly and staying true to one's self, turning personal threats into opportunities, broadening the impact through negotiation, leveraging small wins, and organizing collective action" (Carducci, 2011, p. 467). Elaine intentionally and methodically pursues steady incremental change (Lindbloom, 1959), rather than undertaking instantaneous and dramatic actions such as leaking unseemly shelter practices to the public, which would further alienate Elaine from the dogcatcher. Creating a special bed for a poodle, opening windows to allow fresh air into the shelter, or sponsoring adoption outreach programs exemplify this strategy in action.

Elaine forges unique one-on-one, not superficial or generic, interactions with the dogs. She does not simply walk them; she walks *with* them, guiding rather than controlling interactions, favoring rewards rather than penalties. She intends the walks for exercise and teaching, acclimating the dogs to a world beyond the shelter. Posting modest victories is the goal, such as facilitating one adoption at each Saturday excursion. The politics of this animal shelter could easily lead one to believe that Elaine would not have a dog's chance of accomplishing her agenda. And that would be doggone wrong.

Teaching Old Dogs New Tricks

> Too often, sociologists want to offer some possible solutions but we hardly stop to think about people's own narratives; we so easily discard the narratives of people we interview if they don't match our own narratives. This is what Thomas Kuhn called normal science—we are just confirming what we already think. (Mooney, 2012, para. 14)

I'm not a "normal science" kind of guy. From the outset I intended to include in this book modest solutions to address the concerns I witnessed during fieldwork, rather than simply recount and then analyze stories. I also wanted to tell my stories *and* make transparent how custodians affirmed and challenged my preconceived notions about their culture. Custodians influenced my fieldwork, narratives, interpretations, and recommendations. The shelter story exemplifies this aspiration by recounting a fieldwork experience and revealing how Elaine both confirmed and challenged my preconceived perceptions about, for example, how to challenge dominant cultural norms and advocate for those on the margins. As a metaphorical old dog, I learned a few new tricks from Elaine.

In the remainder of this chapter I summarize insights I gained from Elaine that provide a roadmap for change of sorts for four campus subcultures: (a) departmental administrators and supervisors; (b) high-level university administrators; (c) faculty, students, and staff; and (d) custodians.

Mad Dogs: Custodial Department Administrators and Supervisors

Custodial supervisors and administrators from HU and Compton University (CU) exist in a betwixt-and-between state. Organizationally they are sandwiched between custodians and high-level university administrators. Most members of this enclave are former custodians. In their supervisory role, their power and influence are greater than those of custodians but far less than those of members of the high-level administrator enclave. Being in between, these transitional midmanagers assume roles such as liaisons, mediators, implementers, buffers, and bearers of bad news. The term *mad dog* generally conveys anger or contempt or signals that a conflict is about to commence. These mad-dog midmanagers become lightning rods for the ire of their supervisors as well as their supervisees. When conflict arises, they are usually at the epicenter. These dynamics influence how supervisors and departmental administrators act on the job and influence the kind and scope of recommendations I propose.

Custodial supervisors and administrators are acutely aware of ways to improve the quality of life for custodians, yet their perception of having insufficient institutional clout to challenge authority (whenever necessary) curbs their advocacy instincts. Following Elaine's lead, they might consider implementing a wide array of (not-so-fear-inducing) tempered radical strategies that will yield incremental organizational change and allow them to act and remain under the proverbial radar screen of their bosses.

For CU custodial supervisors and administrators, action steps could involve nudging student affairs colleagues to modify judicial sanctions mandating that wayward students work side by side with custodians like Mone, which signals to students that if they do something wrong, the punishment will be custodial work. For HU administrators and supervisors, an action step might be to devise a plan that ensures the safety of both their vice president and the larger campus community. Or they might advise the president's staff to select employee gifts that are both special and practical, to accommodate the diverse needs of gift recipients.

Following Elaine's lead, supervisors and administrators might purpose-fully find ways to make the custodial subculture more visible and under-standable to the larger community. HU supervisors and administrators could assume an advocacy role and petition the Department of Human Resources to allow custodians to enroll in a professional development seminar, for example, even if they deem seminar content tangential to custodians' work responsibilities.

For CU supervisors and administrators, action steps might include mod-ifying departmental policies that would allow job candidate interviewers to provide specific feedback to job candidates, like Zoe, which would affirm the university's commitment to education. Or the intervention might involve sponsoring professional development workshops that provide custodians with essential human relations and communication skills to share their wis-dom with the larger campus community—following in the footsteps of Vida, Lee, and Samuel. Ben Bernanke, the former chair of the Federal Reserve, said during a commencement speech,

> I think most of us would agree that people who have, say, little formal schooling but labor honestly and diligently to help feed, clothe, and edu-cate their families are deserving of greater respect—and help, if necessary—than many people who are superficially more successful. . . . They're more fun to have a beer with, too. (Kurtz, 2013, para. 7)

Respect and support are of paramount importance to custodians. Mod-eling Elaine's actions and heeding Bernanke's advice, CU departmental supervisors and administrators could directly confront individuals who give custodians like Mone *the look* or confront people who direct microaggres-sions toward custodians like Calvin. Another possibility is to move away from the current one-size-fits-all inspection model and customize inspection schedules based on performance (similar to Elaine's efforts to treat each dog uniquely based on past interactions). Customized plans would decrease the frequency of inspections for exemplary workers. Occasionally offering high-performing workers mementos of appreciation, such as gift cards, would also symbolically convey that good work matters.

HU supervisors and administrators could formally recognize and pub-licly praise workers who add value to the university by reinstituting larger and more formal recognition ceremonies and programs that honor custodians for a job well done, like Margaret (Miss October). Altering existing supervisor-supervisee relationships so that supervisors *work with* custodians rather than expecting custodians to *work for* supervisors (similar to what Elaine does when walking dogs) would benefit supervisors and administrators as well as custodians.

> The treatment of low-wage workers on campus is an issue that flies below the public radar, is ignored by public-policy officials and college trustees, and is dismissed by college administrators as little more than a nuisance. (Eisenberg, 2012b, para. 10)

These recommendations invite departmental supervisors and administrators to engage in small acts of self-expression that will allow them to enact personal values to counter individuals with more power and opposing ideologies. In addition, these recommendations provide the larger community invaluable opportunities to recognize and appreciate the unique contributions of members of the campus's invisible custodial caste. Admittedly, these suggestions are hardly radical, yet they intentionally represent interventions that are within the comfort zone of administrators as well as supervisors and will benefit custodians and those with whom they interact.

Meaner Than a Junkyard Dog: High-Level University Administrators

> More than 700,000 employees at American colleges—gardeners, security guards, cleaning crews, janitors, food-service personnel, etc.—do not earn a living wage, the bare-bones amount sufficient to provide a minimally decent standard of living for their families. This is a disgrace to our system of higher education and a sad reflection on the moral leadership of our colleges. . . . Their work is an essential ingredient of college life; without them, campuses couldn't function. Why are they so poorly valued and treated? (Eisenberg, 2012b, para. 1)

Elaine's assessment about the current state of affairs for custodians is considerably less dire and dramatic than Eisenberg's appraisal. For Elaine and many coworkers, being employed and underpaid is better than being unemployed. She would rather be malnourished than bite the proverbial hand of those who do not sufficiently feed her. Elaine's current job is considerably better than jobs she has held since graduating from high school. She appreciates job mobility, such as moving from a building custodian to a rover. When unfair policies and procedures arise, she expresses her concerns, acting on her convictions. When her boss encouraged her to apply for the crew-chief position that did not include a salary increase, she stood her ground and opted not to apply. Elaine's salary hovers slightly above the living-wage threshold, but her wages coupled with her spouse's earnings as a landscaper ensure that they "get by," which, from Elaine's perspective, is good enough.

Elaine disagrees with Eisenberg's assertions that higher education's modus operandi is disgraceful and campus leaders are morally bankrupt, even though the high-level administrators' approach to management seems remarkably similar to the dysfunctional style of leadership of the dogcatcher, whom Elaine is quick to criticize.

On the animal shelter front, Elaine is aware and distraught that local counties and municipalities across the United States have banished hundreds of thousands of animals to deplorable and underfunded rescue shelters that provide subpar support to animals, despite the dedicated efforts of volunteers. These facilities reflect poorly on local and state government leaders. The dogcatcher acts like a junkyard dog—a vicious, rough, aggressive individual; he brazenly does what he believes needs to be done to ensure his domain remains intact, subscribes to a top-down model of decision making, shuns counsel from others (such as volunteers), provides bare-bones services, and seldom interacts with the animals and volunteer staff unless forced to. His disregard for the sanctity of animals (demonstrated by a preference for shooting them if they remain too long at the shelter, in the spirit of ensuring a lean and efficient operation) goes unchallenged because few organizational checks and balances exist. He is unaccountable for his actions because this animal shelter subculture is invisible to the surrounding community.

A slightly modified version of these junkyard descriptors could easily apply to high-level administrators at HU. Elaine is a highly competent evaluator and critic but only selectively uses these skills. I suspect this inconsistency has something to do with fear. Elaine can afford to risk getting fired from her volunteer job; she would simply volunteer somewhere else. She can't afford to get fired from the job that pays the bills.

Although she is reluctant to criticize those with power, she and many of her colleagues use clichés to convey how the actions of those in power harm them and how they cope. When a custodian says, "Any job is better than no job," the subtext of this comment is, "I'm screwed, but I don't have any other options, so I just suck it up." The message is that in this dismal economy few job prospects exist. As "the [employed] chosen few," custodians must remind people they are "blessed" and express gratitude to be employed. They are willing to do anything, such as not criticizing bosses, to ensure that they will continue to provide for their family. Simply stated, employment trumps everything else.

The phrase, "Don't bite the hand that feeds you," is a custodial euphemism for, "My bosses are crazy. I know it, but I can't say it." The subtext is that there are consequences for complaining, criticizing, and appearing ungrateful. The phrase, "You gotta do what you gotta do," is custodians' way of politely saying, "This place is a dysfunctional insane asylum, but don't worry, I have the strength and political savvy to get by." These messages do not portray administrators as the Darth Vaders of higher education; rather, they imply that the highest priority for these campus leaders is to protect the university, not members of the custodial caste.

Many custodians follow Elaine's lead and refrain from public critique of high-level campus leaders. In private they express concern about high-level administrators' junkyard-dog propensities, such as being hard-nosed, aggressive, and threatening. Each day Elaine challenges the behaviors of the junkyard-dog dogcatcher, with the hope that someday he will change. Challenging the junkyard dog–like behaviors of administrators remains on her to-do list.

The impressions I gleaned from custodians' dog-whistle phrases and private conversations match the impressions that I formed as a result of fieldwork. I never witnessed a single administrator mistreating subordinates, nor did I ever interpret their intentions or policies as retaliatory or punitive. However, I did not encounter high-level administrators behaving like champions of working-class campus castes, nor did I stumble upon administrators who regularly interacted with or "really knew" working-class caste members—except for the custodians who cleaned their offices.

I also took time to solicit from high-level administrators their impressions of custodians. They conveyed their respect and admiration for custodians and possessed a basic and broad understanding of some of their struggles, but few nuances. They are more definitive about why these problems and injustices persist. They subtly imply that they are powerless to dramatically alter custodians' work lives, such as by increasing wages, because the landscape of higher education has dramatically changed and is constantly in flux.

These administrators note that American higher education is in transition and will never again resemble the idyllic, family-like universities of yesteryear. As part of this transition, CU and HU have gradually transformed themselves into big businesses; corporate managerialism has become the ideology of choice to guide these universities through these difficult transitions.

HU's perpetual state of economic and fiscal restlessness contributes to custodians' perceptions that the university is vulnerable, politically unstable, and not transparent. The endless state of uncertainty has influenced high-level administrators' decision to go all in and implement a corporate managerial ideology as the primary means of surviving the crises and again thriving.

The contentious employee strike in 2004 resulted in a minuscule raise for employees and huge headaches for senior administrators, strikers and nonstrikers, and unions. Today, worker-management strife persists. More contemporary cost-cutting initiatives—such as the promotable employee plan (proposing to hire custodians for a few years, provide them training, then return them to the job market to compete for higher-paying jobs elsewhere)—add to the existing disharmony. Custodians remain skeptical because they will ultimately be forced to return to a job market that historically has been unkind to them. High-level administrators are relieved because projected personnel cost-savings (by continually hiring entry-level custodians at low salaries) are considerable.

HU's decade-long history of dwindling external fiscal support, minimal salaries, downsizing, and outsourcing contributes to a dog-eat-dog atmosphere, pitting campus subcultures against each other. In skirmishes such as these, members of the custodial caste seldom fare well. Overcoming labor-management mistrust is complicated nowadays.

CU is more stable fiscally and politically compared to HU. Protecting and growing its healthy financial portfolio, consolidating services to become more nimble, shedding unnecessary programs and personnel, and protecting its academic reputation represent a few long-term institutional goals. CU's gradual and continual creep toward corporate managerialism is the means by which the university intends to become even more elite and prosperous.

Building new residence halls and expanding the university's summer conference program exemplify new campus-wide initiatives aimed at increasing revenues to sustain its fiscal stability. Corporate-influenced initiatives such as these further complicate custodians' work lives by, for example, expanding their work responsibilities, condensing the time they have to complete non-negotiable tasks, and lowering staff morale. These new responsibilities contribute to custodians' feelings of uncertainty, as the institution's short-term plans are not as obvious and transparent as they had hoped. As one custodian noted, "If CU is worried, I should be, too."

History and context matter and influence both CU and HU high-level administrators' relationships with custodians. High-level administrators offered assurances that "if they could, they would" (a) increase custodians' wages and decrease their out-of-pocket health care expenses, (b) minimize downsizing and outsourcing, (c) find time to solicit input from custodians about policies and involve custodians more regularly and substantively in departmental governance, and (d) identify ways to more regularly and substantively interact with custodians. I suspect that if custodians *could* believe this rhetoric, they *would*.

Martin Scorsese, the acclaimed film director, once said, "There's no such thing as simple. Simple is hard." This is especially true when contemplating recommendations for high-level administrators to address wage-related injustices, which is the first recommendation. It is difficult because the recommendation must take into consideration the two distinct institutional cultures (each exercising a unique brand of corporate managerialism) as well as custodians' on-the-job frustrations and coping strategies. Presenting a detailed action plan that addresses living wage–related issues for each institution is beyond the scope of this book, yet conceptual and practical issues—modeled by Elaine—would go a long way toward addressing contested wage-related issues.

Elaine views her volunteer work as both technical and moral. High-level administrators would be wise to follow her lead. This might involve high-level administrators viewing living wage–related matters through analytical *and* moral prisms. CU and HU high-level administrators, privileging the analytical, scrutinize competitors' compensation packages and devise ones that are at least as good as, and usually slightly better than, competitors'. This is a positive step toward ensuring that their universities will recruit and retain employees.

"What salaries will the market allow?" is the question undergirding these wage-related decisions. What if these administrators, following the logic of Elaine's first recommendation, augmented economic questions such as this one by posing moral questions such as, "Who is advantaged and disadvantaged by the current wage structure?"; "Why are service workers so poorly valued and treated?" (a question Eisenberg [2012b] raised); and "What salary scale can both the university and its employees live with, ensuring that both remain financially secure and content?" Posing and answering both data-driven analytical and moral questions would reveal masked ideologies that regulate the allocation of wages and provide opportunities to initiate dialogue about class, power, and race issues central to the wage-related tensions.

The second recommendation centers on income disparity. Custodial wages are low and stagnant, and the gap between custodians' salaries and those of elite faculty and staff continues to widen. Tierney argued, "Those making the largest salaries versus those who are making the least . . . the average between the two has grown over the last 20 years" (cited in Fox, 2014, para. 8). This is not a public relations problem. It is a question of values.

The quintessential example of income disparity in the academy appeared in Chapter 7. The Ohio State University president earned an annual salary of $6.1 million (Associated Press, 2014), which is approximately $2,932 per hour. In 2012, the annual starting salary for a newly hired OSU custodian was $10.28 per hour, or an annual salary of $21,382. High-level administrators in the corporate university must appease elite faculty (usually by raising salaries) and not tarnish the institution's brand. Meanwhile, service workers remain perennially undercompensated. Dynamics such as these call into question espoused democratic values of our higher education system. Equity, compassion, fair play, and justice have given way to not-so-transparent insatiable greed.

The third recommendation for high-level administrators is to make public these disparities and begin to lessen the gap. Like Elaine, it means shifting their mantra of "If I could, I would" to a new and improved (that staple of corporate America) mantra, "I can, and I will." Often these seemingly impossible and politically dangerous acts are, in fact, doable and politically safe. Paying for these increases usually represents only a small percentage of a university's operating budget. For example, in 2010, Georgetown University increased the salaries of nearly 500 service workers so that they would finally earn living-wage salaries. This initiative cost approximately $2 million of the university's $900 million budget (Eisenberg, 2012b).

In 2015, over two dozen Kentucky State University workers received a substantial pay increase because the acting president relinquished nearly $90,000 of his own six-figure salary (Fox, 2014). This magnanimous (and probably short-term) act not only improved the wages and lives of the underpaid and underappreciated service workers, but also symbolically communicated that if complex problems such as wage inequity are to be solved, those with power must also sacrifice.

At St. Mary's College, the faculty senate proposed a plan that would ensure the wages of their lowest-paid staff members would keep pace with inflation by directly linking presidential pay to that of the lowest-paid employees (Rivard, 2014). The institution would achieve its goal of equity by cutting salaries for those at the top of the wage scale or mandating raises for those at the bottom. Although this proposal is not likely to be ratified, it brings to the forefront of the entire campus community this "invisible" issue and provides forums to talk and brainstorm about what to do.

For high-level administrators, these three exemplars contain several useful reminders or suggestions about ways to ease income disparity on their respective campuses: First, raise wages wherever possible, even if the raises are not across the board like at Georgetown. Second, insist that high-level administrators sacrifice and share the pain, as the Kentucky State University president did. Third, disseminate and debate proposals, even those that will not likely become policy, as faculty and staff at St. Mary's did.

Pervasive college campus misperceptions include those of administrators as junkyard dogs and service workers as ignorant, incompetent, apathetic, lazy, and slow (Paules, 1991). The fourth Elaine-influenced recommendation is for high-level administrators to more regularly interact with custodians in their work environments to model and foster border crossings, provide opportunities for individuals to teach and learn from each other, and amend their misperceptions of the Other.

During my fieldwork, the multitude of campus subcultures I encountered on both campuses did not surprise me. However, the insular and segregated nature of these subcultures did. When discussing these observations with senior administrators, they expressed frustrations with federal and state mandates as well as compliance regulations that virtually tether them to their desks and limit their ability to wander the campus, which contribute to others' perceptions that they are inaccessible and uncaring. Despite these challenges, these policy architects influence workers' quality of life. They must substantively interact with, listen to, and learn from these laborers.

Data derived from these kinds of face-to-face encounters are qualitatively different from data contained on a spreadsheet that might reveal, for example, the increase of out-of-pocket health care expenses for employees. A high-level administrator interacting with Samuel would learn about how he postponed his surgery because he could not initially afford to pay his portion of the hospital bill and used his credit card to pay the hospital bill (despite knowing that he would barely have sufficient funds each month to pay the interest, let alone the principal). As a 25-year employee whose salary is at the high end of the custodial pay scale, he remains mindful of costs associated with purchasing even a birthday cake for his mother, opting for the least expensive cake, even if it is not her favorite.

The qualitative data resulting from these interactions are not intended to eclipse other data that administrators use in wage-related policies. Instead, these data augment them, revealing negative effects that seemingly innocuous policies have on marginalized campus enclaves. Ongoing and substantive dialogue about the politics and social functions of higher education is an intended by-product of this recommendation. In the current long-term crises in academia, we desperately need these kinds of conversations.

At CU, numerous custodians spoke with reverence about a high-level administrator who recently died. This administrator single-handedly extended the university's mantra of knowing every student to include knowing every service worker. To date, no CU senior administrator has stepped up to fill this void. At HU, the retirement of a senior associate vice president marked the end of an era where at least one champion for the campus underclass worked in the administration building.

The fifth and final Elaine-influenced recommendation for high-level administrators is to ensure that specific members of the high-level administrator caste understand and have the political clout to advocate for the interests of service workers—someone on their side. Such an advocate would make certain that the university does not offer custodians like Kathyleen—with extensive previous work experience—an entry-level starting salary. These advocates would also work with service offices such as benefits and personnel to extend their responsibilities to include advocacy, not simply accountability, compliance, and accounting.

Corporate managerialism, stagnant low wages, widening income disparity, insular high-level administrators, and the dwindling number of advocates are but a few challenges that high-level administrators must tackle. Looking to custodians like Elaine for advice is wise. Taking such actions would lessen custodians' feelings that they are being left behind and would teach junkyard-dog administrators some new management tricks.

Watchdogs: Faculty, Students, and Staff

In a manuscript documenting findings from an ethnographic study I conducted about a residential college in the mid-1990s, I wrote,

> One evening around Halloween, three students catapulted flaming pumpkins (they were stuffed with paper towels soaked with lighter fluid) out of third-floor windows. As one might imagine, the pumpkins made a colossal mess on the sidewalk and roadway. Students ignored their mess, leaving it for the housekeeping staff. In a discussion about the incident, I noted that during class sessions, students described themselves as activists for the oppressed and the less powerful. Yet their actions suggested otherwise. I pointed out that housekeepers were local examples of the oppressed and less powerful, yet student behaviors did little to support them.
>
> My comments provoked debate and discussion but in this instance did not have the outcome I desired. One student, responding to my challenge about the pumpkin incident, assured me that in the future he would aim his flaming pumpkins toward the grassy knolls rather than the roadway, thus alleviating the housekeepers' burden. (Magolda, 2000, p. 224)

Immediately following this student's response, I knew this was not one of my more potent teachable moments. Yet 15 years later, the song remains the same. Despite collegians' sincere desires to act as social justice advocates, they continue to overlook injustices occurring in their own backyards.

While not always the most attentive watchdogs sniffing out local injustices, once students recognize them, they act. During the past decade, students have been highly successful in protesting on behalf of marginalized campus employees who live in or close to poverty, including custodians. These fair-pay demonstrations have persuaded universities to increase salaries and benefits of low-wage employees, and persuaded workers, in some instances, to mobilize and unionize. Harvard University's (Van Der Werf, 2001) and the University of Miami's (Capriccioso, 2005) protracted living-wage protests were the most contentious and highest-profile examples of activism that resulted in major concessions benefiting low-wage employees. While these campaigns were successful locally and regionally, they have yet to morph into a force to be reckoned with nationally.

Still, these campaigns have provided students with opportunities to lead their universities and persuaded university communities to ponder important questions that are neither frequently asked nor answered, such as: What is the mission of the university? What does it mean to be a socially responsible university? What principles should guide the allocation of scarce resources in severe economic times? Is this university a good place to work or the only place to work? Are stagnant salaries a campus-wide or custodial issue? Does the low starting salary suggest that recruiting and retaining the best possible custodians is a low priority? Southhampton College's crisis in 1998 revealed the impact of posing and answering questions such as these:

> In the winter of 1998, however, a Southhampton College decision to contract out its custodial work instigated a crisis concerning the structure and nature of the entire campus community. . . . The outsourcing of custodial work suddenly forced students, faculty, and staff to question what kind of community the college was and ought to be; what kind of responsibilities an institution has to its employees and the surrounding community; and what role students and other campus groups should play in the decision-making process that impacts their surroundings. (Dolgon, 2000, p. 343)

Student activism, then and now, has been successful in provoking economic, political, and moral reflections that challenge and sometimes upend several sacred corporate managerial principles, such as autocratic decision making, top-down policy formulation, and conservative risk-management strategies. In these negotiations, high-level administrators learn to share power and control over matters typically deemed under their purview: budgeting, employment, and campus operations. Student-initiated protests model ways for campus subcultures to forge alliances, as well as model ways for service workers to mobilize effectively. Dolgon (2000) revealed benefits resulting from these alliances:

> The more students, faculty, and custodians worked together, talked together, argued and fought together, the more socially constructed barriers were challenged. This isn't to say that race and class prejudices and divisions did not remain salient; they were always with us. But by openly confronting them, we began the long process of reshaping their contours and meaning. (p. 356)

While students have been at the forefront of the living-wage debate, faculty members have been more active monitoring and challenging efforts aimed at corporatizing higher education (Aronowitz, 1995, 1997). Giroux and Myrsiades (2001) made explicit the dangers of not keeping a watchful eye on how this ideology is enacted. They acknowledged that universities must generate revenues to operate and survive but warned against reducing the academy to crass entrepreneurial functions. They advocated that faculty and staff remain vigilant watchdogs so that universities do not dilute or abandon their responsibilities to cultivate civic educators, rather than to simply train students for jobs. They also cautioned faculty, staff, and students to avoid the all-too-familiar and dangerous binary of becoming either "servants of corporate power or detached intellectuals" (p. 1). Huber (2000a) discussed in stark terms what is at stake:

> Faculty have a choice: They can either help the corporate world pervert higher education and destroy many of their jobs, or they can unite with other community members around an explicitly social justice vision for higher education. Because of the momentum and power of the corporate grab for higher education, building this united response is the single most effective way that faculty can act in their own interest and in the interest of all working people in the United States. (p. 136)

Solidarity can persuade and pressure universities to improve the working conditions of their low-wage workers and support staff on the margins. These historical events and activist insights provide some guiding principles and recommendations for faculty and students to remember as they forge alliances and devise and enact emancipatory agendas.

Collaborative efforts to monitor corporate managerialism and rectify low wages are two high priorities. It is also important to both espouse and enact a social justice agenda and to continually seek out and remedy injustices, especially those in our own backyards. One need not travel to faraway places to make a difference. Like Elaine, speaking out, confronting the other, and taking on governing responsibilities are morally, economically, and politically the right thing to do in the short and long term. Tending to issues such as these minimizes inequities and tempers feelings of fear and fatalism.

Underdogs: Custodians

On December 20, 2014, that "damn spot" on Kathyleen's lungs got the better of her, and she passed away. Sitting in the back of a funeral home a few days later, during her memorial service, I cursed that damn spot and wished Kathyleen's medical team had caught it earlier. Kathyleen was, in my view, the quintessential custodian. As I listened to the preacher talk about her life, I could not help but revise my appraisal to add that she was also the quintessential underdog—a fierce competitor on the work and health fronts. She had little chance of surviving a corporate takeover of the struggling company where she worked for over three decades. In her early 50s, she was a long shot to find employment in a rural county amid an economic downturn—overqualified for some jobs and undercredentialed for others. In addition, she was a dark horse in her cancer battle. Despite these seemingly insurmountable challenges and the fears associated with each, Kathyleen was a scrappy fighter. Her underdog status did not deter her from giving her all.

Accepting a job for which she was overqualified and severely undercompensated did not keep her from doing this physically demanding job. She channeled her fears into constructive and positive energy. She could have done the minimum amount of cleaning while on the job and hope nobody noticed, but she didn't. She could have gone home rather than return to work after her chemotherapy treatments, but she didn't. She could have allowed friends and coworkers to feel sorry for her declining health, but she didn't. She could have used her complex life circumstances to decline my invitation to participate in this study and help me out, but she didn't. She was tough, tireless, generous, dedicated, motivating, compassionate, and determined.

I suspect these qualities that I observed during our interactions were the same ones that the HU baseball manager and team observed on a daily basis as she cleaned their locker room, one reason why, in 2013, they named her the honorary team captain. The team honored and publicly recognized Kathyleen during a game, where she threw out the first pitch. Months after her death, the team invited her family to a game where the manager unveiled a framed photograph of Kathyleen with "her baseball boys" that they intend to display in their new locker room. Her daughter threw out the first pitch at that game in honor of her mother. Family mattered most to Kathyleen, and her extended family of baseball boys got to experience what her spouse and children already knew: the sacredness of family.

In the dog-eat-dog world of the corporate university, witnessing Kathyleen—an underdog, fighting hard even when the odds were long and time was short—treat strangers like family and subsequently witnessing a team of young men invite an invisible custodian who lived her work life on the margins to become a central part of their world made me feel hopeful. (Only a few have ever accused me of being an optimist.)

I tell this story to honor Kathyleen, but, more importantly, because it reflects many of the themes showcased in this book and provides insights for all members of the campus community about how to navigate the corporate university and how to navigate life. Like most custodians, Kathyleen's most serious challenges—losing a job, struggling to find a job, working in a thankless job, and battling a debilitating disease—were not a result of her "doing something wrong." She accepted these life-changing events, over which she had no control, in stride. She did not pretend to be fearless, yet she did not allow her fear to cause her to not act or to act badly. She used these life challenges to educate, which is what is supposed to happen in the academy. She taught those with whom she interacted how to be humble, grateful for life's gifts (in Kathyleen's case, family), and realistically optimistic. One evening after working with Kathyleen, I met another custodian for dinner at a Chinese restaurant. My fortune cookie read, "You can make the best of a bad situation—they make diamonds out of coal." The custodian's fortune read, "We make a living by what we get, but we make a life by what we give." Both messages reflect the spirit of Kathyleen and her many coworkers.

Dog-ma

Dogma is a set of principles, the foundations of an ideology or belief system. Rather than concluding with a list of recommendations for custodians, I offer one recommendation and then showcase the dogma that the custodians recommended to me.

My recommendation centers on the need for custodians to mobilize. At both CU and HU, uneasiness with unions is unmistakable. It is unlikely that unions, which assume primary responsibility for mobilizing workers, will become a force to be reckoned with in the near future. While I respect (although disagree with) this decision, I remain convinced that finding alternative ways to mobilize custodians is essential. Workers gain results only after they recognize and exercise their power. Workers who collectively join together are more powerful than individual workers. Mobilization ensures that custodians are educated about issues that confront them and act to address these issues. Mobilization ensures the multidirectional flow of information and negotiations from the management to workers and vice versa. Once custodians understand issues and have mechanisms in place to communicate concerns about these issues, collective action can result. Creating a sense of solidarity within custodian subcultures is a prerequisite to mobilizing with other campus advocates.

While I offer one insight for custodians to consider, I conclude with the insights I gained as a result of my interactions with custodians.

From the CU custodians I learned the following:

- Just because someone thinks you've done something wrong doesn't mean you have—Mone
- So much of what is good is bound up in our love of family—Kichelle
- Keep trying—Zoe
- We start and end with family—Hazma, Elif, Eki, Max, Stafani, Malik, and Suki (the night shift)
- Being visible is not the same thing as being seen—Calvin
- If you have a disagreement with others, talk it out and get over it—Monroe
- Ask the question, "What can I do for you?"—Joanne
- Chaos breeds life—Ajla
- Whatever you do, do it well—Anna
- If you are weak, universities will eat you alive—Peaches
- Be yourself; people will eventually figure you out—Chee-Chee
- Happiness does not have to come from making a lot of money—Vida

From the HU custodians I learned the following:

- The importance of unconditionally accepting life and what it brings—Kathyleen
- The working class has class—George
- The best lessons are learned from past mistakes—Chip
- There is a difference between making a living and having a life—Jonathan
- To build a positive relationship with staff, you have to get to know them—Ben
- To respect the wisdom of elders—Lee
- The virtue of patience—Nita
- The good-old-boy network is alive and well in the academy—Will
- The rising and falling fortunes of a university seldom have much of an impact on custodians; they struggle in good and bad times—Edgar
- In work there is meaning and value—Margaret
- To recognize and monitor my privilege—Samuel
- Just because you work at a university does not mean you understand how it works—Lucy
- Do what is right, not simply what is allowed—Elaine

From my custodian colleagues at my workplace at Miami University and The Ohio State University I learned:

- Learn as if you are going to live forever—Ludmila
- Risk taking is a prerequisite to learning—Dolores
- You don't have to be a person of influence to be influential—Juanita "Pat" Denton

Nowadays when I encounter Dr. Ludmila, the custodian who cleans my campus office, and she asks, "How are you today?" I smile; pause to reflect on this research project; and reply, "I see you."

EPILOGUE

When I [Katrina] came here [the United States] I had a package of clothes, two kids, and maybe 150 U.S. dollars. Believe me, it was really hard. I came to United States as a single mom with two kids. My husband was actually killed in the war. My husband's family wanted me to get all my papers done so I could come here with my kids. I came to the United States. Of course it was not easy to travel with two kids. We came, and we didn't have any money. The kids were sick, and there was a lot of paperwork. The kids started school right away. I applied for a job to start to save a little money and bought a car. Of course my sister-in-law helped with the kids. . . . I didn't have anybody else. I learned that you have to stay strong and stay focused. Nothing can hurt me and my life that I cannot get by.

Since we were hired through a refugee program, they could pay us less than minimum wage. . . . I worked from 7:00 a.m. to 3:30 p.m. and then worked part-time starting at 5:30 p.m. for a cleaning company. I worked five part-time hours, and I was working 13 hours a day. They told me, "You really need more time with your kids." I told her I had to do what I had to do, because I did not have any other income. I have been at Compton University for eight years. I started as [a] floater. I was hired for that job for six months. Next I was a housekeeper for almost four years. Then there was an opportunity to apply for a supervisor position. Our manager always tries to open the position and invite everyone into the door. I talked to a couple of supervisors and they encouraged me to apply for it. I actually got it. I was the youngest supervisor. I was working four years before the supervisor job.— Katrina

Life changes are the norm for custodians like Katrina who stay strong and focused and live their version of the good life. This epilogue contains career and life updates on the custodians featured throughout the book since the conclusion of my fieldwork. Like Katrina's, many of their lives were and continue to be in a constant state of transition and change.

Compton University Staff Updates

Ajla received a promotion to supervisor in 2014 after 16 years as a custodian. She continues to operate her cleaning business during evenings and weekends.

Anna remains a custodial supervisor. Her three children finished college and are employed.

Calvin quit his custodian job. Chronic absenteeism coupled with his discomfort with his work environment contributed to his departure.

Chee-Chee, at age 64, continues to relish her role as custodian. A few health scares have slowed her down a bit, but her love of students and serving others remains strong.

Diane continues to work hard while devoting almost all of her free time to family and church. Her seven children all have families, which keeps Diane busy outside of work.

Eki resigned from his custodial job in 2015 and accepted a job as a truck driver. He remains in close contact with many former coworkers.

Elif continues to work the evening shift, spending free time with her children. She remains centrally involved in their schooling.

Hazma is starting his 11th year as a custodian supervisor. He continues to mentor staff, smoke meats, and cook.

Joanne retired after 37 years as a custodian and supervisor. She spends time with family, travels, and has started a home wig-manufacturing business.

Katrina is starting her third year as a supervisor. At home, she remains active in her community.

Kichelle is starting her 18th year as a custodian. She intends to remain working at CU unless, as she says, "God blesses me with some money."

Lance is in his 18th year as director of custodial operations. He has worked tirelessly the past few years to ensure a smooth departmental transition from the Octagon Cleaning Company to a custodial department within CU.

Malik continues as an evening-shift custodian. When not at work, he spends time with his spouse and two children as well as rehabs homes.

Max remains an evening-shift custodian and a carpet-cleaning expert. In his spare time he enjoys spending time with his two daughters and son as well as playing soccer.

Mone remains happily employed and continues to haul trash and supplies across campus. Watching sports and spending time with family consume his time away from work.

Monroe is starting her 18th year of work and is currently a supervisor. Family remains the epicenter of her nonwork life.

Stafani is still working the evening shift and spends her spare time with family and cooking. One son is in high school, and the other attends college.

Suki continues to work the evening shift and spends his nonwork time with his spouse and daughter. He also does handyman work for family and friends.

Tonya remains a supervisor. She continues to rehab houses and shop online during her free time.

Vida continues her work as a custodian and was the 2015 recipient of the Outstanding Housekeeping Staff award. Her daughter, Nikolina, finished her master's in business administration and is working as a brand manager in the Midwest.

Zoe continues to work as a custodian. She is still working to complete her GED.

Harrison University Staff Updates

Ben retired in 2014 and spends time with family while enrolling in numerous classes aimed at retirees.

Chip retired in 2014 and spends considerable time with family, in addition to working part-time at a local amusement park.

Edgar continues to work at HU, but his spouse retired in 2014. Both spend time with family. Edgar recently lost a considerable amount of weight and is enjoying his new healthy lifestyle.

Elaine works the night shift, waxing floors and cleaning carpets. She continues to volunteer at the local dog shelter and remains a strong animal activist in her home community.

George continues to enjoy retirement, spending most of his time with family.

Hazel continues her work as a campus custodian. In 2015 she was promoted to shift supervisor.

Jonathan continues his work as a custodian and recently earned a theology degree at a local Bible college. He aspires to ministry work.

Kathyleen lost her battle with cancer and died in 2014. HU's Department of Athletics recently honored Kathyleen for her exemplary work supporting numerous sports teams.

Lee is enjoying the retired life. He spends time with his grandchildren and enjoys local travel.

Lucy is currently a custodian working in the chemistry building. She enjoys time with professors and students in her building. At home, she spends time with her two adult children and spouse.

Margaret is starting her 15th year of retirement. She spends time with friends and family. She was recently honored at an HU alumni reunion event.

Nita completed her associate's degree and is still a campus custodian working for the Department of Athletics. Spending time with her grandchildren consumes most of her nonwork time.

Samuel continues to work at HU and manage farm responsibilities with his mother. He hopes to retire in two or three years.

Will completed his bachelor's degree in integrative studies in 2015. Currently he is a custodial supervisor in the campus recreation center. He enjoys ATV racing and spending time with his two children.

Miami University Staff Updates

Dolores is now working the day shift as a custodian. Her son, too, is a campus custodian. In her spare time, Dolores remains a social justice advocate, researching social problems such as human trafficking and work safety issues.

Ludmila, at age 75, is a custodian cleaning offices and classrooms in the College of Education, Health, and Society. She remains an avid reader and healthy-living advocate.

APPENDIX A

Research Methodologies and Methods

Philosophical Foundations

Donella Meadows posited, "Your paradigm is so intrinsic to your mental process that you are hardly aware of its existence, until you try to communicate with someone with a different paradigm" (Leonard, 2010, p. xxiii). This appendix details the philosophical foundations of the research presented in this volume, making explicit the paradigmatic assumptions upon which the study rests as well as documenting research processes, procedures, and methods.

A *paradigm* is "a comprehensive belief system, world view, or framework that guides research and practice in the field" (Willis, 2007, p. 8). Paradigmatic beliefs influence the nature of reality or what we think exists (i.e., ontology), how we come to know reality (i.e., epistemology), and the ways we come to know (i.e., methodology). Paradigms shape how we work and inform the assumptions that undergird what we do.

I situate this ethnographic study within an interpretive worldview (Guba & Lincoln, 2005) with critical theory leanings (Foley & Valenzuela, 2005; Madison, 2012). This emphasis results in (a) soliciting and documenting the multiple realities of the respondents—attending to events that related to social conflict and difference; (b) valuing and attending to local environments and contextual histories; (c) examining how participants interpret ideological, political, and sociohistorical forces that influence their lives; (d) infusing the issue of power into interpretations; (e) using difference and conflict, rather than similarities and consensus, as organizing concepts in the analyses to enrich understanding about human struggles and agency; and (f) celebrating the presence and importance of positionality, power, politics, and subjectivity.

Of particular importance were the "silent workings of structure and power" revealing "how historical conditions and larger social conditions shape current situations" (Charmaz, 2011, p. 362). This study documents "not only how these power relations produce oppressive conditions but also how to imagine rearranging these relations to map new conditions that achieve an ever-expansive notion of equity and opportunity" (Pasque, Carducci, Kuntz, & Gildersleeve, 2012, p. 7). As Tierney and Rhoads (1993) asserted, "One key purpose of research . . . is to create the conditions where the participants gain self-understanding and empowerment" (p. 329).

Ethnography is a particular research methodology nested within an interpretivist paradigm. Schwandt (2001) defined *ethnography* as a

> particular kind of qualitative inquiry distinguishable from case study research, descriptive studies, naturalistic inquiry, and so forth by the fact that it is the process and product of describing and interpreting cultural behavior. . . . Both anthropological and sociological definitions of *ethnography* stress the centrality of culture as the analytic concept that informs the doing of ethnography.
>
> Ethnography unites process, product, fieldwork, and written text. Fieldwork, undertaken as participant observation, is the process by which the ethnographer comes to know a culture; the ethnographic text is how culture is portrayed. There is general agreement that culture is not visible or tangible but is constructed by the act of ethnographic writing. Hence, understanding what it means to "write" culture (i.e., literal representation, inscription, transcription, textualization, and cultural translation) is a critical concern in ethnography. (p. 80; emphasis added)

From the outset, I envisioned this ethnographic study to be, as Schwandt described, both a process and product involving the study of Harrison University (HU) and Compton University (CU). The fieldwork component of the study allowed me prolonged engagement with members of these two custodial departments, which resulted in numerous opportunities to come to know these organizations and their members.

This ethnography is also a product that integrates and synthesizes how I perceive and construct the various campus subcultures. The text reflects the outcome of the ethnographic process and my social constructions. Ethnography centers on the examination of different cultures and complex social phenomena and yields empirical data about the lives of people in specific situations, revealing multiple interpretations.

Influences on Fieldwork Methods

This section includes the details about research parameters as well as the data collection and analyses procedures employed during the fieldwork and writing phases of this study. The aforementioned philosophical foundational beliefs influenced these research practices.

Research Parameters

I received Institutional Review Board (IRB) approval in spring 2012 and began fieldwork in July. I concluded the fieldwork phase of this project in August 2013. The most intense fieldwork took place during the 2012–2013 academic year. Follow-up interviews, debriefings, and member checking with participants occurred for 24 months following the completion of the fieldwork. I wanted two diverse sites based on numerous criteria.

My HU fieldwork involved one to two fieldwork outings and one to two interviews per week throughout the year. I visited CU seven times; each visit lasted usually four or five days. I adopted an emergent research design (Patton, 2002), in which I had no predetermined set of research procedures. Rather, the participants' actions guided the trajectory of the study.

Data Collection

Data collection sources included (a) participant-observations (Angrosino & Rosenberg, 2011), such as working with custodians and attending training sessions; (b) ethnographic interviews (Fontana & Frey, 2005) involving approximately 70 individuals; and (c) analyses of hundreds of written and audiovisual documents (Hodder, 2000), such as manuals, newsletters, and performance evaluation reviews.

Participant-Observation

Sweet (2001), when discussing observations, noted,

> Field observations enable researchers to gain a deep understanding of the ways in which individuals locate themselves relative to other individuals in society. It also enables us to write thick descriptions (Geertz, 1973) of human conduct, detailed portraits of social encounters and assessments of what those encounters mean to individuals participating in them. (p. 135)

The most common strategy for observing participants was working side by side with custodians during their shifts to accelerate the completion of their routine cleaning tasks, which allowed for extended and focused conversations and interviews during their work hours. Snowball sampling (Creswell, 2013) expanded the pool of interviewees to ensure that I gained multiple and diverse perspectives.

During my HU fieldwork, I worked four-hour shifts, which gave me time to gather quality information and build rapport. This approach to fieldwork allowed staff members time each day to work without me being present. CU fieldwork usually included four- to five-hour fieldwork outings. Spradley (1980) defined five degrees of participation for researchers: *complete, active, moderate*, *passive*, and *nonparticipation*. I began my fieldwork as a *passive* participant. Gradually I assumed a highly *active* role.

Prolonged engagement allowed me to get acquainted and recognize the congruence between my words and actions. I gradually learned organizational norms and established rapport with custodial and supervisor subcultures. I heeded the advice of Whyte (1997), who noted, "People need time to get used to having a participant-observer around and to feel that they can trust the researcher not to do anything to harm them" (p. 25).

I documented all observations in a notebook or laptop computer and expanded these notes shortly after each event. I also kept a field journal, in which I recorded my personal experiences, impressions, ideas, problems, questions, and preliminary interpretations and hypotheses. This journal augmented my more factual field notes. Finally, I created an electronic log to chronicle all fieldwork activities. This log included the date, time, and location of events and a list of participants for every event.

Interviews

Patton (1990) identified several variations in ethnographic interviewing, ranging from informal conversational interviews, where questions emerged from the context, to a standardized open-ended interview, where wording and a sequence of questions were predetermined. Custodial interviews were informal, open-ended, unstructured, and conversational (Lincoln & Guba, 1985). Although I did not pose predetermined questions, I acknowledged to interviewees my predetermined domains of interest. This format provided interviewees the freedom to set the agenda and discuss what they deemed important, which was my intention.

During each interview I asked participants to complete three tasks: First, "Tell me a story that might sensitize me to what it is like to be a custodian." Second, "Tell me what I should do to gather quality information about custodians." Third, "Share with me names of people who share your worldview and those who have a different worldview."

The first task solicited stories about custodians' lives and work experiences. I prefer imposing minimal structure on participants during interviews; many custodians prefer clear and instructive guidelines during interviews. My amorphous "tell me a story" invitation unnerved some. Despite acknowledging that they seldom recounted life stories while at work, my request elicited skepticism. If they misunderstood my requests, or if I misunderstood their stories or responses, the miscommunication could harm them (e.g., become estranged from supervisors). Accommodating my research expectations seemed counterintuitive to what custodians have been socialized to believe is normal.

When asked to recommend ways to improve or modify my fieldwork plan, several interviewees professed their belief that their minimal formal education disqualified them from critiquing my research design, ignoring the potency of their life experiences. They understood hierarchies and usually acquiesced to those with more power, which did not serve me well in this context.

The final interview segment enlisted interviewees' assistance to identify diverse and information-rich key informants. My goal was to solicit as many different perspectives as possible. The tight-knit subcultures within custodial communities usually based on age, ethnicity, gender, and seniority made it easier for interviewees to recommend coworkers who shared their views than to recommend people who were different.

Snowball sampling (Creswell, 2013) expanded the pool of interviewees to ensure multiple and diverse perspectives. Open-ended and unstructured interviews usually began with a single question: "What is it like to be a campus custodian?" I structured these encounters to more closely resemble conversations rather than formal interviews. Yet custodians' lack of familiarity with research interviews, consent forms, and concepts such as confidentiality and pseudonyms disadvantaged them. They were not always fully aware that they could decline to answer questions I posed. I feared that if my interview overviews were too basic, I would offend them and reinforce the uneducated-custodian stereotype. If my explanations were too obtuse, I feared I would confuse them and reinforce the elitist-faculty stereotype.

Because of housekeepers' hyperwillingness to defer to authority, I made certain that my status as a faculty researcher did not inadvertently pressure housekeepers to talk about uncomfortable topics or act against their interests. I did not want to be one additional person placing demands on them or exploiting their goodwill. Issues rooted in socialized roles and performances for faculty and custodians were easy to recognize and difficult to address.

Document Analysis

"Records, documents, artifacts, and archives—what has traditionally been called 'material culture' in anthropology—constitute a particularly rich source of information about many organizations and programs" (Patton, 2002, p. 293). I analyzed written and audiovisual documents such as staff manuals, newsletters, public notices, advertisements, announcements, and performance evaluation reviews. Finally, I mapped the physical space where custodians and I worked.

Data Analysis

Throughout the fieldwork and data analysis phases, I intertwined coding and analysis to generate themes that are "integrated, consistent, plausible, [and] close to the data" (Glaser, 1965, p. 437). This process involved the categorization of data and then integration of categories to create theory. LeCompte and Preissle (1993) described this process as perceiving, comparing, contrasting, aggregating and ordering, establishing linkages and relationships, and speculating. Through this process of establishing relationships between data and playing with ideas, theory inductively emerges from the field experience.

Writing

Erickson (1973) argued that the goals of writing are to make the familiar strange and the strange familiar. Schlechty and Noblit (1982) offered a variation of Erickson's framework that involved making the obvious obvious, the obvious dubious, and the hidden obvious. Throughout I heeded Erickson's and Schlechty and Noblit's advice.

Finding the "balance between abstraction and concrete example" (Van Maanen, 2011, p. 29) was of paramount importance when interpreting and writing my stories that captured broad and nuanced aspects of custodians' work. To allow readers to vicariously experience content and context, I drafted narratives for readers to "participate" in the social scenes (Chase, 2005; Clandinin & Connelly, 2000).

Tierney and Rhoads (1993) asserted, "One key purpose of research. . . is to create the conditions where the participants gain self-understanding and empowerment" (p. 329). For insiders, such as custodians, I want the text to make the obvious patently so, the obvious dubious (i.e., make the familiar strange), and the hidden obvious. For readers unfamiliar with this invisible subculture, my aim was to make the unfamiliar familiar.

Goodness Criteria

To address goodness criteria and subjectivity concerns, I triangulated data, utilized peer debriefings, and negotiated findings with respondents (Creswell & Miller, 2000). "The success or failure of either report or full-blown ethnography depends on the degree to which it rings true to natives and colleagues in the field" (Fetterman, 2010, p. 11). To minimize the probability of miscommunication and to calm fears, I regularly consulted with participants (i.e., member checking) to see if I got it right.

I devised different strategies to solicit reactions, correct errors of fact, and ensure that respondents critiqued my tentative conclusions. I gave most interviewees a copy of the story in advance and asked them to read it. I then met with them, one-on-one, to verbally explain the content and my rationale for including the story; I also sought their reactions. In advance, I identified topics that could potentially harm them, such as Mone noting that he illegally parked his trash vehicle on the lawn to avoid walking up steps. In this and similar cases, I explicitly asked whether the story should be included, edited, or deleted.

This revised member-checking process did not necessarily help me get it right, but it allowed me to minimize miscommunication and exploitation fears as well as monitor and, whenever possible, lessen the power gap between participants and me. Although I desired an egalitarian relationship with respondents, I never achieved this aim. Understanding the cultural norms of research participants, institutions, and oneself and negotiating these norms is a way to better level the playing field.

Denzin (1989) identified four kinds of triangulation, which I employed in this study. *Data triangulation*, Denzin's first kind of triangulation, refers to the purposeful and systematic use of different data sources involving different individuals at different times and at different places. I regularly solicited divergent perspectives from HU and CU staff and those they served.

Theory triangulation is a second kind of triangulation in Denzin's schema. I viewed findings through interdisciplinary theoretical lenses (e.g., anthropological, cultural studies theory) to extend the possibilities for generating and disseminating knowledge. I assembled interconnected interpretations, rooted in these various discourses. *Methodological triangulation*, Denzin's third type, involves both within-method and between-method forms of triangulation; I included both forms in my study. When interviewing the same respondent multiple times, I initially employed an open-ended interview protocol. In some subsequent interviews I was more directive in order to collect data about a topic about which I had less understanding. These differing interview protocols, exemplifying methodological triangulation, yielded important nuances. *Investigator triangulation*, Denzin's fourth kind of triangulation, involves the use of multiple researchers to minimize subjectivities of a single researcher. While I was the sole fieldworker for this study, I regularly debriefed with my research associates.

Like custodians trying to please their many supervisors, I had to write to several audiences. I tried to create prose that custodians as well as higher education scholars would read and appreciate. To achieve this aim, I relied on Richardson's (2000) criteria for a well-crafted ethnographic text: (a) *substantive contribution* (Does the writing contribute to a reader's understanding of the custodians and higher education?); (b) *aesthetic merit* (Does the use of creative analytic practices result in an interesting written document, causing readers to pause, reflect, and generate multiple interpretative responses?); (c) *reflexivity* (Is the author's self awareness and self-exposure evident for the readers to judge the goodness of the author's perspective?); (d) *impact* (Does the writing affect the reader emotionally and intellectually, and does it generate new questions for readers and move them to action?); and (e) *expression of reality* (Is the text a credible account of the culture, and does the text embody a sense of lived experiences?).

Interesting, accessible, credible, provocative, moderately disorienting, and educational stories were my goal. I intentionally interjected myself into the narratives and purposefully explicated my values, politics, and subjectivities. I avoided smug findings and interpretations, instead favoring ideas that would spawn new questions, rather than simplistically answer existing ones.

Researchers "often enter collaborative relationships with and for powerless and marginalized groups, and through such relationships provide them with a vehicle for voicing their concerns and aspirations" (Lee, 1993, p. 210). Similarly, Denzin and Giardina (2010) noted, "Qualitative research is about making the world visible in ways that implement the goals of social justice and radical progressive democracy" (p. 14). This research methodology optimized opportunities to achieve these aims.

APPENDIX B

Unsanitized Tales From the Field

Omissions Accomplished

As an academic and educational ethnographer it is normal to review field notes, interview transcripts, and personal fieldwork journal entries and then describe and theoretically interpret data. While analyzing the influences of the corporate university on custodians, I realized that I, too, encountered labor struggles during every phase of the research. Corporate-like policies complicated where and how I conducted my fieldwork, inducing my own feelings of fear and pessimism. Admittedly, it is easier to critique the Other rather than the self. This appendix explores the influences of the corporate university on my fieldwork and on me, focusing on fieldwork issues seldom explicitly discussed in ethnographic texts.

DeVita (1992) clarified the benefits of fieldworker tales of self-reflection:

> There were, in most cases, important lessons embedded in the content of [fieldworkers'] experiences. . . . There were lessons to be learned—lessons about the anthropologists, about the people being studied, and about human experiences in a cross-cultural context. (p. xiv)

Fools Rush in Where Angels Fear to Tread

My evolving recognition of my role as an academic worker reveals the influences of corporate-like power on four fieldwork-related issues I encountered: gaining access, mediating conflict, ensuring accountability, and sharing wisdom. This analysis reveals the inescapable influences that corporate ideals have on educational researchers.

Before proceeding with this fieldworker analysis, I should note that significant differences indeed exist between faculty researchers and custodians, despite both operating within the corporate university. Generally, custodians' fears were more intense than mine because their stakes were higher than mine as a tenured professor with greater job security. We also differed in capacities to respond to fears based on status within the academy. My status as a tenured faculty member allowed me to publicly resist and challenge university policies. Custodians' status on campus, coupled with socialized work roles, tempered their desires to challenge policies with which they disagreed. Understanding these differences is essential to fully appreciate the analyses that follow.

Getting Started

Demonstrating the integrity of my research to an Institutional Research Board (IRB) bred feelings of fear and fatalism. IRB members are de facto gatekeepers who determine the research studies that universities sponsor. IRB policies in the corporate-like university are cumbersome and worrisome for researchers as well as IRB members. Gaining permission from IRBs to conduct research is a stressful and fear-evoking process.

In the early 1990s I submitted my dissertation research proposal to a review board. The IRB categorized my study as "an expedited review of minimal risk research" and approved my proposed ethnographic study within 10 days. The IRB reviewed my protocol, posed thoughtful questions, and offered sage advice. I recall the process as educational and collegial, not legalistic or adversarial.

Compared to my dissertation IRB application, my IRB application for this custodian study was more extensive, formal, legalistic, and politely adversarial. I approached writing my custodial IRB application like a defendant might prepare to testify in a court of law. I was truthful and forthright. I carefully answered questions posed, submitted all required documentation, and provided only information the reviewers requested. Providing too much or too little information, as well as providing detailed summaries, were common tensions that I navigated. I was honest, responsive, polite, and guarded, yet this strategy did not initially gain me the IRB's seal of approval. One IRB concern read as follows:

> Though it is clear that the researcher will obtain consent from departmental supervisors and from individual participants, it probably is unavoidable that members of the same department will know who is and is not participating in the study. For example, how will participant-observations be conducted when one individual working in a group does not consent to participate? Will the others be observed while the non-consenting party is present? It also seems that supervisors will easily be able to determine which of their staff are participating. The IRB would like the researcher to

consider if there are any additional safeguards that could be put in place to protect participant identity.

The board advised me to revise my plan of action to further protect participants' rights, ensure confidentiality, and protect the rights of non-participants who interact with participants. IRB feedback alluded to the importance and improbability of achieving these three aims by implying that conducting fieldwork in public settings complicates efforts to protect participants' privacy rights. For example, when I work with a housekeeper and we encounter another custodian who surmises that the housekeeper with whom I am working is a research participant, the inference is correct.

The IRB also acknowledged that guaranteeing anonymity is almost impossible in a hierarchical organization. When I notify supervisors, in order to respect the department's chain of command, I explicitly inform supervisors which custodians are participants. Finally, the IRB implicitly acknowledged that for me to exclusively observe only the custodians is challenging, because they interact with dozens of individuals each day.

"Ethically sound research requires flexibility and a balancing of factors in decision making" (Levine & Skedsvold, 2008, p. 501). The IRB recognized this need for agility, heeding the advice of Murphy and Dingwall (2001), who noted the dangers of being too prescriptive when addressing research challenges:

> These [ethical] obligations are complex and will not be fulfilled through simple adherence to a prescriptive list of requirements. Indeed, given the diversity and flexibility of ethnography, and the indeterminacy of potential harm, a prescriptive approach may be positively unhelpful. It can fail to protect participants and, perhaps even more importantly, may deflect researchers from reflective pursuit of ethical practices. (p. 347)

The IRB did not prescribe solutions; instead, it identified problems, inferred that no easy solutions existed, and mandated modifications without specific suggestions. The subtext of feedback was: Do more. . . . Remedy problems. . . . We will audit the process but not get entangled in your imperfect solutions, and if problems arise, you are accountable. This modus operandi evoked feelings of fear and pessimism. The IRB's highly controlled, highly regulated risk-aversion plan of action favored a language of critique (identifying problems) rather than a language of possibility (offering solutions). Feedback symbolically communicated the board's intentions to protect human subjects from harm and shield the university from liability. The board's concern for me was far less obvious.

IRB committee members also have much to fear. IRB members are in an unenviable position of staying current about mandated policies aimed at identifying and preventing ethical quagmires. "IRBs are often strapped for resources, mired in paperwork, provided with insufficient staff support, or delegated with tasks that are a distraction from what they are intended to do" (Levine & Skedsvold, 2008, p. 502).

IRBs must guard against researcher violations that could result in severe institutional penalties, such as the loss of federally funded research dollars. Contemporary boards are larger and more diverse in order to ensure broad and divergent critiques. They are centralized to ensure oversight; reaching consensus is difficult. Centralized control is a centerpiece of their action.

Centralized control and hyperauditing agitate fears and foster feelings of powerlessness. If the IRB relinquished centralized control and allowed more local experts such as departmental review boards to make some decisions, the board could make better use of local knowledge. Decentralized boards would also generate formal and informal dialogue among the stakeholders about these complex issues, which could lead to more collaborative and imaginative responses. Ongoing educational dialogues, missing from centralized models, would dissipate some fears, yield better feedback, model collaborative governance, and create a more transparent review system, as well as generate collaborative and satisfying solutions drawn from national laws and regulations, local expert judgments, and common sense. These outcomes would benefit educational researchers and the IRB.

Negotiating Conflict

Reluctantly, I acknowledge that my concerns with equating the university with a corporation contributed to my reluctance to take major risks throughout my research.

At Compton University (CU), I met Wayne, an on-site administrator of a contracted national cleaning agency that cleaned academic buildings. During an hourlong meeting, Wayne and I discussed benefits and risks associated with the study. At the conclusion of the meeting he granted me access to the worksite. One week later I received the following e-mail:

> Hi Peter: I just got word back from our corporate office. At this time, our Employment and Labor Relations Department feels we need to reluctantly bow out of the study. We are in the very near future going into union negotiations and they feel this might cause a potential problem so we are not comfortable with having our employees interviewed. Sorry, Wayne.

Similarly, after a productive meeting with senior administrators of a contracted campus food service company, I sensed that attendees had positive vibes about my research proposal. Weeks later I received an e-mail from Yvonne, the human resources director: "Our legal department asked that I get a bit more clarification surrounding your study on the following items." Immediately I knew that if the corporation granted me access to staff and dining facilities, it would be limited and highly regulated. Future correspondence confirmed this suspicion. I eventually declined their invitation to conduct limited and tightly controlled fieldwork.

Disappointment was my initial reaction to rejection. Wayne and Yvonne accepted a centralized decision-making philosophy that privileged the judgments of powerful members of the company while discounting the local knowledge and professional judgments of on-site managers. Protecting the company and its brand were of paramount importance, and my research posed threats. In this corporate environment, outsiders or initiatives that could disrupt efficiency, damage the brand, or provide venues for staff to reveal feelings and concerns are deemed dangerous threats.

Cynicism, fear, and confrontation avoidance influenced my decision to sustain the status quo. I neither directly contacted corporate decision makers to appeal their decisions nor solicited feedback. I feared that challenging authority could negatively affect my sponsor, who took risks in convincing other CU departments to allow me to conduct my fieldwork. I tempered my actions to minimize harm to others. At least that is how I rationalized my actions to myself.

Higher education aspires to be a place where the free and open exchange of ideas is a treasured ideal and conflict is a natural part of the enlightenment agenda of the academy. Conservative risk management, centralized and absolute power, and minimal opportunities for educational researchers to express their views all breed various strands of fear and cynicism. Fighting against these forces is time-consuming, exhausting, and often futile, yet avoiding conflicts is more costly economically, morally, and politically.

Coping With Accountability

As a researcher I struggled with accountability and auditing issues on two fronts influenced by ideals of the corporate university. First, I was accountable to the multiple research stakeholders (the IRB; Harrison University [HU]; CU; and diverse sponsors, gatekeepers, and participants). Pleasing these multiple and diverse stakeholders challenged me, which induced fear. Being too close to or too distant from a particular subculture (e.g., IRB) could satisfy that subculture but ostracize me from other subcultures.

Second, research respondents perceived me as an auditor of their culture, since being a participant-observer has elements of evaluation and surveillance. Although I do not perceive fieldworkers as analogous to auditors, written fieldwork accounts include evaluative commentary. I have the power to determine which stories and data to include in my writings. Aware of my role as a decision maker (and how normal that role seemed to custodians), I destabilized these norms by explicitly acknowledging my power and subtly conveying my intention to share power with research participants.

The university's corporate-like ideals had a profound influence on my dual roles as auditee and auditor. As the auditee, I assumed the role of the compliant researcher. I was cognizant of the mutual agreement I had forged with the IRB, gatekeepers, and research respondents, and I regularly monitored my actions to ensure that I adhered to agreements. Too often, adhering to nonnegotiable administrative processes necessitated that I focus my time on administrative tasks, not moral issues.

For example, in the aforementioned IRB review, the board expressed concern that custodial supervisors could easily determine which staff members were participating in my study. Conducting fieldwork in a hierarchical organization made it difficult to work with a custodian without the supervisor's permission and knowledge. When brainstorming ways to address this concern, for pragmatic reasons I focused on short-term administrative resolutions to satisfy IRB concerns rather than long-term philosophical issues, such as initiating a discussion about the obvious limits of confidentiality in ethnographic research involving hierarchical organizations and a discussion centering on "what is good." IRB formal appeal processes are so cumbersome that challenging board rulings would have delayed and possibly derailed my research.

A university's emphasis on accountability and auditing complicated my work. After a few months of working with a custodian, he confessed to believing that management hired me as a spy to uncover problems that would make it easier for the university to outsource housekeeping services. This revelation reminded me that even if that person refused to individually collaborate with a spy, I would still be auditing the custodial culture and my findings could cause harm.

Most custodians did not harbor conspiracy theories about me; instead, they recognized that my presence, while a pleasant novelty, slowed them down and added another layer of evaluation and accountability to their already busy workday. Despite these feelings, they graciously participated. Fears dissipated as time passed.

I gradually countered custodians' perceptions of me as a spy by assisting them with their work, rather than simply observing them. Over time, I expanded my fieldworker role to include advocacy, offsetting accountability and audit fears shared by the custodians. I edited and proofread grievance petitions they submitted to human resources offices; I interpreted impenetrable bereavement policies. I knew fears and feelings of fatalism were subsiding when custodians disagreed or challenged my views, joked with me, asked me personal questions, or shared insecurities with me.

The corporate-like organizational structures of HU and CU complicated efforts to invite custodians to audit my work. Because of the academy's caste systems, custodians typically defer to authority. I monitored how my status as faculty/researcher might inadvertently pressure custodians to talk about uncomfortable topics or act against their will. I did not want to be another person making demands or exploiting their good intentions. Thorny issues, rooted in socialized roles for faculty and custodians, were easy to recognize and difficult to address.

Custodians seldom viewed themselves as teachers or educators, even though I did. When asked to recommend ways to improve my fieldwork plan, several interviewees stated that their minimal formal education disqualified them from critiquing my research design, ignoring the potency of their life experiences. They understood university hierarchies and usually acquiesced to those with more power, which disadvantaged me. I failed to upend these learned behaviors. Although I marginally succeeded in dissipating power differences stemming from different positionalities and power exerted during my fieldwork, monitoring my auditing power after my fieldwork concluded induced uncertainty and fear.

For many good and not-so-good reasons, higher education is deeply entrenched in auditing, accountability, and surveillance activities—dubiously cloaked in the guise of commonsense administrative practices aimed at rational improvement. It is important to think uniquely and differently about technical and moral aspects of doing good ethnographic work without creating the illusion of rigor and fueling fears and feelings of defeatism.

Getting Closure

The postfieldwork phase of my research provided me sufficient distance from my fieldwork to reflect upon the issue of getting closure by disseminating knowledge. As I analyzed data and began to write, I wanted to be honest and constructive. Still, I feared that some might view me as higher education's Chicken Little—a paranoid, jaded, cynical, and hysterical academician predicting that the corporatization of the university meant imminent demise. I am concerned but cautiously optimistic. This fieldwork has revealed to me both the greatness of and threats to ethnographic research.

I wonder about the future of educational researchers—in particular, ethnographers. Although custodians and managers expressed genuine, ongoing interest in my work and findings, the interest of more senior administrators was minimal, at best. Admittedly, ignoring my work irked me, but the greater annoyance was the insularity of these administrators, who unilaterally decide what is best for the organization without seeking broad input from diverse constituents. I have no delusions about the importance of ethnographic work in solving higher education challenges, but a modest benefit of this kind of research is the representation of diverse perspectives.

This work provides a much-needed critique and captures institutional memory that reveals nuanced insights about campus subcultures, diverse conceptualizations of respect, and the wisdom of those whose voices are seldom heard. While chancellors struggle to find time to spend a few minutes a year with folks like me—to learn firsthand about our jobs, joys, and frustrations—ethnographic work can efficiently inform busy administrators about the other, whoever that may be, and how the other views their actions, especially the ways in which administrators' intended good deeds may breed mistrust, suspicion, and fear. Ethnographic work can reveal hidden insights and provide multiple visions about ways to prepare higher education and research communities for the future.

Conclusion

Decisions to adopt corporate ideals are commonplace in the academy. Aspects of the corporate university highlighted in this appendix are not likely to be dismantled and replaced anytime soon. Universities are hardly neutral and operate according to the ideologies of the dominant class. Carefully examining and mobilizing to challenge the influences of these ideals on various campus subcultures are rare and necessary steps, since an ongoing conversation about the nature and social function of higher education is the exception, not the rule (Nelson, 1997).

REFERENCES

Altenbaugh, R. J. (2003). *The American people and their education: A social history.* Upper Saddle River, NJ: Merrill/Prentice Hall.

Angrosino, M. V., & Rosenberg, J. (2011). Observations on observation: Continuities and challenges. In N. K. Denzin & Y. S. Lincoln (Eds.), *The Sage handbook of qualitative research* (pp. 467–478). Thousand Oaks, CA: Sage.

Anzaldúa, G. (1999). *Borderlands / La frontera.* San Francisco, CA: Aunt Lute Books.

Aronowitz, S. (1995). Higher education: The turn of the screw. *Found object, 6,* 89–99.

Aronowitz, S. (1997). Academic unionism and the future of higher education. In C. Nelson (Ed.), *Will teach for food: Academic labor in crisis* (pp. 181–214). Minneapolis, MN: University of Minnesota Press.

Associated Press. (2014, May 19). *9 public college presidents' pay topped $1 million.* Retrieved from http://www.columbiamissourian.com/news/higher_education/public-college-presidents-pay-topped-million/article_acf563ca-1c40-5df5-83ae-12928880229b.html

Associated Press. (2014, May 27). Median CEO pay rises. *Hamilton Journal-News,* p. A-8.

Banda, E. (2014). *Transformative learning and student empowerment: Zimbabwean graduate students' immersion into the United States.* Unpublished doctoral dissertation. Miami University, Oxford, OH.

Bearman, P. S. (2005). *Doormen.* Chicago, IL: University of Chicago Press.

Berger, C. (2015, July 13). An agentic approach to democratic engagement in higher education. *UMBC Breaking Ground.* Retrieved from https://umbcbreakingground.wordpress.com/2015/07/13/an-agentic-approach-to-democratic-engagement-in-higher-education/

Bogle, K. A. (2008). *Hooking up: Sex, dating, and relationships on campus.* New York, NY: New York University Press.

Bowen, H. R. (1977). *Investment in learning: The individual and social value of American higher education.* San Francisco, CA: Jossey-Bass.

Bringle, R. G., Games, R., & Malloy, E. A. (Eds.). (1999). *Colleges and universities as citizens.* Boston, MA: Allyn & Bacon.

Burstein, M. (2015, March 7). The unintended consequences of borrowing business tools to run a university. *The Chronicle of Higher Education.* Retrieved from http://chronicle.com/article/The-Unintended-Consequences-/190489/

Capriccioso, R. (2005, November 29). Dirty business? *Inside Higher Ed.* Retrieved from http://www.insidehighered.com/news/2005/11/29/miami

Carducci, R. (2011). Tempered radicals: Managing risks in negotiating differences. In P. Magolda & M. B. Baxter Magolda (Eds.), *Contested issues in student affairs: Diverse perspectives and respectful dialogue* (pp. 466–471). Sterling, VA: Stylus.

Carlson, D. (1994). Gayness, multicultural education, and community. *Educational Foundations, 8*(4), 5–25.

Charmaz, K. (2011). Grounded theory methods in social justice research. In N. K. Denzin & Y. Lincoln (Eds.), *The Sage handbook of qualitative research* (pp. 359–380). Thousand Oaks, CA: Sage.

Charon, J. M. (2002). *The meaning of sociology.* Upper Saddle River, NJ: Prentice Hall.

Chase, S. (2005). Narrative inquiry: Multiple lenses, approaches, voices. In N. K. Denzin & Y. S. Lincoln (Eds.), *The Sage handbook of qualitative inquiry* (pp. 651–682). Thousand Oaks, CA: Sage.

Chomsky, N. (2014, February 28). How America's great university system is being destroyed. *Alternet.* Retrieved from http://www.alternet.org/print/corporate-account ability-and-workplace/chomsky-how-americas-great-university-system-getting

Cipolle, S. B. (2010). *Service-learning and social justice: Engaging students in social change.* Lanham, MD: Rowman & Littlefield.

Clandinin, D. J., & Connelly, F. M. (2000). *Narrative inquiry: Experience and story in qualitative research* (1st ed.). San Francisco, CA: Jossey-Bass.

Clark, B. R. (2008). *On higher education: Selected writings, 1956–2006.* Baltimore, MD: Johns Hopkins University Press.

Colby, A. (2003). *Educating citizens: Preparing America's undergraduates for lives of moral and civic responsibility.* San Francisco, CA: Jossey-Bass.

Colby, A., Beaumont, E., Ehrlich, T., & Corngold, J. (2007). *Educating for democracy: Preparing undergraduates for responsible political engagement.* San Francisco, CA: Jossey-Bass.

Colby, A., Ehrlich, T., Beaumont, E., & Stephens, J. (2003). *Educating citizens: Preparing America's undergraduates for lives of moral and civic responsibility.* San Francisco, CA: Jossey-Bass.

Creswell, J. W. (2013). *Qualitative inquiry and research design: Choosing among five traditions.* Thousand Oaks, CA: Sage.

Creswell, J. W., & Miller, D. L. (2000). Determining validity in qualitative inquiry. *Theory Into Practice, 39*(3), 124–130.

Denton, J. M. (2014). *Living beyond identity: Gay college men living with HIV* (Unpublished doctoral dissertation). Miami University, Oxford, OH.

Denzin, N. K. (1989). *Interpretive interactionism.* Newbury Park, CA: Sage.

Denzin, N. K., & Giardina, M. D. (2010). Introduction. In N. K. Denzin & M. D. Giardina (Eds.), *Qualitative inquiry and human rights* (pp. 13–41). Walnut Creek, CA: Left Coast Press.

DeVita, P. R. (1992). *The naked anthropologist: Tales from around the world.* Belmont, CA: Wadsworth Publishing.

Dolgon, C. (2000). Justice for janitors. In G. D. White & F. C. Hauck (Eds.), *Campus, Inc.* (pp. 342–357). Amherst, NY: Prometheus Books.

Duneier, M. (1994). *Slim's table: Race, respectability, and masculinity.* Chicago, IL: University of Chicago Press.

Eckel, P. D., & Kezar, A. J. (2003). *Taking the reins: Institutional transformation in higher education.* Westport, CT: Praeger.

Ehrenreich, B. (2002). *Nickel and dimed: On (not) getting by in America.* New York, NY: Henry Holt.

Ehrlich, T. (2000). *Civic responsibility and higher education.* Westport, CT: Oryx Press.

Eisenberg, P. (2012a, September 4). The caste system in higher education. *Huffington Post.* Retrieved from http://www.huffingtonpost.com/pablo-eisenberg/caste-system-higher-education_b_1853917.html

Eisenberg, P. (2012b, September 14). A living wage for campus workers. *The Chronicle of Higher Education,* p. 19.

Ellison, R. (1965). *The invisible man.* London: Penguin Books.

Epstein, D. (2005, April 25). Sit-in at Wash. U: "It's over." *Inside Higher Ed.* Retrieved from http://www.insidehighered.com/news/2005/04/25/washu

Erickson, F. (1973). What makes school ethnography ethnographic? *Council on Anthropology and Education Newsletter, 4*(2), 10–19.

Essig, C. (2013, December 19). Refreshing or restricting? Ohio State's $32M deal with Coca-Cola brings up questions of transparency. *The Lantern.* Retrieved from http://thelantern.com/2013/12/refreshing-restricting-ohio-states-32m-deal-coca-cola-brings-questions-transparency-costs-vs-benefits/

Etzkowitz, H., Webster, A., & Healey, P. (1998). Introduction. In H. Etzkowitz, A. Webster, & P. Healey (Eds.), *Capitalizing knowledge: New intersections of industry and academia* (pp. 1–17). Albany, NY: State University of New York Press.

Fetterman, D. M. (2010). *Ethnography: Step-by-step.* Thousand Oaks, CA: Sage.

Fields, A. B., & Feinberg, W. (2001). *Education and democratic theory: Finding a place for community participation in public school reform.* Albany, NY: State University of New York Press.

Foley, D., & Valenzuela, A. (2005). Critical ethnography: The politics of collaboration. In N. K. Denzin & Y. S. Lincoln (Eds.), *The Sage handbook of qualitative research* (pp. 217–234). Thousand Oaks, CA: Sage.

Fontana, A., & Frey, J. H. (2005). The interview: From neutral stance to political involvement. In N. K. Denzin & Y. S. Lincoln (Eds.), *The Sage handbook of qualitative research* (pp. 695–727). Thousand Oaks, CA: Sage.

Fox, H. (2014, August 5). College president takes pay cut to give low-wage campus workers raise. *TakePart.* Retrieved from http://www.takepart.com/article/2014/08/05/kentucky-state-university-president-gives-90000-his-own-salary-so-low-paid#.U-KO5DjzMgo.mailto

Ganz, M. (2009, March). Why stories matter. *Sojourners.* Retrieved from http://sojo.net/magazine/2009/03/why-stories-matter

Ghidina, M. J. (1992). Social relations and the definition of work: Identity management in a low-status occupation. *Qualitative Sociology, 15*(1), 73–85.

Ginsberg, B. (2011). *The fall of the faculty: The rise of the all-administrative university and why it matters.* Oxford: Oxford University Press.

Giroux, H. (1992). *Border crossings: Cultural workers and the politics of education.* New York, NY: Routledge.

Giroux, H. (2005, March/April). Academic entrepreneurs: The corporate take-over of higher education. *Tikkun.* Retrieved from http://www.tikkun.org/article .php/Giroux-AcademicEntrepreneurs

Giroux, H. A. & Myrsiades, K. (2001). *Beyond the corporate university: Culture and pedagogy in the new millennium.* Lanham, MD: Rowman & Littlefield.

Glaser, B. G. (1965). The constant comparative method of qualitative analysis. *Social Problems, 12,* 436–445.

Glauberman, L. (2013, February 9). The transformational power of storytelling. *Huffington Post.* Retrieved from http://www.huffingtonpost.com/lloyd-glauber man-phd/storytelling_b_2254110.html

Goffman, E. (1952). On cooling the mark out: Some aspects of adaption of failure. *Psychiatry, 15*(4), 451–463.

Gold, R. L. (1964). In the basement: The apartment-building janitor. In P. L. Berger (Ed.), *The human shape of work* (pp. 1–49). New York, NY: MacMillan.

Golden, S. (2009, September 2). Unexpected philosophers. *Inside Higher Ed.* Retrieved from http://www.insidehighered.com/news/2009/09/02/kings

Gould, E. (2003). *The university in a corporate culture.* New Haven, CT: Yale University Press.

Granovetter, M. S. (1974). *Getting a job: A study of contacts and careers.* Cambridge, MA: Harvard University Press.

Green, A. (2008, October 20). How to get feedback when you're rejected. *U.S. News and World Report.* Retrieved from http://money.usnews.com/money/blogs/out side-voices-careers/2008/10/20/how-to-get-feedback-when-youre-rejected

Guba, E., & Lincoln, Y. S. (2005). Paradigmatic controversies, contradictions, and emerging confluences. In N. K. Denzin & Y. S. Lincoln (Eds.), *The Sage handbook of qualitative research* (pp. 191–215). Thousand Oaks, CA: Sage.

Hammonds, K. H., Jackson, S., DeGeorge, G., & Morris, K. (1997). The New U. *BusinessWeek* (3558), 96–102.

Harris, M. (1981). *America now: The anthropology of a changing culture.* New York, NY: Simon & Schuster.

Harrison, M. D. (2002). *Narrative-based evaluation: Wording toward the light.* New York, NY: Peter Lang.

Heathfield, S. M. (2014, December 16). Must employers tell applicants why they weren't hired? *About.com.* Retrieved from http://humanresources.about.com/ od/selectemployees/qt/must-employers-tell-applicants-why-they-werent-hired .htm?p=1

Hebdige, D. (1979). *Subculture: The meaning of style.* London: Routledge.

Hodder, I. (2000). The interpretation of documents and material culture. In N. K. Denzin & Y. S. Lincoln (Eds.), *The Sage handbook of qualitative research* (pp. 703–715). Thousand Oaks, CA: Sage.

hooks, b. (1994). *Teaching to transgress: Education as the practice of freedom*. New York, NY: Routledge.

Huber, S. (2000a). Faculty workers: Tenure of the corporate assembly line. In G. D. White & F. C. Hauck (Eds.), *Campus, Inc.: Corporate power in the ivory tower* (pp. 119–139). Amherst, NY: Prometheus Books.

Huber, S. (2000b). Tough customers: Business' plan to corner the student market. In G. D. White & F. C. Hauck (Eds.), *Campus, Inc.: Corporate power in the ivory tower* (pp. 106–118). Amherst, NY: Prometheus Books.

Insider Higher Ed. (2014). 2014 survey of college and university chief business officers. Retrieved from http://go.pardot.com/webmail/27982/859526129/5e888fe17010 24e6868725840b2ab35d

Jones, R. L. (2004). *Black haze: Violence, sacrifice, and manhood in Black Greek-letter fraternities*. Albany, NY: State University of New York Press.

Jones, S. R. (2002). (Re)writing the word: Methodological strategies and issues in qualitative research. *Journal of College Student Development, 43*(4), 461–473.

Kaufman, A. C. (2014, May 28). Millionaire WalMart CEO says he's just another associate. *Huffington Post*. Retrieved from http://www.huffingtonpost .com/2014/05/28/walmart-ceo-associate_n_5406017.html?view=print&comm _ref=false

Kelley, R. (1997). Proletariat goes to college. In C. Nelson (Ed.), *Will teach for food: Academic labor in crisis* (pp. 145–152). Minneapolis, MN: University of Minnesota Press.

Kreuter, G. V. L. (1996). *Forgotten promise: Race and gender wars on a small college campus*. New York, NY: Alfred A. Knopf.

Kreuter, H. (2011, June 13). Respect departmental staff. *Inside Higher Ed*. Retrieved from http://www.insidehighered.com/advice/tyro/essay_on_how_to_treat_depa rtmental_staff

Kreuter, N. (2014, February 27). Customer mentality. *Inside Higher Ed*. Retrieved from https://www.insidehighered.com/views/2014/02/27/essay-critiques-how-stu dent-customer-idea-erodes-key-values-higher-education

Kuh, G. D., Kinzie, J., Schuh, J., & Whitt, E. (2005). *Student success in college: Creating conditions that matter*. San Francisco, CA: Jossey-Bass.

Kuh, G. D., Schuh, J. H., Whitt, E. J., & Associates. (1991). *Involving colleges: Successful approaches to fostering student learning and development outside the classroom*. San Francisco, CA: Jossey-Bass.

Kurtz, A. (2013, June 3). *Bernanke's 10 hilarious tips for Princeton grads*. Retrieved from http://money.cnn.com/2013/06/02/news/economy/bernanke-princeton-speech/

LeCompte, M. D., & Preissle, J. (1993). *Ethnography and qualitative design in educational research*. San Diego, CA: Academic Press.

Lee, H. (1960). *To kill a mockingbird*. New York, NY: HarperCollins.

Lee, R. M. (1993). *Doing research on sensitive topics*. Newbury Park, CA: Sage.

Leonard, A. (2010). *The story of stuff: How our obsession with stuff is trashing the planet, our communities, and our health—and a vision for change*. London: Constable.

Levine, F. J., & Skedsvold, P. R. (2008). Where the rubber meets the road: Aligning IRBs and research practice. *PS: Political Science & Politics, 41*(3), 501–505.

Lincoln, Y. S., & Guba, E. G. (1985). *Naturalistic inquiry*. Newbury Park, CA: Sage.

Lindbloom, C. (1959). The "science" of muddling through. *Public Administration Review, 19*, 79–88.

London, S. (2010). *Doing democracy: How a network of grassroots organizations is strengthening community, building capacity, and shaping a new kind of civic education*. Washington, DC: Kettering Foundation.

Lustig, R. J. (2010). Corporate miseducation and the liberal arts response. In S. J. Rosow & T. Kriger (Eds.), *Transforming higher education: Economy, democracy, and the university* (pp. 3–35). Lanham, MD: Rowman & Littlefield.

Madden, R. (2010). *Being ethnographic: A guide to the theory and practice of ethnography*. London: Sage.

Madison, D. S. (2012). *Critical ethnography: Method, ethics, and performance* (2nd ed.). Thousand Oaks, CA: Sage.

Magolda, P. M. (2000). Accessing, waiting, plunging in, wondering, and writing: Retrospective sense-making of fieldwork. *Field Methods, 12*(3), 209–234.

Marks, J., & Nermon, M. (2013, August 9). Campus custodian wages are an insult to Berkeley values. *Daily Californian*. Retrieved from http://archive.dailycal.org/article.php?id=22559

Matthews, A. (1997). *Bright college years: Inside the American campus today*. New York, NY: Simon & Schuster.

McAdams, D. P. (2006). *The redemptive self: Stories Americans live by*. New York, NY: Oxford University Press.

Meyerson, D. E. (2008). *Rocking the boat: How to effect change without making trouble*. Boston, MA: Harvard Business Press.

Miller, S. M., & Reissman, F. (1961). The working class subculture. *Social Problems, 9*(1), 86–97.

Moffatt, M. (1989). *Coming of age in New Jersey: College and American culture*. New Brunswick, NJ: Rutgers University Press.

Mooney, M. A. (2012, November 14). When is suffering transformative? Sullivan's "Living faith: Everyday religion and mothers in poverty." *Patheos*. Retrieved from http://www.patheos.com/blogs/blackwhiteandgray/2012/11/when-is-suffering-transformative-insights-form-sullivans-living-faith/

Muoio, A. (1998, June/July). My greatest lesson. *FastCompany*. Retrieved from http://www.fastcompany.com/34136/my-greatest-lesson

Murphy, E., & Dingwall, R. (2001). The ethics of ethnography. In P. Atkinson, A. Coffey, S. Delamont, J. Lofland, & L. Lofland (Eds.), *Handbook of ethnography* (pp. 339–351). Thousand Oaks, CA: Sage.

Nagle, R. (2013). *Picking up: On the streets and behind the trucks with the sanitation workers of New York City*. New York, NY: Farrar.

Nathan, R. (2005). *My freshman year: What a professor learned by becoming a student*. Ithaca, NY: Cornell University Press.

National Task Force on Civic Learning and Democratic Engagement. (2012). *A crucible moment: College learning and democracy's future.* Washington, DC: Association of American Colleges and Universities.

Nelson, C. (1997). Introduction—Between crisis and opportunity: The future of the academic workplace. In C. Nelson (Ed.), *Will teach for food: Academic labor in crisis* (pp. 3–31). Minneapolis, MN: University of Minnesota Press.

Newman, K. S. (1988). *Falling from grace: The experience of downward mobility in the American middle class.* New York, NY: Free Press.

Ng, C. (2012, May 11). Custodian to graduate from Columbia University after 19 years. *ABC News.* Retrieved from http://abcnews.go.com/US/custodian-gac-filipaj-graduate-columbia-university-19-years/story?id=16311041#.UGNQx_lNbaM

Nixon, J. (2011). *Higher education and the public good: Managing the university.* New York, NY: Continuum International Publishing Group.

Pasque, P. A., Carducci, R., Kuntz, A.M., & Gildersleeve, R. E. (2012). *Qualitative inquiry for equity in higher education: Methodological innovations, implications, and interventions.* Hoboken, NJ: John Wiley & Sons.

Parnes, H. S. (1954). *Research on labor mobility: An appraisal of research findings in the United States.* New York, NY: Social Science Research Council.

Patel, E. (2007). Religious diversity and cooperation on campus. *Journal of College & Character, 9*(2), 1–8.

Patel, E., & Meyer, C. (2009). Engaging religious diversity on campus: The role of interfaith leadership. *Journal of College & Character, 10*(7), 1–8.

Patel, E., & Meyer, C. (2010). Defining religious pluralism: A response to Professor Robert McKim. *Journal of College & Character, 11*(2), 1–4.

Patton, M. Q. (1990). *Qualitative evaluation and research methods.* Newbury Park, CA: Sage.

Patton, M. Q. (2002). *Qualitative research and evaluation methods.* Thousand Oaks, CA: Sage.

Paules, G. F. (1991). *Dishing it out: Power and resistance among waitresses in a New Jersey restaurant.* Philadelphia, PA: Temple University Press.

Perry, S. E. (1978). *San Francisco scavengers: Dirty work and the pride of ownership.* Berkeley, CA: University of California Press.

Pierce, S. R. (2009, November 4). Advice for the new administrator. *Inside Higher Ed.* Retrieved from http://www.insidehighered.com/advice/2009/11/04/pierce

Pirsig, R. M. (1974). *Zen and the art of motorcycle maintenance.* New York, NY: Bantam.

Reich, R. B. (2014, February 5). Why there's no outcry over inequality. *Detroit Free Press.* Retrieved from http://www.freep.com/article/20140205/OPINION05/302050021/Robert-B-Reich-Why-there-s-no-outcry-over-inequality?utm_content=bufferf4179&utm_medium=social&utm_source=twitter.com&utm_campaign=buffer

Richardson, L. (2000). Evaluating ethnography. *Qualitative Inquiry, 6*(2), 253–255.

Rivard, R. (2014, February 20). The president and the paupers. *Inside Higher Ed.* Retrieved from https://www.insidehighered.com/news/2014/02/20/tying-col lege-presidents-wages-salaries-cooks-and-janitors

Rosow, S. J., & Kriger, T. (2010). *Transforming higher education: Economy, democracy, and the university.* Lanham, MD: Lexington Books.

Ruben, M. (2000). Penn and inc.: Incorporating the University of Pennsylvania. In G. D. White & F. C. Hauck (Eds.), *Campus, Inc.: Corporate power in the ivory tower* (pp. 194–217). Amherst, NY: Prometheus.

Saffran, M. (2007, May 27). *Clinton delivers academic convocation address.* Retrieved from http://www.rit.edu/news/story.php?id=45658

Saldana, J. (2011). *Fundamentals of qualitative research.* New York, NY: Oxford University Press.

Sanday, P. R. (1990). *Fraternity gang rape: Sex, brotherhood, and privilege on campus.* New York, NY: New York University Press.

Schlechty, P., & Noblit, G. (1982). Some uses of sociological theory in educational evaluation. In R. Corwin (Ed.), *Policy research* (pp. 283–306). Greenwich, CT: JAI.

Schrecker, E. (2010). *The lost soul of higher education: Corporatization, the assault on academic freedom, and the end of the American university.* New York, NY: New Press.

Schwandt, T. A. (2001). *Dictionary of qualitative inquiry.* Thousand Oaks, CA: Sage.

Scott, J., & Leonhardt, D. (2005). Shadowy lines that still divide. In *New York Times* (Eds.), *Class matters* (pp. 1–26). New York, NY: Times Books.

Seaman, B. (2005). *Binge: Campus life in an age of disconnection and excess.* Hoboken, NJ: John Wiley & Sons.

Shen, P. (Director), & Bennick, G. (Producer). (2009). *The philosopher kings* [motion picture]. United States: Transcendental Media.

Shipler, D. K. (2005). *The working poor: Invisible in America.* New York, NY: Vintage Books.

Spradley, J. (1980). *Participant observation.* New York, NY: Holt, Rinehart and Winston.

Stuber, J. M. (2011). *Inside the college gates: How class and culture matter in higher education.* Lanham, MD: Lexington Books.

Sweet, S. (2001). *College and society: An introduction to the sociological imagination.* Boston: Allyn & Bacon.

Tannenbaum, S. C. (2008). *Research, advocacy, and political engagement: Multidisciplinary perspectives through service learning.* Sterling, VA: Stylus.

Tierney, W. G. (1993). *Building communities of difference: Higher education in the twenty-first century.* Westport, CT: Bergin & Garvey.

Tierney, W. G., & Rhoads, R. A. (1993). Postmodernism and critical theory in higher education: Implications for research and practice. In J. C. Smart (Ed.), *Higher education: Handbook of theory and research*, vol. 9 (pp. 308–343). New York, NY: Agathon.

Troman, G. (2001). Tales from the interface: Disseminating ethnography for policy making. In G. Walford (Ed.), *Ethnography and educational policy* (pp. 251–273). New York, NY: JAI.

Tuchman, G. (2009). *Wannabe U: Inside the corporate university*. Chicago, IL: University of Chicago Press.

Van Der Werf, M. (2001). How much should colleges pay their janitors? *The Chronicle of Higher Education, 47*(47), A27–A28.

Van Maanen, J. (2011). *Tales of the field: On writing ethnography*. Chicago, IL: University of Chicago Press.

Weis, L., & Fine, M. (2000). *Speed bumps: A student-friendly guide to qualitative research*. New York, NY: Teachers College Press.

Whyte, W. (1949, January). The social structure of the restaurant. *American Journal of Sociology, 54*, 302–310.

Whyte, W. F. (1997). *Creative problem solving in the field: Reflections on a career*. Walnut Creek, CA: AltaMira Press.

Wilding, M. (2014, November 13). 7 Signs Your Workplace Is Toxic. *Psych Central*. Retrieved from http://psychcentral.com/blog/archives/2014/11/13/7-signs-your-workplace-is-toxic/

Williams, J. J. (2001). Franchising the university. In H. Giroux & L. Myrsiades (Eds.), *Beyond the corporate university: Culture and pedagogy in the new millennium* (pp. 15–28). Lanham, MD: Rowman & Littlefield.

Willis, J. (2007). *Foundations of qualitative research: Interpretive and critical approaches*. Thousand Oaks, CA: Sage.

Witherell, C., & Noddings, N. (Eds.). (1991). *Stories lives tell: Narrative and dialogue in education*. New York, NY: Teachers College Press.

Young, I. M. (1990). *Justice and the politics of difference*. Princeton, NJ: Princeton University Press.

Zusman, A. (1999). Issues facing higher education in the 21st century. In P. G. Altbach, R. O. Berdahl, & P. J. Gumbert (Eds.), *American higher education in the 21st century: Social, political, and economic challenges* (pp. 109–148). Baltimore, MD: Johns Hopkins University Press.

stereotypes of African American,
104–5
as stressing for success, 82–84
subculture border crossings lacking
for, 158
subculture of invisible campus, xvii
subculture scripts reaffirming low
status of, 173
supervision and discipline of, 69,
85–91
supervision and evaluating quality of,
79–81
teaching and cleaning intertwining
by, 177
tuition waivers and educational
journeys of, 162–63
upward mobility and conformity of,
43–44
upward mobility conundrum and,
44–46
upward mobility of, 42–46
work days in lives of, 63–84
work hour changes concerning,
67–68
working supervisors preferred by, 89
work shift consolidation of, 146

Daisy
in subjective I and eye stories, 33–34
data
fieldwork methodology and analysis
of, 221–22
fieldwork methodology and
collection of, 219–20
as insular and segregated on
subcultures, 205
participant-observation in collection
of, 219–20
triangulation, 223
death, 208–9
decision-makers, 11, 230
interviews and, 41–42
leadership and, 142
workers and non-involved, 94, 96
democracy, 129, 168, 187–88

demographics, custodial operations',
19, 24
Denzin, N. K., 223–24
Department of Housing (DOH),
22–23, 72, 143, 174
Department of Human Resources, 94
Department of Physical Facilities
(DPF), 19, 28, 65, 98, 103,
146, 149
in custodian's life, 47, 65
supervisors and, 93
DeVita, P. R., 225
Dingwall, R., 227
Dirty Albert, in subjective I and eye
stories, 33
discipline, 69, 92
disorientation, 101–3
diversity, 37, 95, 128, 190
OCC prioritizing ethnic, 23–24
document analysis, methodology
influenced by, 220–21
dogma, 210–12
dogs
custodial department administration
and mad, 197–99
custodian and operations at shelter
for, 192–95
custodians' giving all as under-,
208–10
faculty, students, staff as watch-,
206–8
high-level administrators meaner
than junkyard, 199–206
as invisible animal subculture shelter,
195–96
teaching new tricks to old, 196–210
DOH. *See* Department of Housing
Dolgon, C., 152, 207
domains, 116–21
dominant cultures, 105–6
*Don't Try to Put Yourself in Housekeeper's
Shoes,* case study, 174–78
doormen, 55–56
double standards, 127
downsizing, 28–29, 143

Also available from Stylus

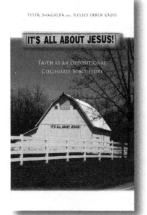

PETER MAGOLDA and KELSEY EBBEN GROSS

IT'S ALL ABOUT JESUS!

FAITH AS AN OPPOSITIONAL
COLLEGIATE SUBCULTURE

It's All About Jesus!
Faith as an Oppositional Collegiate Subculture
Peter M. Magolda and Kelsey Ebben Gross

"A resounding success."—*The Review of Higher Education*

"Magolda and Gross intend not only to enrich understanding of a particular student organization but also to spark intellectual discourse about the value of faith-based organizations within public higher education. . . . This is a must-read for researchers, administrators, faculty, and students."—*Choice*

"The authors give voice to the characters, tell richly descriptive stories, and come forward to offer perspectives and interpretations. And before it's done, important lessons are learned about student culture, higher education, and qualitative research methodology. . . . The authors fill a void in higher education which, while not being hostile, has been indifferent to the presence of faith-based student organizations; perhaps largely [because of a] misunderstanding of the important role they can play in students' lives. Though focused on a specific student organization, the authors offer broader lessons about religion in higher education, cocurricular pedagogy, student culture, and student learning. . . . *It's All About Jesus!* not only immerses the reader in this unique collegiate subculture but also serves as an instructive ethnographic study for those considering or conducting qualitative research."
— *Journal of College Student Development*

"If after picking up *It's All About Jesus!*, you feel motivated and equipped to begin an ethnography of a nearby religious community, you are not alone. It is a sign of their success that Magolda and Gross are able to captivate their readers early and to hold their attention firmly. . . . In the end, *It's All About Jesus!* challenges public and private, secular and religiously affiliated institutions to recognize that dialogue about religion and spirituality is 'essential to students' identity development and essential to living out American higher education standards'."—*Teaching Theology and Religion*

Sty/us

22883 Quicksilver Drive
Sterling, VA 20166-2102   Subscribe to our e-mail alerts: www.Styluspub.com